Getting Started with Competition Math

Limitless Math

L UKE Y ANG

Contents

1 ALGEBRA!   **3**

1.1   Introduction 3

1.2   Linear Equations with One Variable 3

    1.2.1   Introduction 3

    1.2.2   We have that $x - 5 = 3$. Solve for the value of x. 4

    1.2.3   I have 4 toy cars. My friend James has 5 more toy cars than me. How many toy cars does James have? 4

    1.2.4   Solve the equation $4z - 7 = 15$ for y. 5

    1.2.5   Find the value of x in $\frac{3(x-3)}{5} = \frac{7}{4}$. 5

    1.2.6   Solve the equation $7x = 10x + 43 - 3x$ for x. 6

    1.2.7   Find any and all value(s) of a that make the following equation true: $7a - 3a + 48 = 4a - 23 + 71$ 6

    1.2.8   What value(s) of x make the equation $4\sqrt[3]{x} - 6 = \sqrt[3]{x}$ true? . . . 7

    1.2.9   Conclusion 7

    1.2.10 Practice 8

1.3   Graphing Lines (Linear Equations) 9

    1.3.1   Introduction 9

    1.3.2   Graph the equation $y = 2x - 3$. 9

    1.3.3   Plot the graph of the equation $x + y = 2$ 11

    1.3.4   Graph the equation $y = 5$. 13

    1.3.5   Graph the equation $x = 1$. 15

    1.3.6   Find the equation of the following graph. 18

    1.3.7   Find the equation of the line that passes through the points $(1, -3)$ and $(2, 4)$. 20

    1.3.8   Is there anything interesting about the shape that the intersection of the lines $y = 3x + 1$ and $x + 3y = 4$? 23

    1.3.9   Conclusion 26

    1.3.10 Practice 26

1.4   Inequalities Part 1 29

    1.4.1   Introduction 29

    1.4.2   If $x > y$ and n is negative, how do the quantities xn and yn compare? 29

1.4.3   We have that $x > y$. If x and y are both positive, will $\frac{1}{x}$ or $\frac{1}{y}$ be larger? What if x and y are both negative? 30

1.4.4   Solve the following inequality: $3x - 4 > -1$. 31

1.4.5   Solve the following inequality chain: $4x + 5 > 2x - 6 \geq 4$. 32

1.4.6   Solve the inequality chain $3x - 10 > 2x + 5 < 11$. 32

1.4.7   Jamie is on a road trip. She has driven somewhere between 250 and 300 miles, and has used exactly 8 gallons of gas. Calculate the range of values that her car's gas mileage, in miles per gallon, can fall in. 33

1.4.8   Graph the solutions to the inequality $2x - y < -4$. 34

1.4.9   Conclusion 35

1.4.10   Practice 36

1.5   Ratios, Percents, and Proportions 37

1.5.1   Introduction 37

1.5.2   We have a car dealership where the ratio of cars to trucks is 4 to 5. There are 108 cars and trucks at the dealership, in total. How many of the 108 are cars? 37

1.5.3   We have a bag containing marbles of each color of the rainbow, with the ratio red : orange : yellow : green : blue : indigo : purple being $3 : 4 : 7 : 2 : 5 : 1 : 5$. The total number of marbles in the bag is 189. How many of the marbles are either yellow or blue? 37

1.5.4   What is the ratio of x to y if $\frac{10x-3y}{13x-2y} = \frac{3}{5}$? *(Source: MATH-COUNTS)* 38

1.5.5   A soccer team lost $\frac{3}{14}$ of its games this past season. If the number of games lost was 16 less than the number of games won, how many games did the team play in total during the season? 38

1.5.6   What number is 40% of 250? 39

1.5.7   The state income tax where Kristin lives is charged at the rate of $p\%$ of the first $28,000$ of annual income plus $(p + 2)\%$ of any amount above $28,000$. Kristin noticed that the state income tax she paid amounted to $(p + 0.25)\%$ of her annual income. What was her annual income? *(Source: AMC 12)* 39

1.5.8   If x and y are directly proportional and $x = 2$ when $y = 8$, when what is y when $x = 6$? What would y be if they were indirectly proportional and $x = 6$? 40

1.5.9 6 people can paint a wall in an hour. How long would it take 24 people to paint the same wall, assuming that all the people work at the same rate? 41

1.5.10   Conclusion 42

1.5.11   Practice 42

1.6   Introduction to Quadratics 44

1.6.1   Introduction 44

1.6.2   What values of x satisfy the equation $x^2 = 25$? 44

1.6.3   What values of x satisfy the equation $3x^2 - 363 = 0$? 44

1.6.4   Solve the equation $x^2 - 8x = 0$ for x. 44

1.6.5   Expand the expression $(x + 2)(x + 3)$. 45

1.6.6   What are the solutions to the equation $x^2 + 5x + 6 = 0$? 45

1.6.7   Factor the expression $x^2 + 4x + 3$ into the form $(x + r)(x + s)$. What are the solutions to the equation $x^2 + 4x + 3 = 0$? 46

1.6.8   Find the roots of the equation $x^2 - 15x + 56 = 0$. 46

1.6.9   Find all roots to the following equation: $x^2 + 6x - 16 = 0$. . . . 47

1.6.10   Find the roots to the equation $2x^2 + 7x + 6 = 0$. 47

1.6.11   Find all roots to the equation $6x^2 + 9x - 15 = 0$. 47

1.6.12   Expand the products $(x + 2)^2, (x + 3)^2$, and $(3x + 4)^2$. 48

1.6.13   Factor the quadratics $x^2 - 1, x^2 - 4, and x^2 - 81$. 49

1.6.14   Calculate $16^2 - 4^2$. 50

1.6.15   Find all pairs of integers x and y that satisfy the equation $xy - 7x + 3y = 70$. 50

1.6.16   Conclusion 51

1.6.17   Practice 51

1.7   Complex Numbers 53

1.7.1   Introduction 53

1.7.2   Simplify each of the following expressions: 53

1.7.3   Find all solutions to the following equation: $x^2 = -36$. 53

1.7.4   Simplify the following expression: $(75 + 37i) - (56 - 4i)$. 54

1.7.5   Expand the following product: $(2 - 3i)(8 + 2i)$. 54

1.7.6   Expand the following product: $(2 + 3i)(2 - 3i)$. 54

1.7.7   Conclusion 54

1.7.8   Practice 55

1.8   More Quadratics! 56

1.8.1   Introduction 56

1.8.2   Find all solutions to the equation $x^2 - 14x + 51 = 0$. 56

1.8.3   Solve the following equation by completing the square: $4x^2 - 16x + 19 = 0$. 57

1.8.4   Find the roots to the following equation: $x^2 - 4x + 1 = 0$. . . . 57

1.8.5   Conclusion 58

1.8.6   Practice 58

1.9   Graphing Quadratics 60

1.9.1   Introduction 60

1.9.2   Plot the graph of the quadratic equation $y = x^2$. 60

1.9.3   Graph the quadratic equation $y = 3x^2$. 62

1.9.4   Graph the quadratic equation $y = \frac{x^2}{3}$. 63

1.9.5   Graph the quadratic equation $y = -2x^2$. 64

1.9.6   Graph the quadratic equation $y = x^2 + 3$. 66

1.9.7   Graph the quadratic equation $y = (x - 2)^2$. 68

1.9.8   Conclusion 70

1.9.9   Practice 70

1.10 Functions 72
    1.10.1 Introduction 72
    1.10.2 For the function $f(x) = 4x+2$, find the following values: $f(1), f(3)$, and $f(-5)$. 72
    1.10.3 Find the value of x for which $f(x) = 4x + 2$ has a value of 34. . 72
    1.10.4 For the function $f(x) = 3x^2 + 5$, what is the domain? What is the range? 73
    1.10.5 $f(x) = 4x + 3$ for $2 \leq x \leq 4$. What is the range of f? 74
    1.10.6 For $f(x) = x + 5$ and $g(x) = 5x - 2$, compute $f(g(5))$. 75
    1.10.7 For the same $f(x)$ and $g(x)$ as in problem 1.10.6, find a general form for $f(g(x))$. 75
    1.10.8 Find the inverse of the function $f(x) = 3x - 5$. 76
    1.10.9 Does the function $f(x) = x^2$ have an inverse? 76
    1.10.10 Conclusion 77
    1.10.11 Practice 77
1.11 Exponential Functions and Their Graphs 78
    1.11.1 Introduction 78
    1.11.2 Graph the function 2^x. What is its range? 78
    1.11.3 What is the range of the function $f(x) = 4 \times 3^x + 5$? 79
    1.11.4 If $6^x = 2$, then what does 6^{3x+2} equal? 79
    1.11.5 Find all values of x such that $5^{2x+4} = 125^{x+1}$. 80
    1.11.6 Conclusion 80
    1.11.7 Practice 80
1.12 Absolute Value Functions and Their Graphs 82
    1.12.1 Introduction 82
    1.12.2 Graph the equation $y = |x|$. 82
    1.12.3 For what values of x is the equation $|3x + 4| = 1$ true? 83
    1.12.4 For what values of x is the equation $|2x + 4| + |x - 3| = 5$ true? 84
    1.12.5 Conclusion 85
    1.12.6 Practice 85
1.13 Polynomials 86
    1.13.1 Introduction 86
    1.13.2 Add the following two polynomials: $3x^3 + 4x^2 - 7x + 3$ and $9x^7 + 4x^5 + x^2 - 5$. 86
    1.13.3 Multiply the following two polynomials: $(2x^2 - x + 1)$ and $(4x^3 + x^2 - 2x + 4)$. 87
    1.13.4 Conclusion 87
    1.13.5 Practice 87
1.14 Sequences and Series 88
    1.14.1 Introduction 88
    1.14.2 In the sequence $-28, -19, -10, -1, 8, 17...$, find the 8th, 9th, and 11th terms. 88
    1.14.3 Given that $3, x_1, x_2, x_3, x_4, x_5, x_6, 24$ is a finite arithmetic sequence, find the value of x_5. 89

1.14.4 Add all the integers from 1 to 100, inclusive. 89

1.14.5 Find the sum of the following arithmetic series: $-4, -1$,
2, 5, 8, 11, 14, 17. 90

1.14.6 Given the sequence $3, 6, 12, 24, 48, 96...$, find the $7^{th}, 8^{th}$, and 9th
terms. 90

1.14.7 Given the geometric sequence $4, x_1, x_2, x_3, 64$, find all possible
values of x_1, x_2, and x_3. 91

1.14.8 For a geometric series with first term a, common ratio r, and n
terms, find a formula for the sum of the series. 91

1.14.9 Conclusion 92

1.14.10 Practice 92

2 GEOMETRY!   95

2.1 Introduction 95

2.2 Triangle Congruence 103

2.2.1 Introduction 103

2.2.2 In the diagram below, $AB = CD$ and $AD = BC$. Are triangles
$\triangle ABC$ and $\triangle ACD$ congruent? Why or why not? 105

2.2.3 In the diagram below, we have that $AB = BC = 5$, and $AD =
CD = 10$. Prove that $\angle ABD \cong \angle CBD$. 105

2.2.4 Which, if any, of the following four triangles are congruent? . . . 106

2.2.5 Which, if any, of the following four triangles are congruent? . . . 107

2.2.6 Conclusion 108

2.2.7 Practice 108

2.3 Triangle Similarity 110

2.3.1 Introduction 110

2.3.2 Given the following figure and its given properties, find DE. . . . 110

2.3.3 Given $AC = 4, CD = 5$, and $AB = 6$ as in the diagram, find
BC if the perimeter of $\triangle BCD$ is 20. (Source: Mandelbrot) . . . 111

2.3.4 In the diagram, $BDEF$ is a square. $AB = 9$ and $BC = 15$. Find
the side length of square $BDEF$. 112

2.3.5 Conclusion 112

2.3.6 Practice 113

2.4 Right Triangles and Their Properties 115

2.4.1 Introduction 115

2.4.2 Given the following diagram, prove that $a^2 = cd, b^2 = ce$, and
finally that $a^2 + b^2 = c^2$. 115

2.4.3 For the following triangles, find the lengths of the missing sides.
(Figures may not be drawn to scale.) 116

2.4.4 In the following diagram, $\triangle ABC$ is an isosceles right triangle.
From the given information, find all angles and side lenghts of
$\triangle ABC$. 117

2.4.5 For the following diagram of equilateral triangle ABC, find the
area of $\triangle ABC$. 118

2.4.6   In the previous problem, we discussed an equilateral triangle that had been cut in half. Now, we'll explore the properties of each half-triangle, known as $30 - 60 - 90$ triangles. If the original equilateral triangle had side length $2x$, what would the length of both legs be? 119

2.4.7   Conclusion 120

2.4.8   Practice 120

2.5 Special Parts of Triangles 123

2.5.1   Introduction 123

2.5.2   Find the circumcenter of a right triangle, using the diagram below. What is the circumradius of the triangle? 128

2.5.3   In the diagram below, prove that $\frac{AB}{AE} = \frac{CB}{CE}$. 129

2.5.4   Prove that the centroid of any triangle divides each median in a $2 : 1$ ratio, with the longer portion consisting of the segment from the centroid to the vertex. 130

2.5.5   Conclusion 131

2.5.6   Practice 131

2.6 Area and Perimeter 132

2.6.1   Introduction 132

2.6.2   The length of one side of a rectangle is 5 more than twice the length of an adjacent side. Keeping in mind that the perimeter of the rectangle is 58, find the area of the rectangle. 132

2.6.3   What is the area of an equilateral triangle if its perimeter is 48? . 133

2.6.4   A square poster is replaced by a rectangular poster that is 2 inches wider and 2 inches shorter. What is the difference in the number of square inches between the area of the larger poster and the smaller poster? (Source: MATHCOUNTS) 133

2.6.5   In the following diagram, the area of $\triangle ABE$ is 24, the area of $\triangle BCE$ is 15, and the area of $\triangle CDE$ is 10. Find the area of triangle ADE. 134

2.6.6   Conclusion 134

2.6.7   Practice 135

2.7 All About Quadrilaterals! 136

2.7.1   Introduction 136

2.7.2   Given that $ABCD$ is a parallelogram, find the values of a and b, and find the measure $\angle D$. 138

2.7.3   Parallelogram $ABCD$ is formed as shown, with the relationships as shown in the diagram. Find the area of $ABCD$, and find the distance between sides $\overline{AB}$ and $\overline{CD}$. 139

2.7.4 $ABCD$ is a rhombus with diagonals $AC = 16$ and $BD = 8$. Find the area and perimeter of $ABCD$. 140

2.7.5   The width of a rectangle is 2 less than half its length. If the perimeter of the rectangle is 26, find its area. 141

2.7.6   Find the area and perimeter of a square with diagonals of length 10. 141

2.7.7   In trapezoid $ABCD$, we have that $\overline{BC}\|\overline{AD}, \angle B = 160°$, and $\angle C = 70°$. Find $\angle A$ and $\angle D$. 142

2.7.8   For trapezoid $ABCD$, $\overline{AD}\|\overline{BC}, \angle B = \angle C$, and $\angle B < 90°$. Prove that $AB = CD$. 142

2.7.9   Conclusion 143

2.7.10 Practice 143

2.8   All About Circles! 144

2.8.1   Introduction 144

2.8.2   A certain circle has area 121π. What is its diameter? 144

2.8.3   A $120°$ arc of a circle has length 18π. What is its area? 144

2.8.4   For the following circle with center O, chord $\overline{AB}$ has a length of 15. The circumference of the circle is 30π. What is the length of arc AB? 145

2.8.5   A farmer has 30 meters of fence, with which they want to enclose a semicircular space adjacent to a barn. The barn will form one side of the enclosure. What is the area of the space enclosed by the barn and the fence? 145

2.8.6   Circle O has radius 6. The region within the circle formed by segments OA and OB in combination with arc AB is called a sector. The shaded region between chord $\overline{AB}$ and the circle is called a circular segment. Find the area of the shaded circular segment. 146

2.8.7   When an inscribed angle cuts off a $180°$, it is inscribed in a semicircle. Using the following diagram, prove that all such inscribed angles are right angles. 150

2.8.8   Prove that for all angles ACB such that the center of the circle, O, is inside $\triangle ABC$, $\angle ACB$ is half the measure of arc AOB. . . . 151

2.8.9   Given that $\angle AOB = 2x, \angle ACD = x$, and arc $BC = x$, find the value of x. 152

2.8.10 Chords $\overline{CD}$ and $\overline{AB}$ intersect at B. Arc DE is equal to x, and arc AC is equal to y. Find an algebraic formula for $\angle DEB$ in terms of x and y. 153

2.8.11 In the diagram below, arc EF and DC have measures a and b, respectively. Prove that $\angle B = \frac{b-a}{2}$. 154

2.8.12 Conclusion 155

2.8.13 Practice 155

2.9   3-D Figures 157

2.9.1   Introduction 157

2.9.2   Prims 157

2.9.3   Pyramids 160

2.9.4   Cylinders 161

2.9.5   Cones 162

	2.9.6	Spheres	163
	2.9.7	Conclusion	163
	2.9.8	Practice	163

3 COMBINATORICS & PROBABILITY!   **165**

3.1	Introduction	165
3.2	Let's count things!	166
	3.2.1	Introduction	166
	3.2.2	Count the number of integers in the following list: $1, 2, 3,$ $4, 5, 6, 7, 8, 9, 10, 11, 12.$	166
	3.2.3	Count the number of integers in the following list: $10, 11,$ $12, 13, 14, 15, 16, 17, 18, 19, 20, 21, 22, 23, 24, 25, 26, 27.$	166
	3.2.4	Count the number of multiples of 5 between 13 and 166.	166
	3.2.5	In a parking lot, there are 30 vehicles, which are all either sedans or SUVs, and either red or blue. 11 are sedans, and 16 are red. 4 are red sedans. How many blue SUVs are there?	167
	3.2.6	In an ice cream shop, there are 3 choices for the ice cream flavor and 2 choices for the size. How many different ice cream combinations of flavor and size can you create?	167
	3.2.7	How many different outfits can you make from a choice of 4 shirts, 3 pairs of pants, 2 pairs of socks, and 5 pairs of shoes, if you must include one of each element in the outfit?	168
	3.2.8	You have 6 different books. You want to place 3 of them on a shelf. How many different ways can you arrange 3 books in this manner?	168
	3.2.9	A club has 15 members. There are four officer positions: president, vice president, secretary, and historian. How many ways can the four officer be chosen if each member can hold at most one officer position? What if each member can hold any number of officer positions?	169
	3.2.10	Conclusion	169
	3.2.11	Practice	169
3.3	Counting Strategies	171
	3.3.1	Introduction	171
	3.3.2	In a particular language, the alphabet has 7 letters. Each word has at most 4 letters in it. There is no word with 0 letters. How many words are possible in this language?	171
	3.3.3	How many pairs of positive integers (x, y) are there such that $x^2 + y \le 25$?	171
	3.3.4	How many three digit numbers are not multiples of 5?	172
	3.3.5	You have 7 books that you want to arrange on a shelf. 4 of them are about math, and 3 of them are about science. How many ways can you arrange the books so that at least 2 math books are next to each other?	173

3.3.6 In how many four digit numbers is there exactly one zero? 173

3.3.7 Your school's math club has 15 members and 3 officer positions. However, John is best friends with Jane, and will only serve as an officer if Jane also has a position. How many ways can we fill the offices? 174

3.3.8 Conclusion 174

3.3.9 Practice 174

3.4 Overcounting 176

3.4.1 Introduction 176

3.4.2 How many distinct arrangements can possibly be made from the letters in the word "$tree$"? 176

3.4.3 How many distinct arrangements can possibly be made from the letters in the word "$tatter$"? 177

3.4.4 How many distinct arrangements can possibly be made from the letters in the word "$mamma$"? 177

3.4.5 In a round-robin tennis tournament, each player plays every other player exactly one time. How many matches will be held during a 6-person round-robin tennis tournament? 177

3.4.6 How many ways can 8 people be seated around a round table? . 178

3.4.7 Conclusion 178

3.4.8 Practice 179

3.5 Combinations and Combinations and More Combinations 180

3.5.1 Introduction 180

3.5.2 How many ways can a President and Vice President be chosen from a group of 4 people if they cannot be the same person? How many ways can a committee of two people be chosen from a group of four people if the order in which they are chosen does not matter? 180

3.5.3 How many ways can a 3-person committee be chosen from a group of 8 people? 180

3.5.4 In a group of n people, how many ways can we choose a committee of r people from those n people? 181

3.5.5 Compute $\binom{8}{3}$, $\binom{10}{5}$, and $\binom{7}{2}$. 182

3.5.6 Compute $\binom{7}{2}$ and $\binom{7}{6}$, then compute $\frac{9}{2}$ and $\frac{9}{7}$. 182

3.5.7 Compute $\binom{10}{8}$ and $\binom{13}{10}$. 183

3.5.8 Conclusion 183

3.5.9 Practice 184

3.6 Basic Probability 185

3.6.1 Introduction 185

3.6.2 A fair, six-sided die has the integers 1 through 6 painted on its sides. It is rolled once. What is the probability that it lands on a side that is a prime number? 185

3.6.3   In a row at a particular parade, there are 4 different red cars and 5
         different blue cars. If the row has been arranged randomly, what
         is the probability that the first two cars are both blue?   186

3.6.4   Two fair, six-sided dice have the integers 1 through 6 painted on
         their sides. They are each rolled once, at the same time. What
         is the probability that the two numbers they land on have a sum
         of exactly 8?   186

3.6.5   If a fair coin is flipped a total of 7 times, what is the probability
         that at least 4 of the flips come up heads?   186

3.6.6   A standard deck of cards consists of 4 suits, each containing 13
         cards (for a total of 52 cards). The four suits are hearts, diamonds,
         spades, and clubs. Hearts and diamonds are painted red, while
         spades and clubs are black. The 13 cards in each suit are made
         up of the integers from 2 through 10, one ace, a jack, queen, and
         king. A card is chosen from a standard deck of 52 cards. What
         is the probability that the card is a 10 or in the suit of hearts (or
         both)?   187

3.6.7   If we roll three fair six-sided dice at the same time, what is the
         probably that they won't all show the same number?   188

3.6.8   If 5 coins are flipped, what is the probability of getting at least 1
         head?   188

3.6.9   Two fair six-sided dice, one black and one white, are rolled simul-
         taneously. What is the probability that the black die shows a 3
         on its top face, and the white die shows a 5?   189

3.6.10   A fair, six-sided die is rolled 6 times. What is the probability that
         an even number is shown in exactly 4 of the 6 rolls?   189

3.6.11   Two cards are drawn from a standard deck of 52 cards. What is
         the probability that the first card drawn is from the suit of hearts,
         and the second is from the suit of spades?   189

3.6.12   A bag contains 6 red candies and 3 blue ones, all of identical size
         and shape. A candy is selected and not replaced. A second candy
         is then selected. What is the probability that both candies are the
         same color?   190

3.6.13   Conclusion   190

3.6.14   Practice   190

3.7   Expected Value   192

3.7.1   Introduction   192

3.7.2   Calculate the expected value of the roll of a fair six-sided die. . .   192

3.7.3   In a game, a weighted coin is used. It has a $\frac{1}{3}$ chance of landing
         on heads, which will win the player ten dollars, and a $\frac{2}{3}$ chance
         of landing on tails, which will lose the player five dollars. What is
         the expected value of a single coin toss in this game?   193

3.7.4   A group of race cars each have numbers on their roofs. There are 12 cars in total. Some of the cars in the group have a 2 on their roofs, while all the others have a 7. If the expected value for a number on a random car selected is 3.25, how many of the cars have a 7? 193

3.7.5   Conclusion 193

3.7.6   Practice 193

4   NUMBER THEORY!   **195**

4.1   Introduction 195

4.2   Multiples and Divisors 199

4.2.1   Introduction 199

4.2.2   Find all of the positive divisors of 24 and 30. What positive divisors do they have in common? 199

4.2.3   Abbie has 42 blue marbles, which she divides into piles that each have n marbles in them. She also has 56 red marbles, which she also divides into n piles with an equal number of marbles in each pile. What is the largest possible value of n? 199

4.2.4   Find all the common multiples of 6 and 15 between 1 and 100, inclusive. 200

4.2.5   Find the least common multiple (LCM) of 9 and 24. 200

4.2.6   Explain why the difference between any two multiples of 7 is also a multiple of 7. 200

4.2.7   Conclusion 201

4.2.8   Practice 201

4.3   Prime Factorizations 202

4.3.1   Introduction 202

4.3.2   Find the prime factorization of 20. 202

4.3.3   Find the prime factorization of 120. 202

4.3.4   Find a relationship between the prime factorizations of all positive multiples of 12. 203

4.3.5   Using prime factorizations, find $\mathrm{lcm}(15,36)$. 204

4.3.6   Find $\mathrm{lcm}(8,12,20)$. 205

4.3.7   Find $\gcd(36,48)$. 205

4.3.8   Find $\gcd(56,84)$. 205

4.3.9   Conclusion 206

4.3.10 Practice 206

4.4   Counting Divisors 207

4.4.1   Introduction 207

4.4.2   How many positive integer divisors does 100 have? 207

4.4.3   How many positive integer divisors does 160 have? 207

4.4.4 n is a number with prime factorization $n = x_1^{y_1} x_2^{y_2} x_3^{y_3} ... x_a^{y_a}$. Find a formula for the number of positive divisors of n. 207

4.4.5   Conclusion 208

	4.4.6	Practice	208
4.5	Base Numbers	209
	4.5.1	Introduction	209
	4.5.2	Write the decimal (base 10) number 66 in base 8.	209
	4.5.3	Convert the decimal number 40 into base 2.	210
	4.5.4	Convert the decimal number 200 into base 6.	210
	4.5.5	Write the decimal number 35 in base 12.	210
	4.5.6	Write the base 6 number 555_6 in base 10.	210
	4.5.7	Write the base 11 number $A385_{11}$ in base 10.	210
	4.5.8	Write the base 8 number 5764_8 in base 5.	211
	4.5.9	Conclusion	211
	4.5.10	Practice	211
4.6	The Units Digit	212
	4.6.1	Introduction	212
	4.6.2	What is the units digit of the sum $7 + 17$?	212
	4.6.3	What is the units digit of the sum $7 + 27$? $7 + 37$? $7 + 47$? $7 + 57$? $7 + 67$? $7 + 77$? $7 + 87$?	212
	4.6.4	What is the units digit of $97 - 3$?	212
	4.6.5	What is the units digit of $97 - 13$? $97 - 23$? $97 - 33$? $97 - 43$? $97 - 53$? $97 - 63$? $97 - 73$? $97 - 83$?	213
	4.6.6	What is the units digit of 7×3?	213
	4.6.7	What is the units digit of 7×13? 7×23? 7×33? 7×43? . . .	213
	4.6.8	Find the units digit of 14^{80}.	214
	4.6.9	The product of two positive integers has a units digit of 3. One of the integers has a units digit of 9. What must be the units digit of the other integer?	214
	4.6.10	Conclusion	215
	4.6.11	Practice	215
4.7	Divisibility Rules	216
	4.7.1	Introduction	216
	4.7.2	Divisibility by 0	216
	4.7.3	Divisibility by 1	216
	4.7.4	Divisibility by 2	216
	4.7.5	Divisibility by 3	216
	4.7.6	Divisibility by 4	216
	4.7.7	Divisibility by 5	217
	4.7.8	Divisibility by 6	217
	4.7.9	Divisibility by 7	217
	4.7.10	Divisibility by 8	217
	4.7.11	Divisibility by 9	217
	4.7.12	Divisibility by 10	217
	4.7.13	Divisibility by 11	217
	4.7.14	Divisibility by 12	217
	4.7.15	Conclusion	217

CONTENTS

    4.7.16 Practice 218

5 **Solutions**   **221**

Preface

At Limitless Math, we believe that a quality education in the world of mathematics is one of the most valuable gifts that anyone can receive. In particular, competition-style math promotes a mindset based on critical thinking, logic, and mental adaptation, as opposed to one focused on formulaic memorization. This book contains many of the fundamental ideas and topics essential to excelling in competition math, spread across four categories: algebra, geometry, combinatorics, and number theory.

Each category contains numerous subsections, each dealing with a particular topic within the category. Included in these subsections are detailed explanations of example problems that dive into key ideas, tricks, and formulas that can be applied to other problems of the same topic. After each section is group of practice problems which should be done as practice. Solutions can be found at the end of the book.

It is our hope that this book proves useful for students looking to jump-start their journey in competition math, and instills them with knowledge of how to approach problems that can be applied not just in math, but far beyond as well.

Acknowledgements

- A special word of thanks goes to Professor Don Knuth (for TEX) and Leslie Lamport (for LATEX).

- For my parents, without whom this book would not have existed.

- For Christina, Abbie, Isa, Alexa, Daniel, and all the other friends without whom I would have quit this book before making it past Algebra.

- For my students, who are more special to me than they will ever know. Thank you for filling me with hope for how you kiddos will change the world.

Luke Yang

2   *CONTENTS*

Chapter 1

ALGEBRA!

1.1 Introduction

Ah yes, the dreaded algebra. Soon you'll see there's nothing to fear, and in fact, everything to love. Algebra is arguably one of the most basic tools of mathematics, next to counting on your fingers. Seeing the alphabet in math can appear daunting at first, but once you get used to it, you'll wonder how you ever lived without it.

1.2 Linear Equations with One Variable

1.2.1 Introduction

The linear equation: $y = mx + b$, or sometimes $Ax + By = C$, or even $y - y_1 = m(x - x_1)$. Knowing how to solve these equations opens the door to solving countless problems; there are very few problems in which the principles used to solve linear equations cannot be applied. In fact, many problems that appear extremely complicated on the surface can often be reduced down to a simple linear equation.

So what do we mean when we say "solve" a linear equation? In essence, it means to find the value(s) of the variables present that will make the equation true. The word "linear" signifies that all variables present in the equation are simply some constant times the variable raised to the first power.

Examples of linear equations:

- $x + 4 = y$
- $1 = 57z - 346$
- $4.5a = 13a + 4$

Examples of NONLINEAR equations:

- $x^2 + 4 = y$
- $\sqrt{a - 36} + 4 = b^2$
- $\frac{45}{r+72} + 18r = 4$

The fundamental method for solving a linear equations is to isolate the variable you want the value for. We'll see an example of how to do so in the following problem.

1.2.2 We have that $x - 5 = 3$. Solve for the value of x.

You might be able to immediately see that if $x = 8$, then the equation is true, because $8 - 5 = 3$. Even so, let's break that process down so we can replicate it for more complicated problems.

To solve the equation, we need to move things around until we have it in the form of $x = $ some value. Essentially, we need to have x by itself on one side of the equation. We can accomplish this goal by simply adding 5 to both sides of the equation.

> IMPORTANT: What you do to one side of an equation, you must do to the other, as well. If you add 3 to one side, you must add 3 to the other.

$$x - 5 = 3$$
$$(x - 5) + 5 = (3) + 5$$
$$x = 8$$

This concept of manipulating both sides of the equation to isolate the variable we want to solve for is the basis of solving linear equations. Let's do another example.

1.2.3 I have 4 toy cars. My friend James has 5 more toy cars than me. How many toy cars does James have?

At first glance, this problem might not appear to be anything remotely similar to a linear equation. However, we'll soon see that it is!

> IMPORTANT: Many problems (word problems especially) may not appear as though they can be solved using a linear equation. In fact, many of them can be: think about what your variable could be, and build your equation from there.

For this problem, what we're looking for is the number of toy cars that James has. Let's set this value equal to x.

$$x = \text{the number of toy cars that James has}$$

We know that James has 5 more toy cars than me, and I have 4. This is the same thing as saying that I have 5 fewer cars than James; if he were to throw away 5 cars, he would have the same number as me, which is 4. Thinking about the problem this way allows us to build the equation

$$x - 5 = 4.$$

From here, we apply the same thinking as we did in the previous problem. What can we do to isolate x? Adding 5 to both sides will give us

$$(x - 5) + 5 = 4 + 5,$$

which simplifies to $x = 9$ once we perform the addition. We now know that James has 9 toy cars.

1.2.4   Solve the equation $4z - 7 = 15$ for y.

We begin this problem just like we did for the others: try to isolate our variable, which in this case is z. A good first step to take would be to add 7 to both sides, which gives us

$$(4z - 7) + 7 = 15 + 7.$$

Once we combine like terms, we are left with

$$4z = 22.$$

Here is where we take an additional step to solve this problem that we didn't have to do for the others: we don't quite have z by itself on one side; it's still being multiplied by a factor of 4. What can we do to make it just z? We can divide by 4, which gives us

$$\frac{4z}{4} = \frac{22}{4},$$

which simplifies to

$$z = \frac{11}{2}.$$

> IMPORTANT: Isolating the variable entails using whatever mathematical operation is necessary to get the variable in question by itself. Addition, subtraction, multiplication, division, roots, exponents, whatever is necessary. Just remember to apply the operation to both sides.

1.2.5   Find the value of x in $\frac{3(x-3)}{5} = \frac{7}{4}$.

Taken at face value, this problem appears a bit more complicated than the others, and indeed it is. Still, the same idea of isolating the variable applies.

Our first step is to multiply both sides by 5 to get rid of the fraction that x is in, leaving us with

$$3(x - 3) = \frac{35}{4}.$$

Next, we divide both sides by 3, giving us

$$x - 3 = \frac{35}{12}.$$

Finally, we just add 3 to both sides, giving us a final answer of

$$(x - 3) + 3 = \frac{35}{12} + 3 \longrightarrow x = \frac{35}{12} + 3 = \frac{35}{12} + \frac{36}{12} = \frac{71}{12}.$$

Up to now, every equation we dealt with had one solution. Let's explore some other equations which have a different number of solutions.

1.2.6   Solve the equation $7x = 10x + 43 - 3x$ for x.

We'll start this problem like any other: trying to isolate x. On the right side, we notice that we can combine the terms with x, giving us

$$7x = 7x + 43.$$

From here, the next step appears to be to subtract $7x$ from both sides, leaving us with

$$0 = 43.$$

This is an issue, clearly. We have a result that is never true, and looking back, we haven't made any errors in our calculations. Thus, here is an example of a linear equation with no solutions.

> **IMPORTANT: When solving a linear equation results in a false statement, check your work for mistakes. If no mistakes were made, the equation has no solutions.**

1.2.7   Find any and all value(s) of a that make the following equation true: $7a - 3a + 48 = 4a - 23 + 71$

On the left side, we see right off the bat that we can combine $7a - 3a$, giving us

$$4a + 48 = 4a - 23 + 71.$$

Similarly, on the right, we can add $-23 + 71$ to give

$$4a + 48 = 4a + 48.$$

Both sides of the equation are the same, so this equation is always true. In short, all values of a will satisfy the equation, so it has infinitely many solutions.

> **IMPORTANT:** If simplifying a linear equation results in a statement that is always true, no matter the value of the variable, it has infinitely many solutions.

1.2.8   What value(s) of x make the equation $4\sqrt[3]{x} - 6 = \sqrt[3]{x}$ true?

This question looks misplaced. It doesn't seem to be a linear equation at all; our variable x is under a cube root, which doesn't fit with the definition of a linear equation as one containing only variables raised to the first power (taking the cube root is the same as raising a value to the $\frac{1}{3}$ power.)

Turns out, this question is right where it belongs. Let's set $a = \sqrt[3]{x}$. Then our equation becomes

$$4a - 6 = a.$$

We know how to solve that! It's obviously a linear equation. Add 6 to both sides, subtract a from both sides, and we get

$$3a = 6 \longrightarrow a = 2.$$

So we're done? Not quite. Recall that we set $a = \sqrt[3]{x}$, so we stil have to solve for x. Replacing a with 2 gives us $2 = \sqrt[3]{x}$. Cubing both sides gives us

$$2^3 = x \longrightarrow 8 = x.$$

We solved it!

> **IMPORTANT:** Linear equations are often hiding within other, more complicated equations. Making substitutions is often a great way to reveal these camouflaged equations.

1.2.9   Conclusion

So that's the one-variable linear equation. We learned to solve them, i.e. finding the value for which the equation is true.

> **REMEMBER:** To solve linear equations, isolate the variable you want to solve for.

REMEMBER: If the equation can be manipulated into a form that is always true, the equation has infinitely many solutions. If it can be manipulated into a form that is never true, the equation has no solutions.

1.2.10   Practice

1. $2x + 5 = 15$

2. $4x - 7 = 29$

3. $\frac{3x}{5} = x - 8$

4. $3x + 10 = \frac{9x-9}{3} + 13$

5. $0.2x + 5 = 1.2x$

6. $108x - 40 = 36x + 80 - 120 + 72x$

7. For what value of x does the equation $4a + 3x = 10a - 6a + 18$ have infinitely many solutions?

8. My brother is 4 years older than me. In ten years, he will be $\frac{5}{4}$ of my age. How old am I right now?

9. Jenny has a bag full of only pennies and nickels. The bag contains half as many nickels as pennies, and contains a total value of $17.50. How many nickels are in the bag?

10. Find x if $\frac{4}{x^2} + \frac{1}{3} = \frac{7}{x^2}$.

11. Solve for x in the equation $5x^2 + 2x - 7 = 4x - 2x + 38$.

12. The equations $4x + 7 = -13$ and $ax - 30 = 5$ have the same solution x. What is the value of x, and what is the value of b?

13. In a bag, there are an equal number each of pennies, nickels, and quarters. The total amount of money in the bag is a multiple of 50 cents. What is the smallest possible amount of money in the bag? (There is at least one of each type of coin.)

1.3 Graphing Lines (Linear Equations)

1.3.1 Introduction

Now let's talk about how to show these linear equations graphically. We'll be using the Cartesian plane for this textbook.

Linear equations can be graphed on the Cartesian plane by using the information given when the equation is in slope-intercept form.

IMPORTANT: A linear equation in slope-intercept form is of the format

$$y = mx + b,$$

where m is the slope of the line, and b is the y-intercept.

The slope of the graph is the ratio of the difference between the y-coordinates of two points on the line, to the difference between the x-coordinates of the same two points. Take the two points (x_1, y_1) and (x_2, y_2). The slope would be

$$m = \frac{y_2 - y_1}{x_2 - x_1}.$$

The y-intercept of the graph is the y-coordinate at which the graph crosses the y-axis, or put another way, where $x = 0$.

Let's take a look at some examples of how to construct the graph of an equation in this form.

1.3.2 Graph the equation $y = 2x - 3$.

Before we start to draw anything, let's get the information that will tell us how to construct the graph. Considering the form $y = mx + b$, we see that in this case, $m = 2$ and $b = -3$. Thus, the slope of the graph is 2, and the y-intercept is at $y = -3$.

Now we can start to construct the graph. A good place to start is to plot the y-intercept, which in this case has the coordinates $(0, -3)$.

From here, we can choose another point on the graph of $y = 2x - 3$ that we can use to complete our graph. This will allow us to draw a line through the two points, which will be the graph of the equation. Something simple like $x = 1$ will work perfectly; plugging it into our equation gives us

$$y = 2(1) - 3 = 2 - 3 = -1.$$

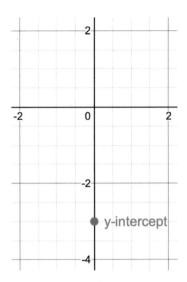

Figure 1.1: y-intercept

Therefore, our point is $(1, -1)$. Plotting that gives us this:

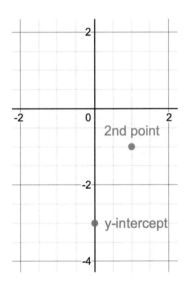

Figure 1.2: y-intercept and 2nd point

Finally, we can draw a line between the two points, giving us that the graph of $y = 2x - 3$ looks like:

IMPORTANT: When drawing the graph of a linear equation given its equation, pick two points on the line, graph them, and draw a line through them. It's often easier to pick one of the points to be the y-intercept.

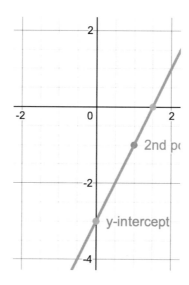

Figure 1.3: Completed graph of y=2x-3

1.3.3   Plot the graph of the equation $x + y = 2$

Right off the bat, this equation looks different from the previous one; the y isn't alone on the left side! In fact, this equation is in **standard form**.

IMPORTANT: Standard Form of a linear equation:

$$Ax + By = C,$$

where $A, B,$ **and** C **are constants and** A **and** B **are not both** 0.

Let's try to get this equation into the familiar slope-intercept form. All we have to do is subtract x from both sides, giving us

$$(x + y) - x = 2 - x \longrightarrow y = -x + 2.$$

Now, we can start the problem just as we did for the last one: try to find the information we need to graph it. We see that our slope, m, is -1. This time, our slope is negative, while in the previous problem, it was positive. We'll see the difference this creates in our graph in a moment. Continuing on, our y-intercept is 2.

Now we're ready to build our graph. Starting once again with our y-intercept, we plot it on our graph, giving us:

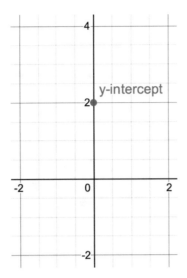

Figure 1.4: y-intercept

Just like before, our next step is to find a second point. We can use any value for x, but a convenient point such as the one at $x = 1$ is close to our y-intercept and easy to work with. Plugging $x = 1$ into the equation gives us

$$y = -(1) + 2 = -1 + 2 = 1.$$

Graphing it gives us:

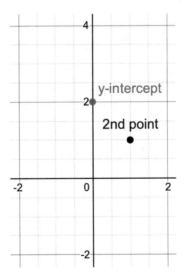

Figure 1.5: y-intercept and 2nd point

To finish it off, we draw the line through the two points, leaving us with:

Here is where we can spot the difference that the negative slope made. Whereas the values on the line in the previous problem **increased** from left to right, the ones on the graph of $y = -x + 2$ **decrease** from left to right.

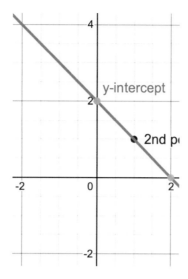

Figure 1.6: Completed graph of y=-x+2

> **IMPORTANT: Equations with positive slopes increase from left to right, while equations with negative slopes decrease from left to right.**

Now we've seen examples of graphs with positive and negative slopes. Next come the graphs that have a slope of 0, because yes, they exist.

Thinking about the definition of the slope of a line, what does a slope of 0 mean? Well, it means that as the x values change, the y values stay exactly the same. Visualizing how that would look on a graph, we might guess that it should be a horizontal, completely flat line. Let's do an example and see if our hunch is correct.

1.3.4 Graph the equation $y = 5$.

We know that this graph will have a slope of 0, but if we hadn't been told by the paragraph above, what would give it away? Looking at our equation, there is no term that contains x; all we can tell is that the equation has a y-intercept of 5. In fact, this lack of a term containing x is precisely what lets us know this equation will have a slope of 0.

> **IMPORTANT: Linear equations without a term containing x will have a slope of 0.**

We can also think about it this way: since there is no term containing x, the value of y does not depend on x at all. Essentially, even if x changes, the value of y will not be affected.

We know that the y-intercept of the graph is 5, so one point we could plot is $(0, 5)$.

Doing that gives us:

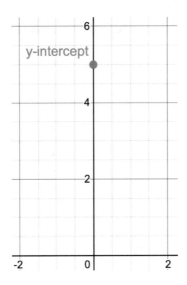

Figure 1.7: y-intercept

What point should we plot next? We can't exactly follow our previous strategy of choosing a different value of x, because the value of y doesn't depend on x... but what does that mean? It means that we can pick whatever value of x we want, and y will still equal 5! We could theoretically go wild and pick $x = 198234$, but let's keep things cool for now and go with $x = 2$, giving us the point $(2, 5)$. Plotting it gives us:

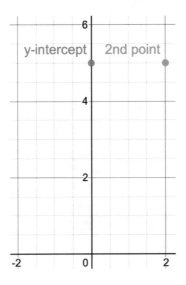

Figure 1.8: y-intercept and 2nd point

Now we can continue as usual, and draw a line between the points:

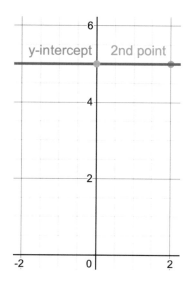

Figure 1.9: Completed graph of y=5

And would you look at that! Our guess was correct: the graph is a horizontal line passing through the y-intercept.

> **IMPORTANT: Linear equations with a slope of 0 are horizontal and have equations of the form $y = n$, where n is some constant. n is also the graph's y-intercept.**

Here, we might think that we're done. We've covered all the possible cases of graphing linear equations! Except we haven't: sometimes, lines can have an undefined slope; one that doesn't exist. Let's take a look at an example.

1.3.5 Graph the equation $x = 1$.

This equation is obviously different from the ones we've dealt with before: this time, there is no term containing y. What does that mean?

Using similar logic as we used in the example with a slope of 0, the lack of a term containing y tells us that the value of x does not depend on y; y can change as much as it wants, and x will still be 1. If x is always 1, no matter what, we can predict that our line might be vertical, passing through every point with an x-coordinate of 1.

We don't have a y-intercept to work with, so what point should we plot first? In this case, we can use the **x-intercept**. Just like the y-intercept is the point at which $x = 0$, where the graph meets the y-axis, the x-intercept is the point at which $y = 0$, where the graph meets the x-axis. We know that $x = 1$ no matter what, and because the point is the x-intercept, $y = 0$, so the coordinates for our point are $(1,0)$. Plotting it gives us:

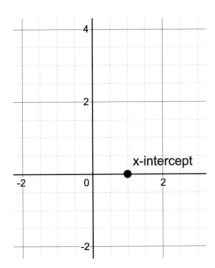

Figure 1.10: x-intercept

Now what should we choose as our second point? It doesn't matter what, x will equal 1, so we can choose any value of y to go with it. Let's go with $y = 2$, which gives us coordinates of $(1, 2)$. The graph now looks like:

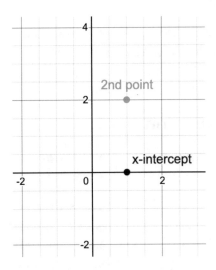

Figure 1.11: x-intercept and 2nd point

Drawing a line between the two points gives us:

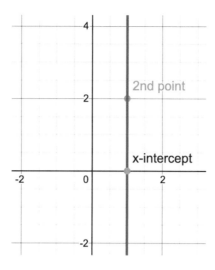

Figure 1.12: Completed graph of x=1

Once again, we were right! We got a perfectly vertical line, with all points having an x-coordinate of 1.

IMPORTANT: **Linear equations with an undefined slope are vertical, with an equation of the form** $x = n$, **for some constant** n. n **is also the x-intercept of the graph.**

Thinking for a moment about the possibilities of vertical graphs, we see that the vast majority of them will never pass through the y-axis. Does this mean that all vertical lines have no y-intercept? Well, no; there is only one that has a y-intercept: the graph of $x = 0$.

IMPORTANT: **Linear equations with an undefined slope have no y-intercept, with the exception of the graph of** $x = 0$.

So far, all of our examples have had us generate a graph from its equation. Let's flip the script, and try to get a line's equation from its graph.

1.3.6   Find the equation of the following graph.

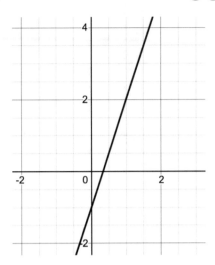

Figure 1.13: Given Graph

To begin, let's look for the features of a graph that we know will give us information relating to its equation: its y-intercept and slope.

The y-intercept is easy to find; we just look for the point where the graph crosses the y-axis. This appears to occur at $y = -1$, for coordinates of $(0, -1)$.

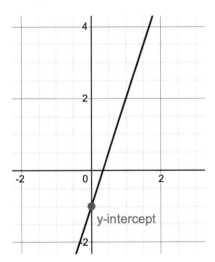

Figure 1.14: y-intercept

Next, we need to find the slope. Recall that the slope of the line, m, is calculated as

$$m = \frac{y_1 - y_2}{x_1 - x_2},$$

where (x_1, y_1) are the coordinates of one point, and (x_2, y_2) are the coordinates of another point that lies to the right of the first point.

We can use the y-intercept of our graph as the first point, but we still need a second. Points with integer coordinates will make our calculations a lot easier, so we look for points on the graph that have integer x- and y- values. A good example would be the point $(1, 2)$, so we can use that.

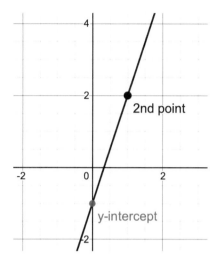

Figure 1.15: y-intercept and 2nd point

We can plug the coordinates of these two points into our equation for slope to find the value of m. Recalling that (x_2, y_2) lies to the right of (x_1, y_1) we see that in this case, $(1, 2)$ should replace (x_2, y_2), and $(0, -1)$ should replace (x_1, y_1).

Substituting these values into our equation for m gives us

$$m = \frac{2 - (-1)}{1 - 0} = \frac{3}{1} = 3.$$

Now we know both the slope and y-intercept of our graph. Using the slope-intercept form of the equation of a line, $y = mx + b$, we can see that the equation of this graph is

$$y = 3x - 1.$$

> **IMPORTANT:** To get a line's equation from its graph, analyze it for features such as the y-intercept and slope. Remember the special conditions for horizontal and vertical lines.

Something else we can try is to get the equation of a line given two of its points. Let's do an example.

1.3.7   Find the equation of the line that passes through the points $(1, -3)$ and $(2, 4)$.

For these types of problems, we can employ a similar approach of finding features such as the y-intercept and slope of the equation. In this case, starting with finding the slope is easier.

Applying the formula for slope of a line, we can see that $(2, 4)$ is to the right of $(1, -3)$, so we'll use $(2, 4)$ as (x_2, y_2). Plugging our values into the equation gives

$$m = \frac{y_2 - y_1}{x_2 - x_1} = \frac{4 - (-3)}{2 - 1} = \frac{7}{1} = 7.$$

Thus, our slope is 7.

Now to find the y-intercept! Using the slope-intercept form of the linear equation $y = mx + b$, we can substitute our slope of 7 in to get

$$y = 7x + b.$$

From here, we can plug in the coordinates of a point that we know for sure are on our line, just like the ones given in the problem: $(1, -3)$ and $(2, 4)$. Let's pick the second one, purely because it might be easier not to deal with the negatives. Substituting the coordinates into our equation gives us

$$4 = 7(2) + b \longrightarrow 4 = 14 + b \longrightarrow 4 - 14 = (14 + b) - 14 \longrightarrow -10 = b.$$

We now have all we need to build our equation: our slope is 7, and our y-intercept is -10. Thus, our equation is

$$y = 7x - 10.$$

IMPORTANT: To find an equation of a graph given two of its points, use the two points to find the slope, then substitute the slope and one set of the given coordinates into the framework of the slope-intercept equation form to find the y-intercept. Put it all together to create the equation!

IMPORTANT: The equation of a graph can be found using any combination of 2 of the following: one point on the graph, another point on the graph, the slope, and the y-intercept.

If you have two known points: Use the method in the box above.

If you have one point and the slope: Plug the slope and the coordinates into the form $y = mx + b$ to solve for the y-intercept.

If you have one point and the y-intercept: Effectively, you have two points on the line! Use the method in the box above.

If you have the slope and the y-intercept: Plug 'em into $y = mx + b$ and you are good to go!

Briefly, let's discuss what happens when we have the graphs of multiple equations, and how they interact. We have three possible cases: the two graphs never intersect, they intersect at one point, or they intersect at all values of x for which they are defined (effectively, they are the same line).

IMPORTANT: These are the ways two lines can interact: *Never intersect:* The two lines are parallel, as shown by the diagram below. By definition of being parallel and within the same plane, they have the same slope.

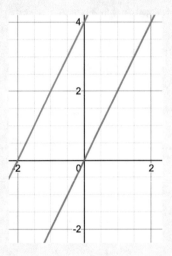

Figure 1.16: Parallel lines: they have the same slope!

Intersect at one point: The two lines meet at exactly one point, meaning that one value of (x, y) is a solution to both of their equations.

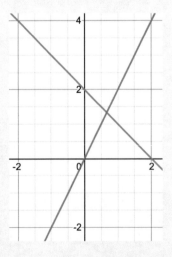

Figure 1.17: Intersecting at one point

Intersect at all points: The two lines are the same and have the same equation.

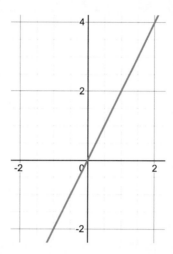

Figure 1.18: Believe it or not, this is the graph of 2 lines. They just have the same equation.

There is one special case of intersecting lines that we need to consider. Let's take a look at the next problem.

1.3.8 Is there anything interesting about the shape that the intersection of the lines $y = 3x + 1$ and $x + 3y = 4$?

Let's start by plotting the lines. We'll begin with $y = 3x + 1$. We know that the y-intercept is 1, so one point we can use to plot the graph is $(0, 1)$.

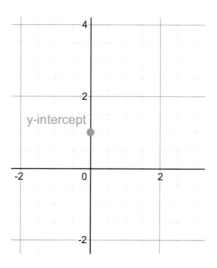

Figure 1.19: y-intercept

Another point on the graph can be found by plugging in $x = 1$, which gives us

$$y = 3(1) + 1 = 3 + 1 = 4 \longrightarrow (1, 4).$$

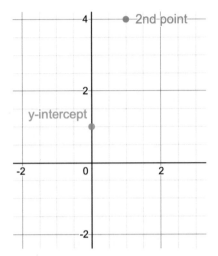

Figure 1.20: y-intercept and 2nd point

Connecting the points gives us this graph:

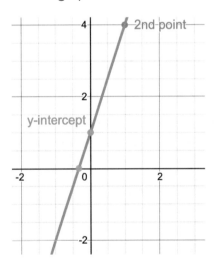

Figure 1.21: Completed graph of $y = 3x + 1$

Now let's start on the second equation. We can start to put it into slope-intercept form by subtracting x from both sides, giving us

$$(x + 3y) - x = 4 - x \longrightarrow 3y = -x + 4.$$

We can then divide both sides by 3, giving us

$$\frac{3y}{3} = -\frac{x}{3} + \frac{4}{3} \longrightarrow y = -\frac{x}{3} + \frac{4}{3}.$$

From here, we can tell that our slope is $-\frac{1}{3}$ and the y-intercept is $\frac{4}{3}$. Plotting the y-intercept gives us:

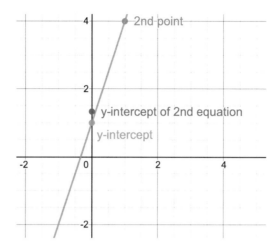

Figure 1.22: y-intercept of 2nd equation

Once again, we can plug a value of x into the equation of the line to get a second point. In an effort to get rid of some of the fractions, let's use $x = 3$, which gives us

$$y = -\frac{3}{3} + \frac{4}{3} = -1 + \frac{4}{3} = \frac{1}{3} \longrightarrow (3, \frac{1}{3}).$$

Plotting this point gives us:

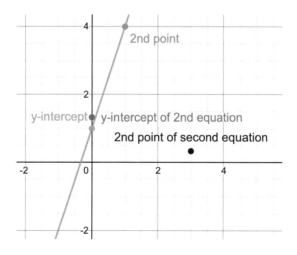

Figure 1.23: y-intercept and 2nd point of second equation

Finally, connecting the two points gives us this picture:

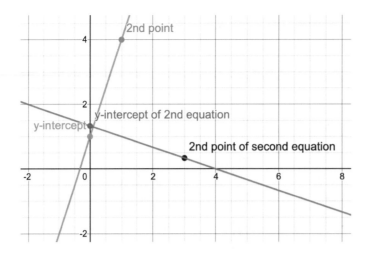

Figure 1.24: Final picture!

Well, would you look at that! The two lines make a right angle!

Coincidence? I think not. Here lies a special case of intersecting lines in which they are perpendicular, and it has everything to do with their slopes. One slope is 3, and the other is $-\frac{1}{3}$. They are special in that the two slopes have a product of -1. More formally, they are **negative reciprocals** of each other.

> **IMPORTANT: Perpendicular lines have slopes that multiply to -1. Said another way, they are negative reciprocals of each other.**

1.3.9   Conclusion

Through this section, we've seen how to graph linear equations using points that lie on their graphs, their slopes, and their x- and y- coordinates. We learned both the slope-intercept and standard form for linear equations, as well as the formula for their slopes. We saw how lines with positive slope increase from left to right, while those with negative slope decrease from left to right. We've seen how horizontal lines have a slope of 0 and are of the form $y = n$, while vertical lines have an undefined slope and are of the form $x = n$. Finally, we learned that lines can either never intersect (parallel), intersect at one point (with a special case being perpendicular lines; their slopes multiply to -1,), or intersect at all points (they're the same line).

1.3.10   Practice

1. Graph the following equations on the empty graph below, and next to each equation's bullet, identify its slope and y-intercept:

   (a) $y = -3x - 5$

(b) $4x - y = 4$

(c) $x = 2$

(d) $2y = 4x + 6$

(e) $y = -5$

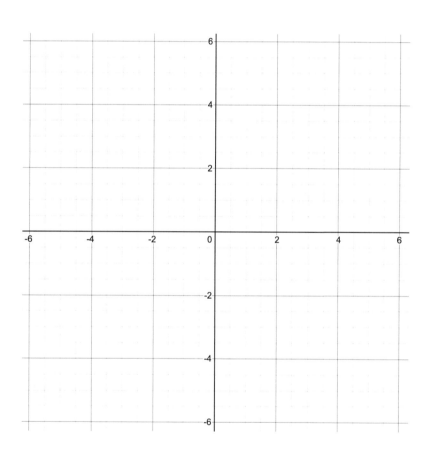

2. Find the equation of the following graph in slope-intercept form:

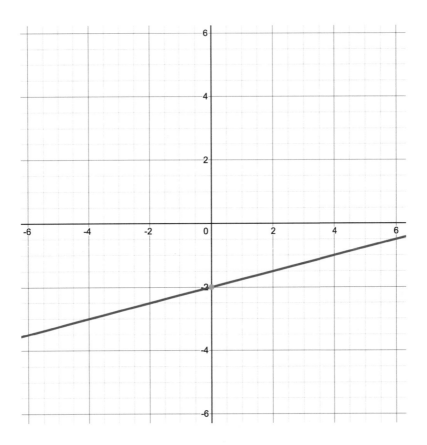

3. Do the following 3 points lie on the same line?

   (a) $(0, 2)$

   (b) $(2, 0)$

   (c) $(4, -3)$

4. Find the equation of the line that passes through $(-1, 3)$ and has slope 3.

5. Are the following two lines perpendicular?

   (a) $2x - y = 3$

   (b) $2x + y = 5$

1.4 Inequalities Part 1

1.4.1 Introduction

Up until now, all that we've worked with has been an expression or an equation. An equation denotes two things that are equal, using the $=$ sign to show equality. Now it's time to work with values that are *not* equal.

Specifically, we're going to deal with inequalities, using the "greater than" ($>$) and "less than" ($<$) signs. Those signs will be used for strict inequalities, denoting that one side *must* be larger than the other. We'll also work with the "greater than or equal to" ($\geq$) and the "less than or equal to" ($\leq$) signs, for nonstrict inequalities, which denote that one side must be greater than *or* equal to the other.

As a head start, here are some facts about inequalities that are logical and don't require too much thought, but are extremely important to understand and us:

IMPORTANT: Properties of Inequalities

If $x > y$ and $y > z$, then $x > z$ as well. Same goes for $x \geq y$ and $y \geq z$; $x \geq z$.

If $x > y$, then $x + n > y + n$ for any real number n. If we know that constants m and n have the relationship $n > m$, we also can say that $x + n > y + m$. Once again, same goes for $x + n \geq y + n$ and $x + n \geq y + m$ if $n \geq m$.

If $x > y$ and n is positive, $xn > yn$. Similarly, if $x \geq y$ and n is positive, $xn \geq yn$.

If x and y are positive with $x > y$, and n is positive, then $x^n > y^n$. By the same token, if $x \geq y$, then $x^a \geq y^a$.

Everything in the box above seems pretty simple. Let's take a look at some cases that require a little more thought.

1.4.2 If $x > y$ and n is negative, how do the quantities xn and yn compare?

It's a little difficult to think about this problem purely conceptually, so let's do a few examples with real numbers to see how things stack up. We can start small, letting $x = 3, y = 2$, and $n = -1$.

$$xn = (3)(-1) = -3, \text{ and } yn = (2)(-1)(-2).$$

Comparing the values, we know that $-2 > -3$, so

$$xn < yn.$$

Interesting. Let's do a couple more to see if the same relationship holds true. Take $x = 5, y = 3$, and $n = -4$. Then we have that

$$xn = (5)(-4) = -20 \text{ and } yn = (3)(-4) = -12.$$

Comparing the values, we see that $-12 > -20$. Once again, we end up with

$$xn < yn.$$

One last example: we have that $x = 4, y = 27$, and $n = -3$. This gives us

$$xn = (4)(-3) = -12, \text{ and } yn = (27)(-3) = -81.$$

Comparing the two, we get $-12 > -81$, so

$$yn > xn.$$

It seems we've figured it out. If $x > y$ and n is negative, $xn < yn$.

> **IMPORTANT:** If $x > y$ and n **is negative,** $xn < yn$. **Essentially, we must reverse the sign of the inequality.**

Now let's see another case where negative numbers can impact our results.

1.4.3   We have that $x > y$. If x and y are both positive, will $\frac{1}{x}$ or $\frac{1}{y}$ be larger? What if x and y are both negative?

Let's start with a visualization. Say we have two pies of equal size. Logically, would you want a slice from one of the pies that was cut into more pieces, or less pieces?

Less pieces, right? Because then each slice would be bigger. That's basically the concept we're looking at here: a smaller denominator in a fraction means larger pieces of the whole.

> **IMPORTANT:** If $x > y$ and they are both positive, $\frac{1}{y} > \frac{1}{x}$.

Let's see if anything is different when it comes to negative x and y. We can start with our given inequality, which is that $x > y$. Dividing both sides by x gives us

$$\frac{x}{x} > \frac{y}{x} \longrightarrow 1 > \frac{y}{x}.$$

Now, we must remember to reverse the sign, giving us

$$1 < \frac{y}{x}.$$

From here, dividing both sides by y gives

$$\frac{1}{y} < \frac{1}{x}.$$

Since y is also negative, we reverse the sign once more, giving us the end result that

$$\frac{1}{y} > \frac{1}{x}.$$

We can see that the statement holds for both positive and negative x and y!

> **IMPORTANT: If $x > y$ have the same sign, $\frac{1}{y} > \frac{1}{x}$.**

Now it's time to take a look at linear inequalities.

1.4.4 Solve the following inequality: $3x - 4 > -1$.

The steps we'll be taking here are extremely similar to what we did to solve linear equations: isolate the variable.

In this case, we see that we can add 4 to both sides, giving us

$$(3x - 4) + 4 > -1 + 4 \longrightarrow 3x > 3.$$

From here, dividing both sides by 3 gives us

$$\frac{3x}{3} = \frac{3}{3} \longrightarrow x > 1.$$

Lucky for us, we don't have to worry about flipping the signs, as we never multiplied or divided by a negative number. That's our final answer: to satisfy this inequality, x must be greater than 1.

> **IMPORTANT: Solve a linear inequality just like you solve a linear equation; isolate the variable. Just be careful about flipping your signs when working with negative numbers.**

1.4.5   Solve the following inequality chain: $4x + 5 > 2x - 6 \geq 4$.

For inequality chains, we can split the inequality up and deal with its pieces separately. First and foremost, we have

$$4x + 5 > 2x - 6.$$

Once again, we isolate our variable, subtracting $2x$ from both sides to get

$$(4x + 5) - 2x > (2x - 6) - 2x \longrightarrow 2x - 5 > -5.$$

From here, we add 5 to both sides, giving us that

$$(2x - 5) + 5 > -5 + 5 \longrightarrow 2x > 0.$$

Dividing both sides by 2 gives us

$$\frac{2x}{2} > \frac{0}{2} \longrightarrow x > 0.$$

Now let's tackle the second part of the inequality chain: $2x - 6 \geq 4$. The first step to isolating x is to add 6 to both sides, giving us

$$(2x - 6) + 6 \geq 4 + 6 \longrightarrow 2x \geq 10.$$

Dividing both sides by 2 gives us

$$\frac{2x}{2} \geq \frac{10}{2} \longrightarrow x \geq 5.$$

To satisfy this inequality chain, we now see that x must both be greater than 0, and greater than or equal to 5. It's easy to see that both conditions can be satisfied by just stating that $x \geq 5$. Therefore, that is the solution!

> **IMPORTANT: When solving inequality chains, break them up into separate inequalities and deal with them separately. Once all inequalities have been solved, find the values for your variable that will satisfy all of them.**

This inequality chain worked out quite nicely for us. Let's see another one where things may not be so simple.

1.4.6   Solve the inequality chain $3x - 10 > 2x + 5 < 11$.

Once again, we start by breaking the inequality chain up into smaller inequalities. Working with the inequality on the left, we must have that

$$3x - 10 > 2x + 5.$$

Subtracting $2x$ and adding 10 to both sides let's us start isolating x, giving us

$$(3x - 10) - 2x + 10 > (2x + 5) - 2x + 10 \longrightarrow x > 15.$$

Now for the other inequality:
$$2x + 5 < 11.$$

Subtracting 5 from both sides gives us

$$(2x + 5) - 5 < 11 - 5 \longrightarrow 2x < 6.$$

Dividing both sides by 2 leaves us with

$$\frac{2x}{2} < \frac{6}{2} \longrightarrow x < 3.$$

So... we must have simultaneously that $x > 15$, and $x < 3$. This simply is not possible. As such, we say that this inequality chain has no solutions.

> **IMPORTANT: If an inequality chain results in conditions for the variable that cannot be simultenously met, the chain has no solutions.**

Now that we've seen how the pure math works, let's see how inequalities might be hiding within some word problems.

1.4.7 Jamie is on a road trip. She has driven somewhere between 250 and 300 miles, and has used exactly 8 gallons of gas. Calculate the range of values that her car's gas mileage, in miles per gallon, can fall in.

As stated in the name of the unit, a car's gas mileage in miles per gallon is the number of miles that it can travel using 1 gallon of fuel.

Keeping that in mind, let's set up an inequality. Say g is the gas mileage of the car. We know that g must be $\frac{\text{some number of miles}}{\text{some number of gallons}}$. That tells us a bit about how to set up our inequality; we were given values for both miles and gallons in the problem.

A minimum value for the car's gas mileage would be if it traveled the least number of miles. As stated in the problem, this minimum number of miles is 250. Similarly, a maximum value of the gas mileage would be if it traveled the largest number of miles, in this case 300. The car used 8 gallons of fuel no matter what, so we don't need to worry about that.

Combining all of our information, our inequality becomes

$$\frac{250 \text{ miles}}{8 \text{ gallons}} \leq g \leq \frac{300 \text{ miles}}{8 \text{ gallons}} \longrightarrow 31.25 \text{ miles per gallon} \leq g \leq 37.5 \text{ miles per gallon}.$$

Therefore, g must be between 31.25 and 37.5 miles per gallon.

> **IMPORTANT:** Keep an eye out for word problems that can make use of an inequality.

Just like linear equations, linear inequalities can be graphed. Let's explore how to do that.

1.4.8   Graph the solutions to the inequality $2x - y < -4$.

To start, we treat the inequality as if it were a linear equation. Getting the inequality into slope-intercept form $(y = mx + b)$ requires us to add y and 4 to both sides, giving us

$$(2x - y) + y + 4 < -4 + y + 4 \longrightarrow 2x + 4 < y.$$

Flipping the inequality around, taking care to flip the sign as well, gives us the final inequality of

$$y > 2x + 4.$$

Continuing on, we graph it as normal. We know the y-intercept is 4, and another point on the line can be found by plugging in 1, giving us

$$y > 2(1) + 4 \longrightarrow y > 6,$$

and coordinates of $(1, 6)$. Plotting the line gives us:

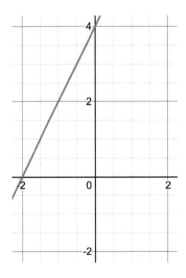

Figure 1.25: Graph of $y = 2x + 4$

Alright. We got the line plotted, but it's time to remember that we're dealing with an inequality. Thinking about what the inequality means, it is essentially saying that for every value of x, the value of y needs to be greater than $2x + 4$. That means all the values of y that are valid lie above the line that we just graphed. The way we represent that fact when we graph inequalities is by shading the area that is valid, as shown in Figure 1.26. Another important detail to note is the dashed line, which is used because the inequality used $>$ and not $\geq$. The dash signifies the fact that the values that lie on the line are not, in fact, solutions to the inequality. If the symbol used were actually $\geq$, the line would be solid.

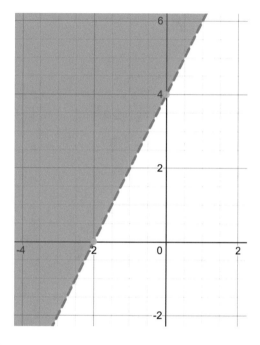

Figure 1.26: Graph of $y > 2x + 4$. Pay attention to the shading and the dashed line.

> **IMPORTANT: Graph an inequality exactly as you would a linear equation. Then analyze what region of the graph, relative to the line, contains solutions to the inequality. Shade those areas. Then consider whether the inequality is strict (uses $<$ or $>$) or nonstrict (uses $\leq$ or $\geq$.) For strict inequalities, dash the line of the graph; for nonstrict ones, make the line solid.**

1.4.9 Conclusion

In this section we learned about the basics of inequalities. There are other types we'll see later on, but this is enough for now. We learned how to use the greater than or less than symbols, what to do if they're strict or nonstrict, and some important properties of inequalities. We analyzed how negative numbers affect our process, and also learned how to solve linear inequalities and graph them.

1.4.10   Practice

1. For each of the following two values, circle which one is greater:

    (a) 7^2 or 5^2

    (b) $\frac{1}{5}$ or $\frac{1}{2}$

    (c) $\sqrt{456789}$ or $\sqrt{456787}$

    (d) $\frac{52633}{52634}$ or $\frac{52635}{52636}$

2. Solve the following inequality: $3x - 4 > 10$

3. Solve the following inequality: $4.5x + 10 \le 55$

4. Solve the following inequality chain: $2x - 4 < 4x + 10 < 3x + 20$

5. Graph the following inequality in the space below: $-3x \le y - 3$

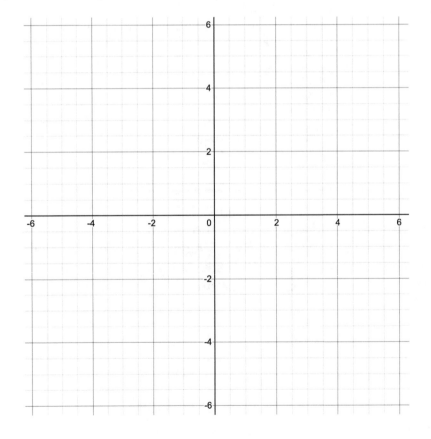

1.5 Ratios, Percents, and Proportions

1.5.1 Introduction

Ratios, percents, and proportions all tell us the relative size of quantities that are being compared. On its own, a ratio does not provide any information about the actual size of the quantities; just how they compare to each other. For example, say we have a car dealership where the ratio of cars to trucks is 4 to 5. This means that for every 4 cars at the dealership, there are 5 trucks. We can write this in a variety of ways, including 4 to 5, $\frac{4}{5}$, or $4:5$. These notations all mean the same thing.

Percent translates to "per hundred," and is a quick way of expressing the ratio of a number to 100. An example would be 50%, which translates to 50 out of 100.

Proportions are another way of expressing how quantities relate to another, but they are best explained through problems, as we'll see later on.

1.5.2 We have a car dealership where the ratio of cars to trucks is 4 to 5. There are 108 cars and trucks at the dealership, in total. How many of the 108 are cars?

This is the same example we presented in the introduction. There are 4 cars for every 5 trucks, so we can think of the entire quantity of vehicles as groups of 9 vehicles, with 4 cars and 5 trucks in every group. There are 108 vehicles in total, so there must be $\frac{108}{9} = 12$ groups in total. We know that for every group, there are 4 cars, and we have 12 groups, so the total number of cars we have must be

$$12 \times 4 = 48.$$

1.5.3 We have a bag containing marbles of each color of the rainbow, with the ratio red : orange : yellow : green : blue : indigo : purple being $3:4:7:2:5:1:5$. The total number of marbles in the bag is 189. How many of the marbles are either yellow or blue?

This problem is a little more complicated, just by the sheer size of the data we're given. Let's work through it step by step.

We can begin as we did the previous problem: separating the total into groups that contain the number of marbles given by the ratio. We can find the size of this group by adding up the elements of the ratio, giving us a size of

$$3 + 4 + 7 + 2 + 5 + 1 + 5 = 27.$$

This gives us that the number of groups in 189 marbles is

$$\frac{189}{27} = 7.$$

We want to find the number of yellow or blue marbles; for every group of 27 marbles, there are $7+5 = 12$ yellow or blue ones. Therefore, the number of yellow or blue marbles we have is equal to

$$7 \times 12 = 84.$$

1.5.4   What is the ratio of x to y if $\frac{10x-3y}{13x-2y} = \frac{3}{5}$?   (Source: MATHCOUNTS)

Let's clean this problem up a little bit by getting rid of the fractions. Multiplying both sides by $(13x - 2y)$ and 5 gives us

$$\frac{10x - 3y}{13x - 2y} \times (13x - 2y) \times (5) = \frac{3}{5} \times (13x - 2y) \times (5) \longrightarrow 5(10x - 3y) = 3(13x - 2y)$$

$$\longrightarrow 50x - 15y = 39x - 6y.$$

Now our objective is to get the variables of each type by themselves, which means getting the x's on one side and the y's on the other. Adding $15y$ to both sides and subtracting $39x$ from both sides will do this for us, giving:

$$(50x - 15y) + 15y - 39x = (39x - 6y) + 15y - 39x \longrightarrow 11x = 9y.$$

We want to get our values in terms of x and y with coefficients of 1, so we can divide both sides by 11 and y, giving us

$$\frac{11x}{11 \times y} = \frac{9y}{11 \times y} \longrightarrow \frac{x}{y} = \frac{9}{11}.$$

We have our answer! The ratio of x to y is simply $\frac{9}{11}$.

1.5.5   A soccer team lost $\frac{3}{14}$ of its games this past season. If the number of games lost was 16 less than the number of games won, how many games did the team play in total during the season?

First off, we must notice that if the team lost $\frac{3}{14}$ of their games, that means they won $1 - \frac{3}{14} = \frac{11}{14}$ of their games. The problem tells us that the number of games lost was 16 less than the number of games won. Let's let the total number of games played equal x. This information gives us that

$$\frac{11}{14}x - \frac{3}{14}x = 16 \longrightarrow \frac{8}{14}x = \frac{4}{7}x = 16.$$

Multiplying both sides by 7 gives us

$$\frac{4}{7}x \times 7 = 16 \times 7 \longrightarrow 4x = 112.$$

Dividing both sides by 4 gives us that

$$\frac{4x}{4} = \frac{112}{4} \longrightarrow x = 28.$$

Therefore, the team played 28 games in total.

> **IMPORTANT:** This problem is a great example of how linear equations play a role in many problems of other types. Knowing how to set up a linear equation is an essential tool for solving many problems, including those involving ratios, percents, and proportions. Know your linear equations!

So far, we've only looked at ratios. Let's try some percentage problems.

1.5.6 What number is 40% of 250?

We know that percent means out of 100, so 40% means 40 out of 100. We can set up some ratios to compare, using x as the value to represent 40% of 250. We have that 40% translates to $\frac{40}{100}$, which is in turn equal to $\frac{x}{250}$. This gives us the equation

$$\frac{40}{100} = \frac{x}{250}.$$

Multiplying both sides by 250 gives us that

$$\frac{40}{100} \times 250 \frac{x}{250} \times 250 \longrightarrow \frac{10,000}{100} = x \longrightarrow 100 = x.$$

Thus, we have that 40% of 250 is 100.

1.5.7 The state income tax where Kristin lives is charged at the rate of $p\%$ of the first $28,000$ of annual income plus $(p+2)\%$ of any amount above $28,000$. Kristin noticed that the state income tax she paid amounted to $(p+0.25)\%$ of her annual income. What was her annual income? *(Source: AMC 12)*

Let's set x equal to the amount over $28,000$ that Kristin's income was. Then we have that the total tax she paid should be equal to

$$\frac{p}{100} \times 28,000 + \frac{p+2}{100}x.$$

The problem tells us that we can set that value equal to $(p+0.25)\%$ of her total annual income, which we know is $28,000 + x$. This gives us that

$$\frac{p}{100} \times 28,000 + \frac{p+2}{100}x = \frac{p+0.25}{100} \times (28,000 + x).$$

Expanding out the values in the equation gives us that

$$280p + \frac{p+2}{100}x = \frac{28,000p + 7,000 + xp + 0.25x}{100}$$

$$\longrightarrow 280p + \frac{p+2}{100}x = 280p + 70 + \frac{xp + 0.25x}{100}.$$

Subtracting $280p$ from both sides gives us

$$(280 + \frac{p+2}{100}x) - 280p = 280p + 70 + \frac{xp + 0.25x}{100} - 280p \longrightarrow \frac{p+2}{100}x = 70 + \frac{xp + 0.25x}{100}.$$

Multiplying both sides by 100 gives

$$(p+2)x = 7000 + xp + 0.25x.$$

Subtracting $(xp + 0.25x)$ from both sides gives

$$(p+2)x - xp - 0.25x = (7000 + xp + 0.25x) - xp - 0.25x \longrightarrow (p+2)x - xp - 0.25x = 7000.$$

Factoring an x from all terms on the left gives us

$$(p + 2 - p - 0.25)x = 7000 \longrightarrow 1.75x = 7000.$$

Dividing both sides by 1.75 gives

$$\frac{1.75x}{1.75} = \frac{7000}{1.75} \longrightarrow x = 4000.$$

Since x is the amount over $28,000$ that Kristin made, her total annual income would be $\$28,000 + \$4,000 = \$32,000$.

That was long! Still, working step-by-step led us to the answer.

That's it for ratios and percents - time to look at proportions. We can start by introducing the two basic concepts we'll be studying:

> *Direct Proportion:* if x and y are directly proportional, then $\frac{x}{y}$ is a constant.
>
> *Indirect Proportion:* if x and y are indirectly proportional, then xy is a constant.

1.5.8 If x and y are directly proportional and $x = 2$ when $y = 8$, when what is y when $x = 6$? What would y be if they were indirectly proportional and $x = 6$?

If x and y are directly proportional, then $\frac{x}{y} = \frac{2}{8} = \frac{1}{4}$. This allows us to set up the equation

$$\frac{6}{y} = \frac{1}{4}.$$

Multiplying both sides by y gives us

$$\frac{6}{y} \times y = \frac{1}{4} \times y \longrightarrow 6 = \frac{y}{4}.$$

Multiplying both sides by 4 gives

$$6 \times 4 = \frac{y}{4} \times 4 \longrightarrow 24 = y.$$

Thus, $y = 24$ when $x = 6$ if the two are directly proportional. We can verify this by calculating their ratio, which is $\frac{6}{24} = \frac{1}{4}$. This is consistent with the original values we were given in the problem, so our answer is correct.

If they are indirectly proportional, we know that xy is a constant value. Using the values given in the problem, we see that

$$xy = 2 \times 8 = 16.$$

This allows us to set up the equation

$$6y = 16.$$

Simply dividing both sides by 6 gives us that

$$\frac{6y}{6} = \frac{16}{6} \longrightarrow y = \frac{16}{6} = \frac{8}{3}.$$

Multiplying $6 \times \frac{8}{3} = 16$ tells us that we got the right answer!

> **IMPORTANT: A great way to check your answers is to plug them back into what you know should be a true statement. If the statement holds, you did it right!**

1.5.9 6 people can paint a wall in an hour. How long would it take 24 people to paint the same wall, assuming that all the people work at the same rate?

We need to analyze the problem a bit to see whether we have a direct or indirect proportion; logically, more workers would mean that the time would decrease. This indicates that it should be an indirect proportion.

> **IMPORTANT: A good clue to whether a relationship is direct or indirect is how the values change relative to each other; if one increases and the other increases as well, it is probably direct. Conversely, if one increases and the other decreases in response, it is probably indirect.**

Now we can set up our proportion. We've identified that this is an indirect proportion, so the product of people $\times$ hours should stay constant. The problem tells us that this value should be $6 \times 1 = 6$. This allows us to set up the equation

$$24t = 6.$$

Dividing both sides by 24 gives us

$$\frac{24t}{24} = \frac{6}{24} \longrightarrow t = \frac{1}{4}.$$

Therefore, it would take 24 people a quarter of an hour to paint the wall.

1.5.10   Conclusion

In this section, we explored ratios, percents, and proportions. The ratio of two quantities shows how they compare relatively to each other, and can be expressed in the form x to y, $x : y$, or $\frac{x}{y}$. A percentage is an easy way to express the ratio of a number to 100. When it comes to proportions, we saw that in direct proportions between x and y, the value $\frac{x}{y}$ is constant. With indirect proportions, xy is a constant.

1.5.11   Practice

1. The ratio of peanuts to almonds in a nut mix is $5 : 7$. There are a total of 96 peanuts and almonds in the mix. How many almonds are in the mix?

2. Mia got 85% of the questions on her test right. If she got 6 questions wrong, how many questions were on the test in total?

3. There are 2 boxes of blocks. 50% of the blocks in the first box are blue, and 10% of the blocks in the second box are blue. The second box has twice as many blocks as the first. What percentage of the total number of blocks are not blue? Round to the first decimal place.

4. A math competition has 5 levels. 20 students compete in the first level, $\frac{1}{5}$ of them compete in the second level, $\frac{1}{4}$ in the third, $\frac{2}{7}$ in the fourth, and $\frac{1}{4}$ in the fifth. How many competitors are there, in total?

5. Each tile measuring 1 square foot costs 24. How much will it cost to tile a 180 square foot floor?

6. Cassandra sets her watch to the correct time at noon. At the actual time of $1 : 00$ PM, she notices that her watch reads $12 : 57$ and 36 seconds. Assuming that her watch loses time at a constant rate, what will be the actual time when her watch first reads $10 : 00$ PM? *(Source: AMC 12)*

7. On a world map, 2 inches represents 35 miles. How long would a real-life distance of 945 miles be on the map, in inches?

8. 30 workers can build 10 cars in 4 days. How long would it take 48 workers working at the same rate to build 15 cars?

9. Isa drove at a rate of 40 miles per hour to her friend's house. On the way home, how fast must she travel in order to average 35 miles per hour for the whole trip?

1.6   Introduction to Quadratics

1.6.1   Introduction

Quadratics are equations of the form

$$ax^2 + bx + c,$$

where a, b, and c are constants, known as the coefficients of the expression. Similarly to how we solved linear equations by isolating the variable, we solve quadratics by getting x on its own. However, it's somewhat more complicated here.

1.6.2   What values of x satisfy the equation $x^2 = 25$?

We can easily isolate x by taking the square root of both sides, giving us

$$\sqrt{x^2} = \sqrt{25} \longrightarrow x = \sqrt{25}.$$

We know the square root of 25 is 5, so we might be tempted to just say that the only solution is $x = 5$. However, when dealing with quadratics, we must always remember to consider the negative values; $(-5)^2$ is also equal to 25. Thus, our two solutions to the equation are $x = -5, 5$.

> IMPORTANT: When taking a square root, never forget the negative root!

1.6.3   What values of x satisfy the equation $3x^2 - 363 = 0$?

Let's try isolating the variable again: adding 363 to both sides gives us

$$(3x^2 - 363) + 363 = 0 + 363 \longrightarrow 3x^2 = 363.$$

Dividing both sides by 3 gives us

$$\frac{3x^2}{3} = \frac{363}{3} \longrightarrow x^2 = 121.$$

Taking the square root of both sides tells us that $x = -11, 11$.

Referring back to our form for a quadratic equation $(ax^2 + bx + c)$, it's clear that isolating the variable works just fine when there is no bx term. What if there was one?

1.6.4   Solve the equation $x^2 - 8x = 0$ for x.

We might think that isolating the variable would work here. Following that approach tells us to add $8x$ to both sides, giving us $x^2 = 8x$. Dividing both sides by x gives us the answer that $x = 8$. However, this is not quite true. Just by guess-and-check, we can see that another solution to the equation is $x = 0$. However, if we follow the same isolation technique with $x = 0$, we have to divide by 0 when taking the step to go from $x^2 = 8x$ to $x = 8$. This is illegal! So what can we do?

Instead, we can take our original equation and factor out the x, giving us

$$x^2 - 8x = x(x - 8) = 0.$$

We know that if two quantities multiply to 0, at least one of them must equal 0. Thus, we have two cases: either $x = 0$, or $x - 8 = 0$. The first case is easy; $x = 0$ is the solution. For the second, we simply solve the linear equation by isolation, adding 8 to both sides to give us

$$(x - 8) + 8 = 0 + 8 \longrightarrow x = 8.$$

Therefore, the two solutions to our equation are $x = 0, 8$.

> **IMPORTANT: The basic approach to solving most quadratic equations is to rewrite the equation as a product of terms that equals 0. Every value that makes one of the terms equal to 0 is a solution to the equation.**

1.6.5   Expand the expression $(x + 2)(x + 3)$.

To expand the expression, we must multiply each term in the first part of the expression by each term in the second part. This process goes as follows:

$$(x + 2)(x + 3) = x(x + 3) + 2(x + 3) = (x)(x) + (x)(3) + (2)(x) + (2)(3)$$

$$= x^2 + 3x + 2x + 6 = x^2 + 5x + 6.$$

> **IMPORTANT: When multiplying expressions that are sums/differences of terms, we multiply every term in the first expression by every term in the second. The sum of the resulting products is the expansion.**

1.6.6   What are the solutions to the equation $x^2 + 5x + 6 = 0$?

We need to rewrite the expression $x^2 + 5x + 6$ as a product, and luckily, the problem above tells us how. We have that $x^2 + 5x + 6 = (x + 2)(x + 3) = 0$. From here, we know that either $x + 2 = 0$ or $x + 3 = 0$, so x must be either -2 or -3.

1.6.7 Factor the expression x^2+4x+3 into the form $(x+r)(x+s)$. What are the solutions to the equation $x^2 + 4x + 3 = 0$?

Let's start by expanding $(x + r)(x + s)$. This gives us

$$(x + r)(x + s) \longrightarrow x(x + s) + r(x + s) \longrightarrow (x)(x) + (x)(s) + (r)(x) + (r)(s)$$

$$\longrightarrow x^2 + sx + rx + rs \longrightarrow x^2 + (s + r)x + rs.$$

Effectively, for a quadratic in the form $x^2 + bx + c$, $r + s = b$, and $rs = c$. Comparing this to our given expression, $x^2 + 4x + 3$, we see that $s + r$ must equal 4, and rs must equal 3. Using guess and check, we need to find two numbers that add up to 4, and multiply out to 3. This gives us that r and s must be 3 and 1, or 1 and 3. Therefore, we can rewrite $x^2 + 4x + 3$ as

$$(x + 3)(x + 1).$$

Now, we must solve the equation

$$(x + 3)(x + 1) = 0.$$

We know that either $x + 3 = 0$, or $x + 1 = 0$, so we have that $x = -3, -1$. These are the solutions to the equation. (Solutions to a quadratic are often also called the **roots**.)

> **IMPORTANT: For a quadratic in the form $x^2 + bx + c$, factored as $(x + r)(x + s)$, we know that $r + s = b$, and $rs = c$.**

1.6.8 Find the roots of the equation $x^2 - 15x + 56 = 0$.

Let's try our hand at factoring again. Using the form $(x + r)(x + s)$ and knowing that $x^2 + (s + r)x + rs = x^2 - 15x + 56$, we can once again use guess and check to find numbers that sum to -15, and multiply out to 56. This tells us that r and s are -7 and -8. Thus, we have that

$$x^2 - 15x + 56 = (x - 7)(x - 8) = 0.$$

$x - 7 = 0$ or $x - 8 = 0$, so we have that $x = 7, 8$.

> **IMPORTANT: If you haven't had much experience working with quadratics before, it might take you a while to do all the factoring and guessing the values of r and s. That's completely ok! This is a skill that comes with practice. Do lots of practice problems for factoring, and you'll master it in due time.**

Let's do one more example here. The rest is up to you to practice!

1.6.9 Find all roots to the following equation: $x^2 + 6x - 16 = 0$.

Once again using the form $(x + r)(x + s)$, we see that $r + 2 = 6$, and $r - 2 = -16$. In this case, we know that either r or s must be negative, but not both. This is because the only way to get a negative product from two numbers is if only one of them is also negative. Using guess and check to assess our options, we see that r and s must be 8 and -2. Therefore, we have that

$$x^2 + 6x - 16 = (x + 8)(x - 2),$$

so the two roots are solutions to $x + 8 = 0$ and $x - 2 = 0$. This gives us roots of $x = -8, 2$.

So far, all of our examples have had $a = 1$ in quadratics of the form $ax^2 + bx + c$. Let's see some examples where $a \neq 1$.

1.6.10 Find the roots to the equation $2x^2 + 7x + 6 = 0$.

In this case, $a = 2$. The only way we can get a product of 2 is if we have 1×2. (We don't need to consider negative numbers in this case.) This gives us a quadratic of the form $(2x + r)(x + s) = 2x^2 + 7x + 6$. Expanding our product gives us

$$(2x + r)(x + s) = 2x(x + s) + r(x + s) = (2x)(x) + (2x)(s) + (r)(x) + (r)(s)$$

$$= 2x^2 + 2xs + rx + rs = 2x^2 + (2s + r)x + rs.$$

This tells us that $2s + r = 7$, and $rs = 6$. Now it's time for more guess and check: from that, we can get that $s = 2$, and $r = 3$. This gives us the factored quadratic

$$2x^2 + 7x + 6 = (2x + 3)(x + 2).$$

From here, we see that our roots are the solutions to the equations $2x + 3 = 0$ and $x + 2 = 0$, which are $x = -\frac{3}{2}$ and -2, respectively. Thus, those are our roots!

> **IMPORTANT: When factoring a quadratic where $a \neq 1$, it's important to check how the relationship between r, s, b, and c changes.**

1.6.11 Find all roots to the equation $6x^2 + 9x - 15 = 0$.

Once again, in this case, $a \neq 1$. Some possible factors that have a product of 6 are 1×6, and 2×3. Since we have a few possible choices, let's generalize our factorization into something of the form $(Ax + r)(Bx + s)$. Expanding this out gives us

$$(Ax+r)(Bx+s) = Ax(Bx+s)+r(Bx+s) = (Ax)(Bx)+(Ax)(s)+(r)(Bx)+(r)(s)$$

$$= ABx^2 + Asx + Brx + rs = ABx^2 + (As + Br)x + rs.$$

From this expansion, we can get several relationships: we now know that

$$AB = 6, rs = -15, \text{ and } As + Br = 9.$$

From the fact that $rs = -15$, we see that both r and s must be odd, and one of them must be negative. We also know that since r and s are odd, and $As + Br$ is also odd, then one of A or B is also odd. These are all important clues that can lead us to the correct factorization.

Let's try $A = 1$ and $B = 6$. This gives us $6x^2 + 9x - 15 = (x + r)(6x + s)$. Expanding the right side gives us

$$(x + r)(6x + s) = 6x^2 + sx + 6rx + rs = 6x^2 + (6r + s)x + rs.$$

We can guess and check for quite some time for values of r and s that satisfy this equation, but unfortunately we won't find any. It's time to try $A = 2$ and $B = 3$. This gives us $(2x + r)(3x + s)$, which expands out to

$$6x^2 + 2sx + 3rx + rs = 6x^2 + (2s + 3r)x + rs.$$

Guess and check this time yields results: $r = 5$ and $s = -3$ work! Finally, we have that

$$6x^2 + 9x - 15 = (2x + 5)(3x - 3).$$

Solving $2x + 5 = 0$ and $3x - 3 = 0$ for x yields the roots: $x = -\frac{5}{2}, 1$.

Alternatively: We could have noticed that we can factor a 3 out of our original equation to get

$$6x^2 + 9x - 15 = 3(2x^2 + 3x - 5) = 0 \longrightarrow 2x^2 + 3x - 5 = 0.$$

We could have taken this approach, and then completed this arguably simpler factorization from that point on. While this is valid, now you have been exposed to a more complex quadratic, and the process through which it can be factored!

Now it's time for an introduction to some special factorizations that are likely to crop up time and again.

1.6.12   Expand the products $(x+2)^2, (x+3)^2,$ and $(3x+4)^2$.

This should be simple. Let's dive in!

$$(x + 2)^2 = (x + 2)(x + 2) = x(x + 2) + 2(x + 2) = (x)(x) + (x)(2) + (2)(x) + (2)(2)$$

$$= x^2 + 2x + 2x + 4 = x^2 + 4x + 4$$

$$(x + 3)^2 = (x + 3)(x + 3) = x(x + 3) + 3(x + 3) = (x)(x) + (x)(3) + (3)(x) + (3)(3)$$

$$= x^2 + 3x + 3x + 9 = x^2 + 6x + 9$$

$$(3x + 4)^2 = (3x + 4)(3x + 4) = 3x(3x + 4) + 4(3x + 4)$$

$$= (3x)(3x) + (3x)(4) + (4)(3x) + (4)(4) = 9x^2 + 12x + 12x + 16 = 9x^2 + 24x + 16)$$

Notice anything special about how those expansions worked out? Turns out, there's a formula that explains these similarities! Taking a closer look at the generalization for the square of some $(a + b)$, we see that

$$(a + b)^2 = (a + b)(a + b) = a(a + b) + b(a + b) = (a)(a) + (a)(b) + (b)(a) + (b)(b)$$

$$= a^2 + ab + ab + b^2 = a^2 + 2ab + b^2.$$

This is the formula for the **square of a binomial**, where a binomial is any expression of the form $(a + b)$ for some a and b.

> **IMPORTANT: The formula for the square of a binomial, $(a + b)$, is $(a + b)^2 = a^2 + 2ab + b^2$. This is incredibly important, as recognizing this relationship makes solving many problems both quicker and easier to do without mistakes. Don't just memorize the formula; understand it's derivation so that you can apply it as effectively as possible.**

1.6.13 Factor the quadratics $x^2 - 1, x^2 - 4, and x^2 - 81$.

Let's tackle these one by one.

$$x^2 - 1 = (x + 1)(x - 1)$$

$$x^2 - 4 = (x + 2)(x - 2)$$

$$x^2 - 81 = (x + 9)(x - 9)$$

We have another pattern! This leads us to another formula in terms of some a and b:

$$a^2 - b^2 = (a + b)(a - b).$$

This formula is known as the **difference of squares**.

> **IMPORTANT: The difference of squares is another formula that is crucial: $a^2 - b^2 = (a + b)(a - b)$. Once again, don't just memorize this formula; understand it and know when to apply it.**

1.6.14   Calculate $16^2 - 4^2$.

At face value, this is quite a simple calculation that we could do, given maybe about half a minute. However, we can do it in seconds if we use the difference of squares.

Using that relationship, we can write

$$16^2 - 4^2 = (16 + 4)(16 - 4) = (20)(12) = 240.$$

And that's it! That's our answer, and that's how quickly we got it. You can see how valuable knowing this relationship and how to use it can be when it comes to speed and accuracy.

Now that we've seen the square of a binomial and difference of squares, let's take a look at one more: Simon's Favorite Factoring Trick!

1.6.15   Find all pairs of integers x and y that satisfy the equation $xy - 7x + 3y = 70$.

To solve this problem, we need to factor the left side. It should end up in the form $(x + a)(y + b)$, where a and b are integers.

The expansion of this product must have a xy term, which it definitely will. It must also have a $3y$ term, which we can get by making a equal to 3. We also need a $-7x$ term, so b has to be -7. This gives us

$$(x + 3)(y - 7).$$

Expanding this gives us

$$(x + 3)(y - 7) = xy + 3y - 7x - 21,$$

and we know that $xy - 7x + 3y = 70$, so $xy + 3y - 7x - 21$ must equal $70 - 21 = 49$. Thus, we have

$$(x + 3)(y - 7) = 49.$$

Now we just need to find integers $x + 3$ and $y - 7$ that multiply to 49. The only possible ways to get 49 as a product of integers is if we have $1 \times 49, (-1) \times (-49), 7 \times 7$, or $(-7) \times (-7)$. We thus have 7 solutions:

$$x + 3 = 49, y - 7 = 1$$

$$x + 3 = -49, y - 7 = -1$$

$$x + 3 = 7, y - 7 = 7$$

$$x + 3 = 1, y - 7 = 49$$

$$x + 3 = -1, y - 7 = -49$$

$$x + 3 = -7, y - 7 = -7$$

Solving these 6 cases gives us the solutions $(x, y) = (46, 8); (-52, 6); (4, 14); (-2, 56);$ $(-4, -42); (-10, 0).$

IMPORTANT: Simon's Favorite Factoring Trick, named for the Art of Problem Solving Member Simon Rubinstein-Salzedo, is a great way to factor expressions that look like they can't be factored "traditionally." It states that

$$ab + ay + bx + by = (a + x)(b + y).$$

1.6.16   Conclusion

In this section, we learned about quadratics: equations of the form $ax^2 + bx + c$. We saw how to expand factored forms, how to factor from expanded form, and special tricks for how to factor, including the square of a binomial, difference of squares, and Simon's Favorite Factoring Trick. Most crucial with quadratics in particular is practice! Solving them is not a skill that comes naturally to many, so practice is so, so important.

1.6.17   Practice

1. Expand the following expressions:

   (a) $(x + 2)(x + 4)$

   (b) $(x + 3)(x - 5)$

   (c) $(x - 2)(x - 6)$

   (d) $(2x - 2)(x + 7)$

   (e) $(3x - 3)(x - 9)$

   (f) $(x + 4)(4x - 3)$

2. Find all solutions to the following equations:

   (a) $x^2 - 3x + 2 = 0$

   (b) $x^2 + 4x + 3 = 0$

   (c) $x^2 - 5x + 6 = 0$

   (d) $x^2 + x - 2 = 0$

   (e) $2x^2 - 5x - 3 = 0$

   (f) $8x^2 - 12x - 8 = 0$

3. Find all solutions to the equation $\sqrt{x + 7} + x = 13$. *(Source: UNCC)*

4. Expand the following expressions:

   (a) $(x + 4)^2$

   (b) $(2x + 5)^2$

   (c) $(x - 16)^2$

5. Factor each of the following expressions:

   (a) $x^2 - 144$

   (b) $x^2 - 289$

   (c) $4x^2 - 121$

6. Calculate the value of $301^2 - 99^2$.

7. Factor each of the folloiwng expressions:

   (a) $xy - 7x + 9y - 63$

   (b) $-xy + 5x + 2y - 10$

1.7 Complex Numbers

1.7.1 Introduction

Before delving into the realm of complex numbers, we must first understand what an imaginary number is. An imaginary number is any number whose square is a real number that is not positive. The most basic of all imaginary numbers is i, where $i = \sqrt{-1}$. This concept can be a bit difficult to understand, so let's do a few examples.

1.7.2 Simplify each of the following expressions:

1. i^2

2. i^3

3. i^{10}

4. i^{100}

1. We know that $i = \sqrt{-1}$, so it follows that $i^2 = (\sqrt{-1})^2 = -1$.

2. We can rewrite i^3 as $i^3 = i \times i^2$. We know that $i^2 = -1$, so $i \times i^2 = i \times (-1) = -i$.

3. We can once again use the fact that $i^2 = -1$, and rewrite i^{10} as $i^{10} = (i^2)^5$. This gives us $i^{10} = (i^2)^5 = (-1)^5 = -1$.

4. i^{100} can be rewritten as $i^{100} = (i^2)^{50} = (-1)^{50}$. We know that $(-1)^2 = 1$, and we can rewrite $(-1)^{50}$ as $(-1)^{50} = [(-1)^2]^{25} = 1^{25} = 1$.

> **IMPORTANT: When working with powers of i, rewriting them in terms of powers of i that we know values of is a good strategy.**

1.7.3 Find all solutions to the following equation: $x^2 = -36$.

Taking the square root of both sides gives us
$$\sqrt{x^2} = \sqrt{-36} = \sqrt{36} \times \sqrt{-1} = 6i \text{ or } -6i.$$
We can rewrite this as the solutions are $\pm 6i$.

Now that we know what imaginary numbers are, we can explore complex numbers. Complex numbers are all numbers that can be expressed as a sum of a real number and an imaginary number. Examples include $2 + 4i, 6 + 5i, 1 + i, and 4 - i$. Additionally, all real numbers as well as all imaginary numbers are included in the definition of complex numbers. This is because real numbers can be expressed as real number $+ 0i$, and similarly, imaginary numbers can be expressed as $0 +$ imaginary number. By convention, the real part of the number goes first. Complex numbers can be added by combining the real numbers and imaginary numbers separately. For example, $(4 + 3i) + (5 - 4i) = (4 + 5) + (3i - 4i) = 9 - i$.

1.7.4   Simplify the following expression: $(75+37i)-(56-4i)$.

As we did above, we can combine the real and imaginary terms separately:

$$(75+37i) - (56-4i) = (75-56) + (37i - (-4i)) = (75-56) + (37i+4i) = 19+41i.$$

1.7.5   Expand the following product: $(2-3i)(8+2i)$.

When multiplying complex numbers, the process is very similar as to expanding a factored quadratic. We simply multiply each term in the first complex number by each term in the second, like so:

$$(2-3i)(8+2i) = 2(8+2i) + (-3i)(8+2i) = (2)(8) + (2)(2i) + (-3i)(8) + (-3i)(2i)$$

$$= 16 + 4i + (-24i) + (-6i^2) = 16 - 20i - 6i^2.$$

But wait! We're not done. We know that $i^2 = -1$, so we can rewrite our final answer as

$$16 - 20i - 6(-1) = 16 - 20i + 6 = 22 - 20i.$$

> **IMPORTANT: Multiplying complex numbers is like expanding a factored polynomial. Make sure to full simplify any terms that contain powers of i.**

1.7.6   Expand the following product: $(2+3i)(2-3i)$.

Expanding, we get

$$(2+3i)(2-3i) = 2(2-3i) + 3i(2-3i) = (2)(2) + (2)(-3i) + (3i)(2) + (3i)(-3i)$$

$$= 4 + (-6i) + 6i - 9i^2 = 4 - 9i^2 = 4 - 9(-1) = 4 + 9 = 13.$$

There's something special about this product; it has no imaginary portion! Our end result was solely a real number. This is not a coincidence.

$2 - 3i$ was the complex **conjugate** of $2 + 3i$, in that the sign of the imaginary part of the original complex number was reversed.

> **IMPORTANT: The conjugate of a complex number $a+bi$ is $a-bi$. The conjugate of a complex number z is denoted as $\overline{z}$. The product of a complex number and its conjugate is always a real number.**

1.7.7   Conclusion

In this section, we learned about complex numbers, which comprise a real and imaginary part. Imaginary numbers are based on i, the square root of -1. We learned how to add complex numbers, multiply them, and how to work with their conjugates.

1.7.8 Practice

1. Find the value of $(2i)^2$.

2. Find the value of $-(3i)^2$.

3. Find the values of $(\frac{i}{4})^3$.

4. Find the value of $(-5i)^4$.

5. Computer i^{994}.

6. Simplify the following expression: $(3 + 40i) + (37 - 4i)$.

7. Simplify the following expression: $(-2 + 8i)(-4 - 2i)$.

8. Simplify the following expression: $(1 + 2i)(1 - 3i)(2 + 8i)$.

1.8   More Quadratics!

1.8.1   Introduction

We've had a nice introduction to quadratics, but now it's time to learn a few more techniques, making use of what we learned in complex numbers.

1.8.2   Find all solutions to the equation $x^2 - 14x + 51 = 0$.

We can try as much as we want, but there is no way to factor this equation in a way that would be useful for us. Here is where we learn a new technique: **completing the square**.

> **IMPORTANT: Completing the square is a technique of adding a constant term to a quadratic term (ax^2) and linear term (bx) so that the result is a perfect square.**

Let's see how to complete the square. We know that

$$(a + b)^2 = a^2 + 2ab + b^2,$$

so let's see where the terms in $x^2 - 14x + 51$ fit into that form. We see that in this case, $a^2 = x^2$, and $-14x = 2ab$. From here, we can see that $a = x$, so $-14x = 2(x)(b) \longrightarrow -14 = 2b \longrightarrow b = -7$. Thus, we see that the square we want to end up with is

$$(x - 7)^2 = x^2 - 14x + 49.$$

However, it's obvious that the expression we have is not exactly the same;

$$x^2 - 14x + 51 \neq x^2 - 14x + 49.$$

What can we do to make the left side equal the right? Well, adding 2 to the right side gives us

$$x^2 - 14x + 51 = x^2 - 14x + 49 + 2.$$

Therefore, we have that $x^2 - 14x + 51 = (x - 7)^2 + 2$. Now, our original equation has become

$$(x - 7)^2 + 2 = 0.$$

Subtracting 2 from both sides gets us

$$(x - 7)^2 = -2.$$

Taking the square root of both sides tells us that

$$x - 7 = \pm\sqrt{-2} = \pm i\sqrt{2}.$$

To finally isolate x, we add 7 to both sides, giving us the final solution that $x = 7 \pm i\sqrt{2}$.

1.8.3 Solve the following equation by completing the square: $4x^2 - 16x + 19 = 0$.

Once again, we can use the form $(a + b)^2 = a^2 + 2ab + b^2$ to guide us. We see that $a^2 = 4x^2 \longrightarrow a = 2x$. Similarly, we know that $2ab = -16x \longrightarrow 2(2x)(b) = -16x \longrightarrow 4b = -16 \longrightarrow b = -4$. This tells us that the binomial we're looking to square is $(2x - 4)$. Expanding the square gives us that

$$(2x - 4)^2 = 4x^2 - 16x + 16.$$

Looking at how this compares to $4x^2 - 16x + 19$, we see that

$$4x^2 - 16x + 16 + 3 = 4x^2 - 16x + 19 \longrightarrow (2x - 4)^2 + 3 = 4x^2 - 16x + 19 = 0.$$

Now we have that $(2x-4)^2+3 = 0$. Subtracting 3 from both sides gets us $(2x-4)^2 = -3$. Taking the square root of both sides gives us $2x - 4 = \pm\sqrt{-3} = \pm i\sqrt{3}$. Adding 4 to both sides gives us $2x = 4 \pm i\sqrt{3}$. Finally, dividing by 2 gives us $x = \frac{4 \pm i\sqrt{3}}{2}$.

Now onto the last technique we'll be exploring for solving quadratics: the quadratic formula!

> **IMPORTANT: For** any quadratic equation $ax^2 + bx + c = 0$, **the roots are equal to** $\frac{-b \pm \sqrt{b^2 - 4ac}}{2a}$. **This equation you should have memorized, but you will likely do so many problems using it that you'll memorize it without any extra effort.**

The quadratic formula can be a very powerful tool to solve quadratics, but it can be relatively time-consuming. As such, it is best not to turn straight to the quadratic formula when confronted with a quadratic equation; mastering the other methods and applying them will likely yield the correct result in a much more efficient manner.

> **IMPORTANT: The quadratic equation should not be the first method to try when solving a quadratic. Other methods, particularly factoring, are often much quicker if you have mastered those skills.**

1.8.4 Find the roots to the following equation: $x^2 - 4x + 1 = 0$.

This equation can't be factored, so let's try using the quadratic formula. Using the form $ax^2 + bx + c$, we see that in our case, $a = 1$, $b = -4$, and $c = 1$. Plugging these into our formula, we get that

$$x = \frac{-(-4) \pm \sqrt{(-4)^2 - 4(1)(1)}}{2(1)} = \frac{4 \pm \sqrt{16 - 4}}{2} = \frac{4 \pm \sqrt{12}}{2} = \frac{4 \pm 2\sqrt{3}}{2} = 2 \pm \sqrt{3}.$$

Now that we've seen the quadratic formula in action, it's time to analyze parts of it that can tell us important information; particularly, the discriminant. The **discriminant** for a quadratic of the form $ax^2 + bx + c$ is equal to $b^2 - 4ac$, or put simply, what is found in the square root in the quadratic formula.

The discriminant can tell us a great deal about the qualities of the roots of the quadratic. If the discriminant is positive, we know that the roots of the quadratic will be real. With no negative square root, there is no possibility of the root having an imaginary portion. Thus, the roots will be real.

Conversely, if the discriminant is negative, we know that the roots of the quadratic will be complex. No matter what, the roots will have an imaginary portion.

That's still not all the discriminant can tell us: if the discriminant is 0, we know yet another piece of information: the quadratic has a **double root**, meaning that both roots are the same. This makes sense logically, as the $\pm$ detail in the formula is what gives the quadratic 2 different roots. Adding or subtracting 0 makes no difference, so the roots will be the same!

The discriminant ($b^2 - 4ac$) of a quadratic equation can reveal useful information about its roots.

Positive discriminant: The quadratic has 2 real roots.

Negative discriminant: The quadratic has 2 complex roots.

Discriminant equal to 0: The quadratic has a double real root; both of its roots are real and the same.

1.8.5   Conclusion

In this section, we saw how quadratics can have complex roots in addition to real roots. We also learned how the discriminant can provide valuable information about the characteristics of a quadratic's roots. The quadratic equation, as we saw, can be a useful tool to solve a quadratic, but factoring and recognizing special quadratics such as differences of squares and squares of binomials should still take precedence.

1.8.6   Practice

1. Solve the following equations for x by completing the square:

    (a) Solve the following equation for x : $x^2 + 6x + 7 = 0$.

    (b) Solve the following equation for x : $9x^2 - 24x + 13 = -6$.

    (c) Solve the following equation for x : $4x^2 + 28x + 45 = -7$.

2. Without solving them, predict how many roots each of the following equations has, and whether or not they will be real:

   (a) $3x^2 - 4x + 7 = 0$

   (b) $5x^2 - 25x + 37 = 0$

   (c) $x^2 + 3x - 2 = 0$

   (d) $x^2 - 12x + 36 = 0$

3. Solve the equations from Question 2 using the quadratic formula.

1.9   Graphing Quadratics

1.9.1   Introduction

Similarly to how linear equations can be graphed on the Cartesian plane, so can quadratics. Quadratics generally take the shape of a **parabola**, which looks a bit like a ⋃, but can also look like ⋂.

1.9.2   Plot the graph of the quadratic equation $y = x^2$.

We don't really know a whole lot about how to graph a quadratic, so let's go back to the basics: we'll plot some points and see where that takes us.

We'll want some points with positive x values as well as negative ones, just so we can see what happens on both sides of the y-axis. The quadratic is simple, so some points we can use that immediately come to mind are $(0,0); (1,1); (-1,1); (2,4); (-2,4); (3,9)$; and $(-3,9)$. Plotting all of these gives us the following graph:

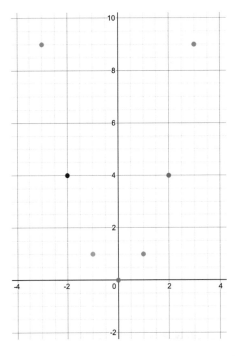

Figure 1.27: Plotted points of $y = x^2$

Drawing lines to roughly connect the points gives us something that looks like this:

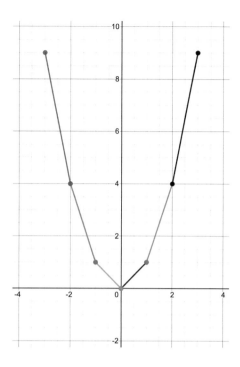

Figure 1.28: Connecting the dots!

Finally, smoothing it out to give us a nice curve leaves us with our final graph:

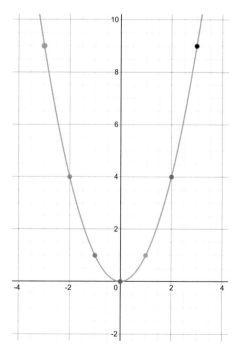

Figure 1.29: Final graph of $y = x^2$

IMPORTANT: When graphing anything, not just lines or quadratics, a good place to start if you're unsure is plotting several points that you know are on the graph.

1.9.3   Graph the quadratic equation $y = 3x^2$.

We'll take a similar approach to this problem: plotting points that we know are on the graph. Noting that compared to $y = x^2$, for every value of x on $y = 3x^2$, the y-value will be 3 times higher. We should expect this to give us a "skinnier" graph, essentially, the same graph as $y = x^2$, except horizontally compressed / vertically stretched. Let's see if what we expect is what we get.

Some points we can plot are $(0, 0)$; $(1, 3)$; $(-1, 3)$; $(2, 12)$; $(-2, 12)$; $(3, 27)$; and $(-3, 27)$. This gives us:

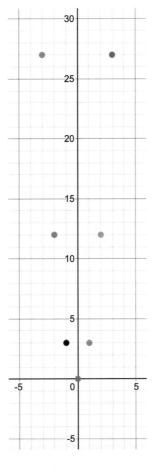

Figure 1.30: Plotted points of $y = 3x^2$

We're already getting what we expected: a horizontally compressed of $y = x^2$. Let's go ahead and try to draw a curve through our points. This gives us:

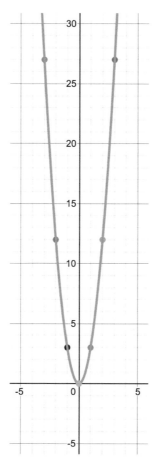

Figure 1.31: Final graph of $y = 3x^2$

As we can see, the end result is what we expected!

> **IMPORTANT: The graph of a quadratic $y = ax^2$ is similar to the graph of $y = x^2$, except the value of a determines the degree to which the graph is horizontally compressed. A higher value of a indicates greater compression, while a lower one indicates lower compression.**

Now we'll see what happens if the coefficient of x^2 is a fraction.

1.9.4   Graph the quadratic equation $y = \frac{x^2}{3}$.

Logically, each y-value for any corresponding x-value will be $\frac{1}{3}$ as great as it would for the same x-value in $y = x^2$, so the graph should be horizontally stretched / vertically compressed. Let's see if this turns out to be true.

Some points we can graph, once again, are $(0,0)$; $(1, \frac{1}{3})$; $(-1, \frac{1}{3})$; $(2, \frac{4}{3})$; $(-2, \frac{4}{3})$; $(3, 3)$; and $(-3, 3)$. Plotting those gives us this outline:

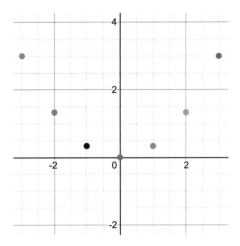

Figure 1.32: Plotted points of $y = \frac{x^2}{3}$

As we can see, the end result is what we expected!

IMPORTANT: For the graph of a quadratic of the form $y = ax^2$, if $0 < a < 1$, the graph is wider compared to $y = x^2$, being horizontally *expanded* instead of compressed.

1.9.5   Graph the quadratic equation $y = -2x^2$.

Ooh, a negative! That's new. Let's see how this changes things. We know from the 2 as a part of the coefficient that this graph should be horizontally compressed compared to $y = x^2$. We can try to guess that the negative would make all y-values on the graph negative. Where did we get this from? Well, squaring anything (real numbers only, of course) results in a positive number, and multiplying a positive number (in this case -2) by a positive number (in this case x^2) is always negative. Therefore, all of our y-values should be negative. Let's see if this holds true.

Our approach remains the same: let's plot some points. Keeping things simple, we have $(0, 0); (1, -2); (-1, -2); (2, -8); (-2, -8); (3, -18);$ and $(-3, -18)$. Plotting these gives us:

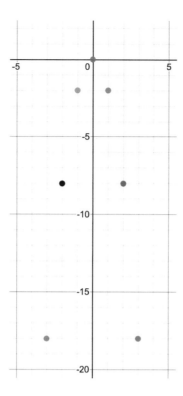

Figure 1.33: Plotted points of $y = -2x^2$

Looks like we might be right! All the points we plotted are below the x-axis, meaning that they have negative y-coordinates. Drawing a smooth curve to connect the dots gives us:

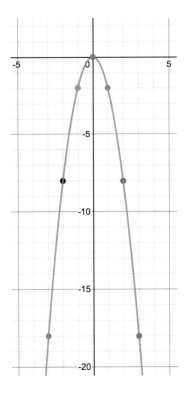

Figure 1.34: Final graph of $y = -2x^2$

As we can see, the negative coefficient of x^2 effectively reflected the graph across the x-axis.

IMPORTANT: For the graph of a quadratic of the form $y = ax^2$, if $a < 0$, the graph will be the same shape as $y = -ax^2$, just reflected across the x-axis.

1.9.6   Graph the quadratic equation $y = x^2 + 3$.

Let's try to guess how this graph is going to look. We know from the x^2 term that our shape should be identical to the graph of $y = x^2$, but what will the $+3$ do? If we think about it, that's going to make every value of y greater by 3 than it would be if the graph were $y = x^2$. As such, we can conjecture that this graph should be the same shape as $y = x^2$, just with all the points shifted up 3 units.

To test our hypothesis, we'll once again plot some points: $(0, 3); (1, 4); (-1, 4); (2, 7);$ $(-2, 7); (3, 12);$ and $(-3, 12)$. Plotting these gives us:

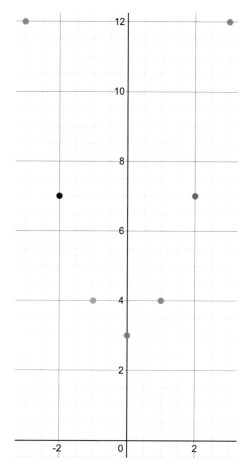

Figure 1.35: Plotted points of $y = x^2 + 3$

We were right! Drawing a smooth curve gives us:

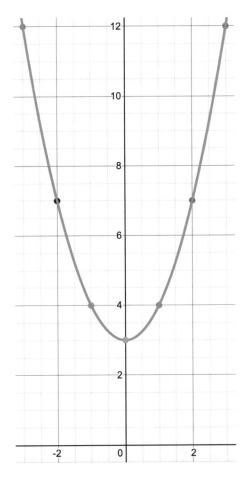

Figure 1.36: Final graph of $y = x^2 + 3$

IMPORTANT: For the graph of a quadratic of the form $y = ax^2 + k$, k denotes a vertical shift of the graph of ax^2, with a larger k indicating a greater magnitude of the shift. A positive k indicates a shift up, while a negative k indicates a shift down.

1.9.7   Graph the quadratic equation $y = (x - 2)^2$.

This will be the last "modification" to the graphs of quadratics that we'll look at. There is a coefficient of just 1 on the x term, so we can expect the graph to hold the same shape as the graph of $y = x^2$. But what will the -2 do?

Well, let's compare to $y = x^2$. Take $x = 2$. On $y = (x - 2)^2$, that will be effectively the same point as $x = 0$ on $y = x^2$. Similarly, for $x = 3$, on $y = (x - 2)^2$, that would map to the same point as $x = 1$ on $y = x^2$. From this, we can guess that the graph might be exactly the same as $y = x^2$, just with all points shifted to the right.

Plotting our points as usual, we get $(0, 4); (1, 1); (2, 0); (3, 1);$ and $(4, 4)$. That gives us these points:

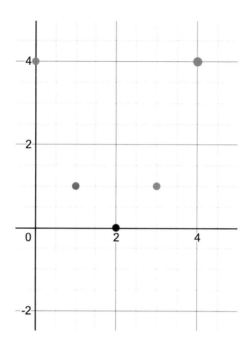

Figure 1.37: Plotted points of $y = (x - 2)^2$

Drawing our smooth curve, we get:

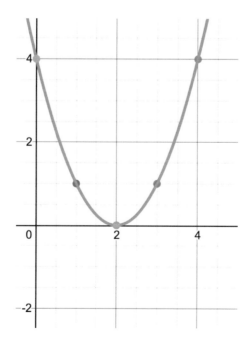

Figure 1.38: Final graph of $y = (x - 2)^2$

We can summarize our findings in one solid set of transformations:

> **IMPORTANT: For the graph of a quadratic equation of the form** $y = a(x - h)^2 + k$, **known as vertex or standard form:**
>
> If a is positive, the parabola opens upward (like a cup); if a is negative, the parabola opens downward (like a rainbow).
>
> The larger a is, the more narrow the graph is.
>
> k denotes the vertical shift of the graph; positive k means an upward shift, while negative k denotes a downward shift.
>
> h denotes horizontal shift. Positive h is a shift to the right, while negative h is a shift to the left. (h, k) is the vertex of the parabola.

1.9.8   Conclusion

In this section, we learned about the graphs of quadratics, better known as parabolas. We saw how these graphs can be transformed, both by stretching them and shifting them.

1.9.9   Practice

1. Graph the following equations on the given graph below:

   (a) $y = (x + 2)^2$

   (b) $y = x^2 - 4$

   (c) $y = -\frac{x^2}{2}$

   (d) $y = 3x^2 - 4$

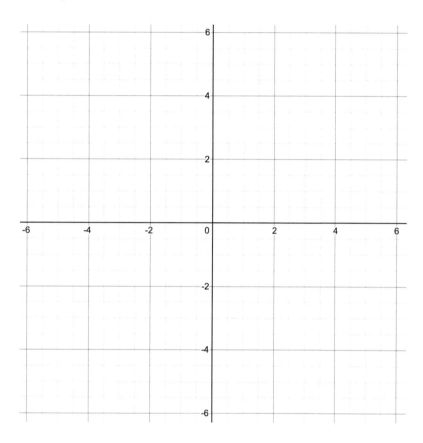

2. Find the vertex of the graph of the following quadratic: $y = 2x^2 - 12x + 22$

1.10   Functions

1.10.1   Introduction

A function is like a vending machine. Depending on what you input on the machine, you get a different item. Similarly, in mathematical functions, for whatever value you input, you get an output by following the process that the function defines. The **domain** of the function is defined as all the values that can be used as input. Conversely, the **range** is defined as the all the values that can be produced as output. To be defined as a function, all inputs must have only one output.

As for notation, equations are usually used to define functions in the following manner:

$$f(x) = 3x + 5.$$

f is the most commonly used label for functions, and $f(x)$ is read out loud as "f of x."

Functions!

Domain: values that you can input into the function

Range: values that can be outputted by the function

1.10.2   For the function $f(x) = 4x+2$, find the following values: $f(1), f(3),$ and $f(-5)$.

To find these values, we simply substitute the given values for x in the function:

$$f(1) = 4(1) + 2 = 4 + 2 = 6$$

$$f(3) = 4(3) + 2 = 12 + 2 = 14$$

$$f(-5) = 4(-5) + 2 = -20 + 2 = -18.$$

IMPORTANT: To find the value of a function for a particular input value, substitute the input value for the variable in the function and solve.

1.10.3   Find the value of x for which $f(x) = 4x + 2$ has a value of 34.

Now we've flipped the script: instead of solving for the output given an input, we need to find the input given an output. We know that for this particular x, $f(x) = 34$. Therefore, we can say that

$$f(x) = 34 = 4x + 2 \longrightarrow 4x + 2 = 34 \longrightarrow (4x+2) - 2 = 34 - 2 \longrightarrow 4x = 32 \longrightarrow x = 8.$$

> **IMPORTANT:** To find the input value that results in a given output, substitute the output for the function name and solve for the variable.

1.10.4 For the function $f(x) = 3x^2 + 5$, what is the domain? What is the range?

For this function, the domain is easy to see: it doesn't matter what value of x we choose. As long as it is real, the function will produce a result according to its definition of $f(x) = 3x^2 + 5$. As such, the domain is all real numbers.

The range is a bit more tricky. We know that $3x^2$ will always be nonnegative, because squaring a real number can never have a negative result. Thus, the least that $3x^2$ can be is 0, resulting in a minimum value of

$$f(x) = 0 + 5 = 5.$$

Our next step must be to see if f can produce an output of all real numbers greater than or equal to 5.

To begin, we can set $y = f(x)$, which gives us $y = 3x^2 + 5$. Now we solve for x in terms of y; in other words, we try to isolate x we can do this by first subtracting 5 from both sides, giving us $y - 5 = 3x^2$. Dividing both sides by 3 gives us $\frac{y-5}{3} = x^2$. Finally, taking the square root of both sides gives

$$x = \pm\sqrt{\frac{y-5}{3}}.$$

Here, we see that if we plug in $y = 5$, we get $x = \pm\sqrt{0}$. If we plugged in anything less than $y = 5$, we would get a square root enclosing a negative value, which would result in no real values. As such, we can say that there are no real values of x that would make it so $f(x) < 5$. For all values of y greater than or equal to 5, we know that $x = \pm\sqrt{\frac{y-5}{3}}$, so we can say that all numbers greater than or equal to 5 compose the range of f.

> **IMPORTANT:** To find the domain of a function, search for restrictions (such as numbers that make the function undefined) and exclude those. To find the range, a good strategy is to set $y = f(x)$ and solve for x in terms of y.

1.10.5 $f(x) = 4x + 3$ for $2 \leq x \leq 4$. **What is the range of f?**

If our domain was all real numbers as it has been previously, it's easy to see that our range would also be all real numbers. However, it's not that simple this time around.

We know that $x \geq 2$, and $4(2) = 8$. Thus, $f(x) \geq 8 + 3 = 11 \longrightarrow f(x) \geq 11$. We also know that $x \leq 4$, and $4(4) = 16$. Thus, $f(x) \leq 16 + 3 = 19 \longrightarrow f(x) \leq 19$. From here, we can see that $11 \leq f(x) \leq 19$, so the range of f is all real numbers from 11 to 19, inclusive.

> **IMPORTANT: Setting up an inequality when given restrictions on a function's domain is a good way to find its range.**

Now we've seen the basics of functions as they relate to their domains and ranges. Let's see how different functions interact with each other. We'll explore adding, multiplying, and dividing functions.

All three of these operations with functions follow logic, which is lucky for us. Here's a quick rundown:

Combining Functions

Addition: If we have two functions, $f(x)$ and $g(x)$, combining $f(x) + g(x)$ is as simple as adding the terms that each function contains. For example, let $f(x) = 3x^2 + 4x - 7$, and $g(x) = 3x + 5$. Adding the two gives us $f(x) + g(x) = (3x^2 + 4x - 7) + (3x + 5) = 3x^2 + 7x - 2$.

Multiplication: Multiplying two functions is similarly simple.   Take $f(x) = x + 5$ and $g(x) = 2x - 7$. Multiplying them gives us $f(x) \cdot g(x) = (x + 5)(2x - 7) = 2x^2 + 10x - 7x - 35 = 2x^2 + 3x - 35$.

Division: Finally, division is also straightforward.   Say $f(x) = 3x$ and $g(x) = x + 7$. We thus have that $\frac{f(x)}{g(x)} = \frac{3x}{x+7}$.

It's important to note that if $f(x)$ and $g(x)$ are functions, then adding them, subtracting them, multiplying them, or dividing them also results in a function. For division, though, there is the extra restriction that the function that is the divisor must be nonzero.

On to new things! It's time to look at function composition.

Function composition is the process of taking the output of one function, and using it as the input for another. An example would be $f(g(x))$, for two functions $f(x)$ and $g(x)$. This means that we compute the output of $g(x)$, and then use that value as input for $f(x)$. Conversely, if we had written $g(f(x))$, we would first compute the output of

$f(x)$, and then use that value as input for $g(x)$. Let's see some problems that deal with composition.

1.10.6 For $f(x) = x + 5$ and $g(x) = 5x - 2$, compute $f(g(5))$.

We work from the inside out. First, let's start with $g(5)$. We have that

$$g(5) = 5(5) - 2 = 25 - 2 = 23.$$

Now, we know that $g(5) = 23$, so we can substitute 23 for $g(5)$ in $f(g(5))$ to get $f(23)$. We have that

$$f(23) = 23 + 5 = 28.$$

Thus, we have that $f(g(5)) = 28$.

IMPORTANT: When working with composite functions, start from the inside and work your way out.

1.10.7 For the same $f(x)$ and $g(x)$ as in problem 1.10.6, find a general form for $f(g(x))$.

We know that $g(x) = 5x - 2$, so we can substitute $5x - 2$ for $g(x)$ in $f(g(x))$. This gives us $f(5x - 2)$. From the definition of $f(x)$, we have that

$$f(5x - 2) = (5x - 2) + 5 = 5x + 3.$$

IMPORTANT: Don't be scared to directly put one function inside another to find a general form. Just be careful that you don't make any computation errors, and you should be good to go!

On to the last topic of functions that we'll cover: **inverse functions**. By definition, an inverse function "undoes" the work of the original function. A standard notation for the inverse function of a function f is f^{-1}. For inverse functions, the following relationship is defined:

Inverse functions

Functions f and f^{-1} are inverse functions if and only if:

$f^{-1}(f(x)) = x$ for all x in the domain of f, and

$f(f^{-1}(x)) = x$ for all x in the domain of f^{-1}.

To find the inverse of a function, there are a set of steps we must follow. Let's see how they come together in the following problem.

1.10.8   Find the inverse of the function $f(x) = 3x - 5$.

Our first step is going to be to replace $f(x)$ with y, giving us $y = 3x - 5$. Next, wherever we see an x, we replace it with a y, and wherever we see a y, we replace it with an x. For this problem, this gives us

$$y = 3x - 5 \longrightarrow x = 3y - 5.$$

From here, all we have to do is solve for y by isolating it. Adding 5 to both sides gives us $x + 5 = 3y$, and dividing both sides by 3 gives us $y = \frac{x+5}{3}$. Finally, we replace y with $f^{-1}(x)$, giving us that our inverse function is:

$$f^{-1}(x) = \frac{x + 5}{3}.$$

IMPORTANT: To find an inverse function of a function $f(x)$:
1. Replace $f(x)$ or whatever the function is named with y.
2. Wherever there is an x, replace it with a y; wherever there is a y, replace it with an x.
3. Solve for y.
4. Once y has been isolated, replace it with $f^{-1}(x)$.
5. Voila! You've found the inverse function!

1.10.9   Does the function $f(x) = x^2$ have an inverse?

Let's start by exploring some values that this function outputs. If we plug in $x = 1$, we get $f(1) = 1$. However, if we plug in $x = -1$, we also get that $f(-1) = 1$. Similarly, if we plug in $x = 2$, we get that $f(2) = 4$, but if we plug in $x = -2$, we get that $f(-2) = 4$. We can immediately see that this introduces a problem; if f were to have an inverse, how would we know if $f^{-1}(4)$ were to equal 2 or -2?

The simple answer is this cannot be true. Remember, by the definition of a function, each input can have only one output. Therefore, there is no way to "choose" which value the inverse function would output. Functions like $f(x) = x^2$ simply do not have inverses.

IMPORTANT: A function that produces the same output for two different inputs does not have an inverse.

1.10.10   Conclusion

This section was a big one: functions. We saw how functions behave a bit like vending machines, spitting out different items for different inputs. Important things to remember include how in a function, each input can have only one output. We learned about their domains and ranges, how functions can be added, subtracted, multiplied, and divided, and how they can be composed. Finally, we learned about their inverses.

1.10.11   Practice

1. For the function $f(x) = 3x^2 + 4x - 5$, find the value of $3f(3) - f(5)$.

2. What is the domain of the function in problem 1? The range?

3. Add the following functions: $f(x) = 3x^2 + 4x - 5$ and $g(x) = 8x + 3$.

4. Multiply the following functions: $f(x) = 2x + 5$ and $g(x) = 3x^3 - 2$.

5. For $f(x) = 3x^2 + x - 4$ and $g(x) = 2x + 3$, find $f(g(x))$.

6. For the same functions as in problem 5, find $g(f(x))$.

7. For $f(x) = 3x - 8$, find the inverse function.

8. For $f(x) = x^2 + 4x + 4$, find the inverse function.

1.11   Exponential Functions and Their Graphs

1.11.1   Introduction

Exponential functions are functions of the form $f(x) = a^x$, where $a > 1$. In this section, we'll explore their characteristics, as well as their graphs. As a refresher, here are the crucial properties of exponential functions that we'll be working with:

Exponential Function Properties:

$$(x^y)^z = x^{yz}$$

$$(x^y)(x^z) = x^{y+z}$$

1.11.2   Graph the function 2^x. What is its range?

We know how to graph unknown things: plot some points. For this graph, let's try to include a mix of both positive and negative x-coordinates, in case the graph behaves weirdly.

Some points we can plot are $(-4, \frac{1}{16}); (-3, \frac{1}{8}); (-2, \frac{1}{4}); (-1, \frac{1}{2}); (0, 1); (1, 2); (2, 4); (3, 8);$ and $(4, 16)$. Plotting these gives us:

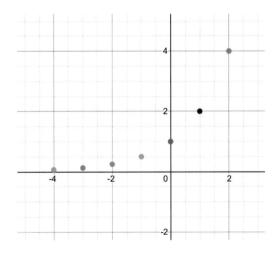

Figure 1.39: Plotted points of $y = 2^x$

Connecting the dots gives us the following graph:

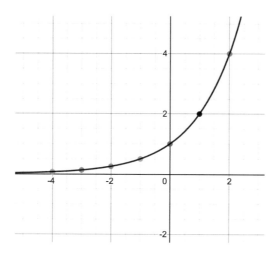

Figure 1.40: Final graph of $y = 2^x$

Let's analyze the graph for features that tell us how to find the range. For one, as x gets more negative, the graph appears to get closer and closer to $y = 0$. It won't ever reach $y = 0$, though. How do we know that? Well, we know that we can never have an output of 0, and 2^x can never be negative, so we can be sure that the graph will never reach $y = 0$.

Conversely, the graph contains y-values of all positive numbers. Thus, we can say that the range is all real numbers above 0, or simply, all positive numbers.

1.11.3   What is the range of the function $f(x) = 4 \times 3^x + 5$?

First, let's analyze the exponential portion: 3^x. We know that this value has a minimum of 0 that it will never reach. Thus, the minimum value of 4×3^x is $4 \times 0 = 0$. Adding $0 + 5 = 5$ gives a minimum value of 5 for $f(x)$. Conversely, 3^x has a maximum value of infinity as x increases, so we can say that the range of this function is all positive numbers greater than 5.

1.11.4   If $6^x = 2$, then what does 6^{3x+2} equal?

Yikes! This problem looks a bit hard... how can we make it easier? Well, we can rewrite it in simpler terms by setting $a = 6^x$. This allows us to say that $a = 2$. As for 6^{3x+2}, rewriting that is a bit more complex. We can say that

$$6^{3x+2} = 6^{3x} \times 6^2 = (6^x)^3 \times 6^2.$$

We have that $a = 6^x$, so this becomes $a^3 \times 6^2 = 36a^3$. Plugging $a = 2$ into the expression, we have that $36a^3 = 36 \times 2^3 = 36 \times 8 = 288$.

> **IMPORTANT:** Sometimes a hard problem is made easier by substituting in a variable for some term in the function.

1.11.5   Find all values of x such that $5^{2x+4} = 125^{x+1}$.

Here, we need to make use of a clever insight: $125 = 5^3$. This allows us to rewrite our original equation as

$$5^{2x+4} = 125^{x+1} = (5^3)^{x+1} = 5^{3(x+1)} = 5^{3x+3} \longrightarrow 5^{2x+4} = 5^{3x+3}.$$

From here, it's a simple matter of setting the two exponents equal to each other:

$$2x + 4 = 3x + 3.$$

To isolate x, we subtract $2x$ and 3 from both sides, giving us $1 = x$. Thus, the value of x that makes our original equation true is 1.

1.11.6   Conclusion

In this section, we briefly explored exponential functions. We saw their graphs, which have the characteristic that they flatten out as x decreases, while increasing dramatically as x increases. We also saw how to work with the properties of exponents in problems involving exponential functions.

1.11.7   Practice

1. On the grid below, graph the equation $y = 2^x - 2$.

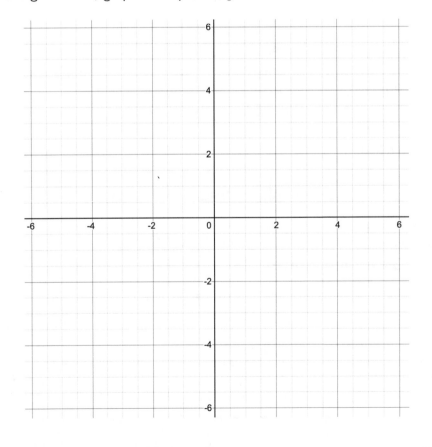

2. For what values of x is the equation $6^{3x-2} = 216$ true?

3. For what values of x is the equation $9^{2x+4} = 27^{x+4}$ true?

4. Find the domain and range of the function $f(x) = 2^x + 4$.

1.12   Absolute Value Functions and Their Graphs

1.12.1   Introduction

The concept of absolute value is a little tricky. The best way to think of the absolute value of a number is its distance from 0 on a number line. Distance can never be negative. The distance between -3 and 0 is the same as that between 3 and 0; it's 3 in both cases. In this way, it makes sense that the absolute value of -3 and 3 is 3 in both cases. We denote absolute value using these symbols: $||$. For example, the absolute value of -10 would be expressed as $|-10|$.

Absolute value can also be used to express distances between numbers that don't include 0 on the number line; for example, $|5 - 4|$ equals the distance between 5 and 4 on the number line, which is 1. As another example, $|3 - (-5)|$ is the distance between 3 and -5 on the number line: 8.

It's important to have this understanding of what absolute value really means, but for the purposes of math, a more simplistic definition is often useful. As a general rule, the absolute value of a quantity can be found by calculating the real value of the quantity, and then taking the positive version of that value. If the value inside the absolute value symbol has a real value of -3, then its absolute value would simply be $+3$, or just 3. if the value inside the absolute value is positive, its absolute value is the same as the real value.

> **IMPORTANT: The absolute value for x if $x \geq 0$ is equal to x. If $x < 0$, then $|x| = -x$.**

1.12.2   Graph the equation $y = |x|$.

Time to graph! Let's plot some points. Just like we did with exponential functions, we'll want points from both negative and positive x values. Let's use $(-3, 3); (-2, 2); (-1, 1);$ $(0, 0); (1, 1); (2, 2);$ and $(3, 3)$. Plotting these gives us:

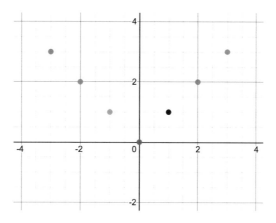

Figure 1.41: Plotted points of $y = |x|$

Connecting the dots gives us this V-shaped graph:

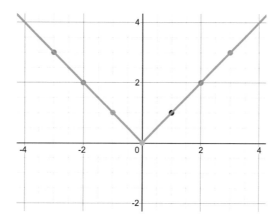

Figure 1.42: Final graph of $y = |x|$

> **IMPORTANT: V-shaped graphs are often related to absolute value.**

1.12.3 For what values of x is the equation $|3x + 4| = 1$ true?

In this problem, we have 2 cases: either $3x + 4$ is positive, and thus $|3x + 4| = 3x + 4$, or $3x + 4$ is negative, and $|3x + 4| = -(3x + 4)$. Let's take a look at them individually.

If $3x + 4$ is positive, then we simply have that

$$|3x + 4| = 3x + 4 = 1 \longrightarrow 3x = -3 \longrightarrow x = -1.$$

If $3x + 4$ is negative, then we have that

$$|3x + 4| = -(3x + 4) = 1 \longrightarrow -3x - 4 = 1 \longrightarrow -3x = 5 \longrightarrow x = -\frac{5}{3}.$$

Thus, our two solutions are $x = -1$ and $x = -\frac{5}{3}$.

1.12.4   For what values of x is the equation $|2x+4|+|x-3| = 5$ true?

Our first instinct might be to try to isolate x, but that could get complex. Instead, let's try to break the problem up into distinct cases, and solve for each case individually.

In the first case, both $2x + 4$ and $x - 3$ are positive. For this to be true, $2x + 4 > 0$ and $x - 3 > 0$. Solving each of those inequalities gives that $2x > -4 \longrightarrow x > -2$, and $x > 3$. To satisfy both of those inequalities, we must have that $x > 3$. Now we can solve the equation we were given: if $x > 3$, then we know that

$$|2x+4|+|x-3| = 5 \longrightarrow (2x+4)+(x-3) = 5 \longrightarrow 3x+1 = 5 \longrightarrow 3x = 4 \longrightarrow x = \frac{4}{3}.$$

Well, $x = \frac{4}{3}$ is not in the interval $x > 3$, so it is not a solution.

The next case is that both $2x + 4$ and $x - 3$ are negative, or less than 0. Solving the inequalities $2x + 4 < 0$ and $x - 3 < 0$ gives us that $2x < -4 \longrightarrow x < -2$ and $x < 3$. To satisfy both of those, we must have that $x < -2$. Using this condition in the original equation, we have that

$$|2x + 4| + |x - 3| = 5 \longrightarrow -(2x + 4) + [-(x - 3)] = 5 \longrightarrow -2x - 4 - x + 3 = 5$$

$$\longrightarrow -3x - 1 = 5 \longrightarrow -3x = 6 \longrightarrow x = -2.$$

We have to check this solution, because recall that our original condition was that $x < -2$, not $x \leq -2$. Plugging $x = -2$ back into our original equation gives us

$$|2(-2) + 4| + |-2 - 3| = 5 \longrightarrow |0| + |-5| = 5 \longrightarrow 5 = 5.$$

Thus, $x = -2$ is a solution.

The last case we must check is if either of $2x + 4$ or $x - 3$ are negative, while the other is positive. From our first two cases, we know that $2x + 4$ is negative when $x < -2$, and positive when $x > -2$. Similarly, $x - 3$ is negative when $x < 3$, and positive when $x > 3$. For one to be positive while the other is negative, then, we must have that $-2 < x < 3$. For this to be true, $2x + 4$ would be positive, while $x - 3$ would be negative. Using these conditions for our original equation gives us that

$$|2x + 4| + |x - 3| = 5 \longrightarrow (2x + 4) + [-(x - 3)] = 5 \longrightarrow (2x + 4) - (x - 3) = 5$$

$$\longrightarrow x + 7 = 5 \longrightarrow x = -2.$$

Well, we know from our second case that this is a solution.

We've tested all the possible cases, and we found that there is just one solution: $x = -2$.

> **IMPORTANT: For problems that involve more absolute values of more than one quantity, it is wise to break the problem into cases where the quantities are different combinations of positive and negative.**

1.12.5 Conclusion

In this section, we explored absolute value functions and a bit about their graphs. We saw how the concept of absolute value can be understood using distance on a number line, and how an absolute value effectively takes the positive value of a quantity, no matter what. For their graphs, we saw the characteristic V-shape of absolute value graphs.

1.12.6 Practice

1. On the grid below, graph the function $f(x) = |2x + 3|$.

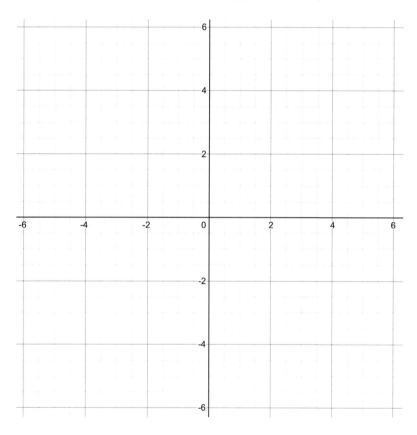

2. Solve the following equation: $|x + 4| + 30 = 36$.

3. Solve the following equation: $|4x - 16| + 6 = 0$.

4. Solve the following equation: $\frac{|x+4|}{2} = 3$.

5. Solve the equation $|3x - 5| + |2x + 4| = 10$.

1.13   Polynomials

1.13.1   Introduction

Up until now, we've seen equations and expressions with variables raised to the first power (linear), and variables raised to the second power (quadratic). What about the equations with variables raised to the third power? Fourth? Fifth? The list goes on - it's literally infinite. These expressions, in general, are called **polynomials**. Formally defined, a polynomial is a sum of terms in which every term consists of a constant times a variable raised to a nonnegative integer power. For example, the following are all polynomials:

> **Examples of polynomials:**
> - $x^7 - 5x^6 + 4x^3 - 2x$
> - $-y^4 + y^3 + 4y^2 - 62y + 42$
> - $z^5 + z^2$

Crucially, the variables cannot be in the denominators of fractions or under square root signs.

One term that we will need to be familiar with is the **degree** of the polynomial.

> **IMPORTANT: The degree of a polynomial is the highest power of the variable in the polynomial. The term containing this power is known as the polynomial's leading term.**

Keeping all that in mind, it's time to explore some basic operations with polynomials: addition, subtraction, and multiplication.

1.13.2   Add the following two polynomials: $3x^3 + 4x^2 - 7x + 3$ and $9x^7 + 4x^5 + x^2 - 5$.

Addition is completely logical: simply add the terms of both polynomials, combining terms with the same degree.

$$(3x^3 + 4x^2 - 7x + 3) + (9x^7 + 4x^5 + x^2 - 5) = 9x^7 + 4x^5 + 3x^3 + (4x^2 + x^2) - 7x + (3 - 5)$$

$$= 9x^7 + 4x^5 + 3x^3 + 5x^2 - 7x - 2.$$

> **IMPORTANT: The sum of any two polynomials is another polynomial!**

1.13.3 Multiply the following two polynomials: $(2x^2 - x + 1)$ and $(4x^3 + x^2 - 2x + 4)$.

To multiply this out, we use the distributive property, just as we did for smaller polynomials.

$$(2x^2 - x + 1)(4x^3 + x^2 - 2x + 4) =$$
$$(2x^2)(4x^3 + x^2 - 2x + 4) + (-x)(4x^3 + x^2 - 2x + 4) + (1)(4x^3 + x^2 - 2x + 4)$$
$$= (8x^5 + 2x^4 - 4x^3 + 8x^2) + (-4x^4 - x^3 + 2x^2 - 4x) + (4x^3 + x^2 - 2x + 4)$$
$$= 8x^5 - 2x^4 - x^3 + 11x^2 - 6x + 4.$$

> **IMPORTANT:** Multiply polynomials using the distributive property, just as we did with polynomials of lesser degree.

> **IMPORTANT:** The product of any two polynomials is another polynomial!

1.13.4 Conclusion

So that's the basics of polynomials! Pretty simple. We learned about the definition of a polynomial, their degrees, and how to perform operations with them.

1.13.5 Practice

1. Add the following two polynomials: $4x^4 + 3x^2 - 1$ and $x^6 + x^5 - 3x^4 + x$.

2. What is the product of the degrees of the two polynomials in problem 1?

3. Multiply the two polynomials from problem 1.

4. What is the degree of the product from problem 3?

1.14   Sequences and Series

1.14.1   Introduction

In its most basic form, a sequence is simply a list of numbers, like $1, 2, 3, 4, 5$. In this chapter, we'll discuss some specific types of sequences, as well as their sums, which are known as series.

We have finite sequences, which have a predetermined, finite number of terms; finite sequences have an end. However, not all sequences end. These are known as infinite sequences, and we denote them with a "..." at the end to indicate that they continue.

In this section, we'll explore arithmetic and geometric sequences and series. Put simply, in an arithmetic sequence, the difference between two consecutive terms is always the same; in a geometric sequence, the ratio of two consecutive terms is always the same.

> **IMPORTANT: In an arithmetic sequence, there is a constant difference between two consecutive terms.**

> **IMPORTANT: In a geometric sequence, there is a constant ratio of two consecutive terms.**

Let's start with arithmetic sequences.

1.14.2   In the sequence $-28, -19, -10, -1, 8, 17...$, find the 8th, 9th, and 11th terms.

We know that this is an arithmetic sequence, because simply looking at the terms given to us shows that each term is 9 greater than the one that came before it. Thus, the terms have a common difference of 9. We have 6 terms given to us, so we can get the 7th by adding 9 to the 6th, and then find the 8th by adding 9 to that, and so on.

Adding 9 to the 6th term of 17 gives us that the 7th term is $17 + 9 = 26$. Adding 9 to that gives us the 8th term, which is $26 + 9 = 35$. Similarly, the 9th term is $35 + 9 = 44$. To get to the 11th term, we can simply see that we'll need to add 9 twice; once to get to the 10th term, and another time to get to the 11th. This gives us that the 11th term is $44 + 2(9) = 44 + 18 = 62$.

From this, it's time to introduce the formula for the nth term of an arithmetic sequence with a as its first term, and d as its common difference. You should be able to analyze this formula and understand logically where it comes from; don't simply memorize it.

> **IMPORTANT:** The formula for the nth term of an arithmetic sequence with first term a and common difference d is:
>
> $$a + d(n - 1).$$
>
> The only part of this formula that might need a little explanation is the $n - 1$ in there. That comes from the number of times that d will need to be added on to the first term of a. To get to the nth term, you will need to add that a total of $n - 1$ times. Think about it: to get from the first term to the second, you need to add d a total of $2 - 1 = 1$ time. To get from the first term to the third, you need to add d a total of $3 - 1 = 2$ times.

1.14.3 Given that $3, x_1, x_2, x_3, x_4, x_5, x_6, 24$ is a finite arithmetic sequence, find the value of x_5.

In this sequence, we have that 3 is the first term, and 24 is the 8th and final term. Using our formula for the nth term of an arithmetic sequence, we can find the common difference. We know the 8th term is 24, giving us the following equation:

$$24 = 3 + d(8 - 1).$$

Isolating d, we get

$$24 = 3 + d(8 - 1) \longrightarrow 21 = d(8 - 1) \longrightarrow 21 = d(7) \longrightarrow d = 3.$$

From here, we can either subtract 3 twice from 24 to get x_5, or plus our new value for d into the formula. Either way gives us that $x_5 = 18$.

Now that we're a bit more familiar with arithmetic sequences, let's look at arithmetic series. We'll start with a classic!

1.14.4 Add all the integers from 1 to 100, inclusive.

That is... quite a lot of numbers to add, to say the least. Adding them all one by one will not only be tedious, but will be so extensive that we're incredibly likely to make a mistake.

Here comes the trick: let's find the final answer as a sum of pairs of terms. We can notice that the sum of the first and last terms is $1 + 100 = 101$. The sum of the second and second-to-last is $2 + 99 = 101$. This pattern continues; we can create exactly 50 pairs in this manner that add up to 101. Therefore, our sum is equal to $50(101) = 5050$.

Using this example, we can explore the general formula for the sum of an arithmetic series.

IMPORTANT: The formula for the sum of an arithmetic series with first term a, common difference d, and number of terms n is

$$\frac{n}{2} \cdot [2a + d(n-1)].$$

This is essentially the same as saying "total number of terms $\times$ sum of first and last terms, all divided by 2," or put more simply, "total number of terms $\times$ average of first and last terms."

1.14.5 Find the sum of the following arithmetic series: $-4, -1, 2, 5, 8, 11, 14, 17$.

Let's apply our formula: our first term is -4, the common difference is 3, and the number of terms is 8. This gives us that the sum should be

$$\frac{8}{2} \cdot [2(-4) + 3(8-1)] = 4 \cdot [-8 + 21] = 4(13) = 52.$$

We can check our answer by manually adding all the terms; sure enough, we're correct!

By doing enough of these practice problems, this formula should make so much sense that you won't even need to memorize it; you'll simply understand it that well. That should always be the goal: to have such a deep understanding of a concept that memorizing its formula is not necessary.

REMINDER: Your goal is to understand the concepts behind formulas, not to memorize the formulas. Memorizing formulas is not learning.

Now it's time to move on to geometric sequences.

1.14.6 Given the sequence $3, 6, 12, 24, 48, 96...$, find the $7^{th}, 8^{th}$, and 9th terms.

We know this is a geometric sequence, because we can see that the common ratio between terms is 2; each term is double the previous one. Thus, doubling the 6th term gives us the 7th, and so on. Following this rule, we get that the following three terms are $192, 384$, and 768.

From this logic is where we derive the formula for the nth term in a geometric sequence:

> **IMPORTANT:** The formula for the nth term in a geometric sequence with first term a and common ratio r is
>
> $$ar^{n-1}.$$

1.14.7 Given the geometric sequence $4, x_1, x_2, x_3, 64$, find all possible values of $x_1, x_2,$ and x_3.

We can begin by finding out how many times we must multiply to go from 4 to 64 with three terms in between. If our common ratio is r, we thus have the equation that

$$64 = 4r^4.$$

Dividing both sides by 4 gives us that $16 = r^4$. Thus, r can be either -2 or 2. Having $r = -2$ gives us $x_1 = -8, x_2 = 16$, and $x_3 = -32$. Having $r = 2$ gives us $x_1 = 8, x_2 = 16$, and $x_3 = 32$.

Now, the formula for geometric series is a bit complex. We'll derive it so you can see how it works.

1.14.8 For a geometric series with first term a, common ratio r, and n terms, find a formula for the sum of the series.

Let's work out an example with real numbers instead of variables, just so we can get an idea of what to expect. Say we have a series

$$S = 1 + 3 + 9 + 27 + 81 + ... + 729 + 2187.$$

We can't use the same pairing-up technique that we used for arithmetic series. What we can do instead is to try to multiply S by 3, as this will give us a new series that shares a bunch of terms with S. This gives us that

$$3S = 3 + 9 + 27 + 81 + 243 + ... + 2187 + 6561.$$

Subtracting S from $3S$ allows many of these terms to cancel, leaving us with

$$3S - S = (3+9+27+81+243+...+2187+6561) - (1+3+9+27+81+...+729+2187)$$

$$= -1 + 6561 = 6560.$$

Dividing by 2 gives us that $S = 3280$.

Now let's do that same process, but with the variables we were given. Our sum is then

$$S = a + ar + ar^2 + ar^3 + ar^4 + ... + ar^{n-2} + ar^{n-1}.$$

Multiplying this series by r give sus that

$$rS = ar + ar^2 + ar^3 + ar^4 + ar^5 + \ldots + ar^{n-1} + ar^n.$$

Subtracting $rS - S$ gives

$$rS - S =$$

$$(ar+ar^2+ar^3+ar^4+ar^5+\ldots+ar^{n-1}+ar^n)-(a+ar+ar^2+ar^3+ar^4+\ldots+ar^{n-2}+ar^{n-1})$$

$$= ar^n - a.$$

We can factor the left side to get

$$S(r - 1) = a(r^n - 1).$$

Isolating S gives us that

$$S = \frac{a(r^n - 1)}{r - 1}.$$

That's it! We found the formula!

IMPORTANT: The formula for the sum of a geometric series with first term a, common ratio r, and number of terms n, is

$$\frac{a(r^n - 1)}{r - 1}.$$

1.14.9   Conclusion

To wrap up the Algebra chapter, we looked at arithmetic and geometric sequences and series. We explored formulas for n^{th} terms in each, as well as sums of both types. It truly cannot be emphasized enough how important it is to try to understand the logic behind these formulas through practice problems. Memorizing the formulas won't do any good in the long run; understanding how they work will allow you to remember them forever.

1.14.10   Practice

1. What are the next two terms in the sequence $37, 41, 45, 49, 53\ldots$?

2. Find the sum of the following series: $24 + 29 + 34 + 39 + 44 + 49 + 54 + 59$.

3. Find the sum of the arithmetic series with first term -21, common difference -2, and 7 terms.

4. Given that the sum of the first 3 terms of an arithmetic series is 60 and the sum of the first 10 terms of the series is 235, what is the first term in the series?

5. What are the next two terms in the sequence $36, 12, 4, \frac{4}{3}$?

6. Find the sum of the following series: $-2 + 4 - 8 + 16 - 32 + 64 - 128 + 256$.

7. Find the sum of the following series: $1296 + 216 + 36 + 6 + 1 + \frac{1}{6} + \frac{1}{36}$.

Chapter 2

GEOMETRY!

2.1 Introduction

Geometry! Fun stuff - shapes, lines, angles, and more. We'll be exploring the properties and ideas related to triangles, quadrilaterals, other polygons, circles, and plenty of three-dimensional figures as well. First, a little housekeeping: the following boxes contain information that you should know as a prerequisite to this chapter. It's important to note that in this chapter, figures are not necessarily drawn to scale.

A point has 0 dimensions; there is no up, down, right, or left. Points are labeled with capital letters, as shown below.

A
•

Figure 2.1: Point A

A line segment is the result of connecting two points. The two points are called the endpoints of the segment, which we use to name the segment: as shown below, the segment that connects points A and B is $\overline{AB}$. To denote the length of the segment, we simply remove the bar from above the letters, which looks like AB.

Figure 2.2: Line segment $\overline{AB}$

The midpoints of a segment lies halfway between the endpoints; it is the same distance from both endpoints. We can show that these distances are equal by putting a tick mark along each half-segment.

Figure 2.3: Midpoint C

A ray is a line segment that extends forever in one direction. The starting point is the origin, or vertex. We denote a ray similarly to a line segment, making sure that the origin point comes first in the name. Instead of a simple line over the letters, we use an arrow.

Figure 2.4: Ray $\overrightarrow{AB}$

A line is a line segment that extends forever in both directions. We denote a line with a line with both arrowheads over the letters.

Figure 2.5: Line $\overleftrightarrow{AB}$

Three or more points that lie on the same line are collinear. If three or more lines pass through one point, the lines are concurrent.

A circle can be defined as the set of all points that are the same distance from a particular point. That point is the center of the circle, and the fixed distance is the radius. A circle is denoted using the symbol $\odot$ and a letter corresponding to its center.

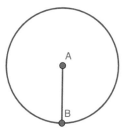

Figure 2.6: $\odot A$ with radius $\overline{AB}$

A line that touches a circle at a single point is tangent to the circle. A line that touches a circle at two points is a secant line. A segment that connects two points on the circle is a chord. A chord through the center of a circle is its diameter.

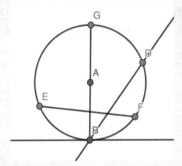

Figure 2.7: $\odot A$ with tangent through B, secant $\overleftrightarrow{BD}$, chord $\overline{EF}$, and diameter $\overline{BG}$

An angle is formed by two rays with a common vertex. An intersection of two lines or lines segments also forms an angle. The common origin of the angle is the vertex, and the rays that form it are called the sides of the angle. The angle below has vertex B and sides $\overrightarrow{BA}$ and $\overrightarrow{BC}$. The angle itself can be called either $\angle ABC$ or $\angle CBA$, but what's important is that the vertex is in the center.

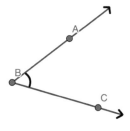

Figure 2.8: $\angle ABC$

An angle that measures less than $90°$ is acute.

An angle that measures between $90°$ and $180°$ is obtuse.

Right angles measure $90°$.

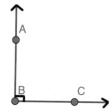

Figure 2.9: Right angle $\angle ABC$

Adjacent angles share a side. In the diagram, $\angle ABD$ and $\angle DBC$ are adjacent.

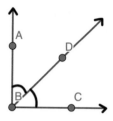

Figure 2.10: Adjacent angles $\angle ABD$ and $\angle DBC$

Straight angles measure exactly $180°$, and reflex angles measure greater than $180°$.

Two angles that add up to $90°$ are complementary.

Two angles that add up to $180°$ are supplementary.

The sum of all three angles in a triangle is $180°$.

For any triangle, the sum of two sides is greater than the third side. This is known as the Triangle Inequality.

When parallel lines are intersected by a transversal (a line that cuts across parallel lines) the angles created have the following relationship:

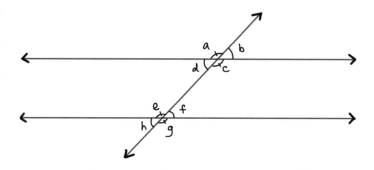

Figure 2.11: Angles created by a transversal

$$a = c = e = g, \text{ and } b = d = f = h.$$

The perimeter of a closed figure is the distance in 1 trip all around its edge. To find the perimeter of polygons, simply add up the lengths of all the sides.

The area of a closed figure can be described as the number of 1×1 unit squares needed to completely cover the figure. Formulas for area that you should already know include the following, where b is the base and h is the height. For circles, r is the radius.

Square / rectangle / parallelogram: $A = b \cdot h$

Triangle: $A = \frac{b \cdot h}{2}$

Trapezoid: $A = \frac{b_1 + b_2}{2} \cdot h$

Circle: $A = \pi \cdot r^2$

The volume of a three-dimensional figure is the amount of space it takes up, measured in $1 \times 1 \times 1$ unit blocks that fit in the figure. Formulas for volume include the following, where b is the area of the base and h is the height. For circles, r is the radius.

Prisms / cylinders: $V = b \cdot h$

Pyramids / cones: $V = \frac{b \cdot h}{3}$

Sphere: $V = \frac{4\pi r^3}{3}$

2.2 Triangle Congruence

2.2.1 Introduction

In general, two figures can be considered congruent (denoted using the symbol $\cong$ if they are exactly the same, not counting orientation. With triangles, there are special shortcuts we can use to prove that two triangles are congruent, without having to explicitly prove that every single side and angle is the same.

SSS Congruence: Two triangles are congruent if the lengths of the sides of one triangle are equal to the lengths of the corresponding sides of another triangle.

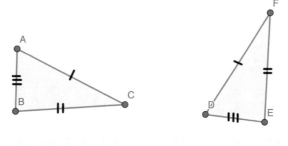

Figure 2.12: SSS Congruence

SAS Congruence: Two triangles are congruent if two sides of one triangle and the angle between them are equal to the corresponding sides and angle of another triangle.

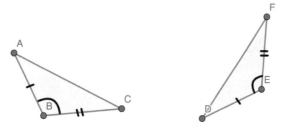

Figure 2.13: SAS Congruence

ASA Congruence: Two triangles are congruent if two angles of one triangle and the side between them are equal to the corresponding angles and side of another triangle.

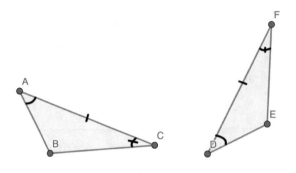

Figure 2.14: ASA Congruence

AAS Congruence: Two triangles are congruent if two angles and one side of one triangle equal the corresponding angles and side in another triangle as shown below.

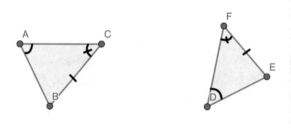

Figure 2.15: AAS Congruence

CPCTC: Corresponding Parts of Congruent Triangles are Congruent.

2.2.2   In the diagram below, $AB = CD$ and $AD = BC$. Are triangles $\triangle ABC$ and $\triangle ACD$ congruent? Why or why not?

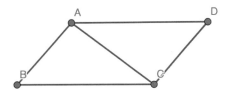

To be congruent, these triangles will need to have some certain angles and/or sides be equal. Let's see what we can find.

Right off the bat, we see that both triangles share $\overline{AC}$ as a side. We don't know much about the angles, so we'll keep looking at sides. The problem tells us that $AB = CD$, so those are another pair of corresponding sides between the two triangles that are equal. Finally, we know that $AD = BC$, which finishes off the conditions necessary for congruence: both triangles have 3 sides of equal length, so they are congruent by SSS.

2.2.3   In the diagram below, we have that $AB = BC = 5$, and $AD = CD = 10$. Prove that $\angle ABD \cong \angle CBD$.

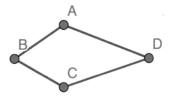

Upon first glance, we might not know how to approach this problem. How are we even supposed to compare $\angle ABD$ and $\angle CBD$ if we can't even visualize them? They don't even appear on the figure!

Here's where we employ one of the most important tactics for solving geometry problems: draw extra lines that will help you find more information.

> **IMPORTANT: When you need more information in a geometry problem, draw in extra line(s) that will give it to you.**

Here, that line happens to be the segment connecting points B and D. Drawing that in gives us the following figure:

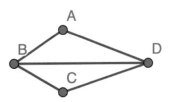

Now let's mark up our drawing with the information we know. We know that $AB = BC$ and $AD = CD$, so we have the following figure:

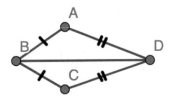

How are we going to know that $\angle ABD \cong \angle CBD$, though? Well, if we can prove that $\triangle ABD \cong \triangle CBD$, we'll have that $\angle ABD$ and $\angle CBD$ are corresponding parts of congruent triangles, so they must also be congruent.

As it turns out, we can prove that $\triangle ABD \cong \triangle CBD$! We already have two pairs of congruent sides as given to us in the problem, and the two triangles also share side BD. Thus, by SSS, the two triangles are congruent. Therefore, by CPCTC, $\angle ABD \cong \angle CBD$.

2.2.4 Which, if any, of the following four triangles are congruent?

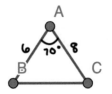
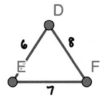
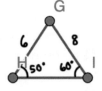
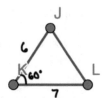

We can compare the triangles one by one. Starting with the first two, we see that $\triangle ABC$ and $\triangle DEF$ share sides of length 6 and 8. However, we don't know anything about the angles in triangle DEF, and we don't know the length of $\overline{BC}$ in $\triangle ABC$. Thus, we cannot say that $\triangle ABC \cong \triangle DEF$.

Let's see about triangles ABC and GHI. Once again, they share sides of length 6 and 8. This time, though, we do know some information about the angles in both triangles. In $\triangle ABC$, we know that $\angle BAC = 70°$. In $\triangle GHI$, we know that $\angle GHI = 50°$, and $\angle GIH = 60°$. We can use this information to find $\angle HGI$, as we know that the angles in any triangle add up to $180°$. Subtracting our two known angles from $180°$ will give us the measure of $\angle GHI$, which turns out to be $180° - (50° + 60° = 180° - 110° = 70°$. Thus, $\angle HGI = 70°$, just like $]angleBAC$. Now we have that a pair of sides and the angle between them are equal in both triangles, so we know that $\triangle ABC \cong \triangle GHI$ by SAS congruence.

Now let's see about triangles ABC and JKL. They share just one side length, and the information we have about their angles is not enough to prove any common angles. Thus, we do not have enough information to say that they are congruent.

For triangles DEF and GHI, it's a similar story. We know that they have at least 2 sides that are the same length, but we know nothing about the angles in $\triangle DEF$. Thus, we cannot say that the two are congruent.

For our second-to-last pair, we have triangles DEF and JKL. Once again, we have two equal side lengths, but not enough information about the angles or third side length to prove congruence.

Finally, we'll check out triangles GHI and JKL. We have two equal sides, but not enough information about the angles to prove congruence.

Thus, the only pair of congruent triangles is $\triangle ABC$ and $\triangle GHI$ by SAS congruence.

2.2.5 Which, if any, of the following four triangles are congruent?

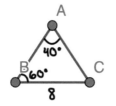 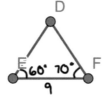 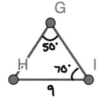 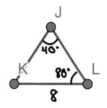

We can go through a similar process as the previous problem. Starting with $\triangle ABC$ and $\triangle DEF$, we see that the triangles share no known side lengths, and the angles are different, as well. Therefore, they are not congruent.

It's a similar story with triangles ABC and GHI. We can do some quick mental math to figure out the last angle in each triangle using the fact that the three angles in each triangle should add up to $180°$. They don't share any angles or known side lengths.

For triangles ABC and JKL, there's some hope! Doing our trick with the $180°$ shows us that the triangles share all three angles, and have a common side length in the same relative position. Thus, we can say that they are congruent, by either ASA or AAS congruence.

The next pair we'll look at will be triangles DEF and GHI. Our $180°$ trick shows us that the corresponding angles within these two triangles are congruent. We also have a shared side length of 9, so we can once again use either ASA or AAS congruence to prove that $\triangle DEF \cong \triangle GHI$.

We don't need to test the remaining pairs, because we've already found all the pairs of congruent triangles that there can be.

> **IMPORTANT:** Sometimes triangles can be proven congruent using more than one shortcut.

2.2.6   Conclusion

In this section, we explored the shortcuts to determining triangle congruence, as well as the idea that corresponding parts of congruent triangles are congruent. The four shortcuts we saw in use were SSS, SAS, ASA, and AAS.

2.2.7   Practice

1. For each of the figures below, identify any pairs of congruent triangles, and explain why the triangles are congruent.

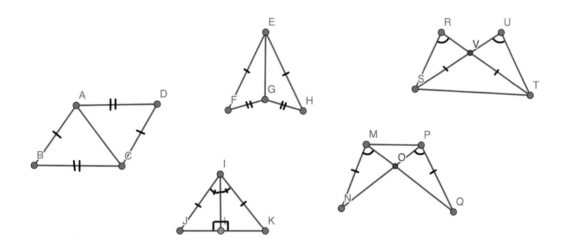

2.3   Triangle Similarity

2.3.1   Introduction

Two fingers can be considered similar (we denote similarity between figures using the $\sim$ sign) if one of them is a scaled-up version of the other. In similar figures, corresponding angles are equal, and the ratio of lengths of corresponding sides is also always the same.

Just like with congruence, there are several shortcuts to use when working with similar triangles.

AA Similarity: Two triangles are similar if at least 2 of the angles of one triangle are equal to the 2 corresponding angles in the second triangle. The reason we don't require 3 angles to be the same is simple: if you know 2 angles, you can easily find the third by using the fact that the three angles add up to $180°$. If you know 2 angles, there is only one possibility for the third angle. Thus, having 2 angles of one triangle equal 2 in another ensures that all 3 will be equal anyway.

SAS Similarity: Two triangles are similar if 2 sides of one triangle are in the same ratio as 2 sides in another triangle, and the angles between the sides equal each other.

SSS Similarity: Two triangles are similar if every side of one triangle is the same constant multiple of the corresponding sides in the other.

2.3.2   Given the following figure and its given properties, find DE.

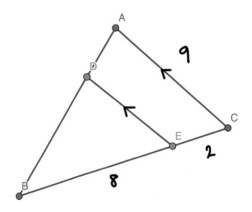

We can easily find DE if we prove that $\triangle ABC \sim \triangle DBE$. Well, the presence of parallel lines with $\overline{DE}$ and $\overline{AC}$ tells us that $\angle BDE \cong \angle BAC$, and $\angle BED \cong \angle BCA$. Marking this gives us the following figure:

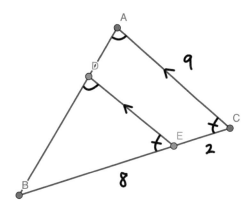

What we've just done is prove that $\triangle ABC \sim \triangle DBE$ by AA similarity! Thus, we can set up the ratio

$$\frac{DE}{AC} = \frac{BE}{BC} \longrightarrow \frac{DE}{9} = \frac{8}{8+2} \longrightarrow \frac{DE}{9} = \frac{8}{10} \longrightarrow 10DE = 72 \longrightarrow DE = 7.2.$$

> **Often, the presence of parallel lines creates congruent angles, which can be used to find similar triangles!**

2.3.3 Given $AC = 4, CD = 5$, and $AB = 6$ as in the diagram, find BC if the perimeter of $\triangle BCD$ is 20. *(Source: Mandelbrot)*

If we look a little bit, we can see that we have a pair of similar triangles here! We can recognize that $\frac{AC}{AB} = \frac{4}{6} = \frac{2}{3}$, and $\frac{AB}{AD} = \frac{6}{9} = \frac{2}{3}$. Therefore, those sides have the same ratio; we can combine this with the observation that both triangles ACB and ABD share angle A to show that $\triangle ACB \sim \triangle ABD$ by SAS similarity.

From this, we can see that the ratio between corresponding sides of $\triangle ABD$ and $\triangle ACB$, in that order, is $\frac{3}{2}$. Thus, we can set up the equation that

$$BD = \frac{3BC}{2}.$$

We know that the total perimeter of $\triangle BCD$ is 20, so we can say that

$$BC + CD + DB = 20,$$

which gives us that

$$BC + 5 + \frac{3BC}{2} = 20 \longrightarrow BC + \frac{3BC}{2} = 15 \longrightarrow \frac{5BC}{2} = 15 \longrightarrow 5BC = 30$$

$$\longrightarrow BC = 6.$$

2.3.4 **In the diagram, $BDEF$ is a square. $AB = 9$ and $BC = 15$. Find the side length of square $BDEF$.**

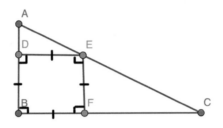

From the sides of the square and the right angles it contains, we can tell that $\overline{EF} \parallel \overline{AB}$, and $\overline{DEF} \parallel \overline{BC}$. Thus, by AA similarity, we know that

$$\triangle ADE \sim \triangle ABC \sim \triangle EFC.$$

Let the length of one side of the square be equal to s. Thus, we have that $AD = 9 - s$, and $FC = 15 - s$. We can now use the properties of similar triangles to solve for s. We can create the equation

$$\frac{AD}{DE} = \frac{EF}{FC}.$$

Substituting in the values we found, we transform that into

$$\frac{6-s}{s} = \frac{s}{10-s} \longrightarrow (10-s)(6-s) = (s)(s) \longrightarrow 60 - 16s + s^2 = s^2 \longrightarrow 60 - 16s = 0$$

$$\longrightarrow 60 = 16s \longrightarrow s = \frac{60}{16} = \frac{15}{4}.$$

2.3.5　Conclusion

In this section, we explored the shortcuts to find similar triangles (AA, SAS, and SSS) and their properties. We saw the importance of parallel lines in creating equal angles that can then be used to find similar triangles. Similar triangles show up in all kinds of geometry problems, so it is crucial to master the skill of knowing how to find them.

2.3.6 Practice

1. Prove that triangles ACD and FEG are similar, given the following angle measures.

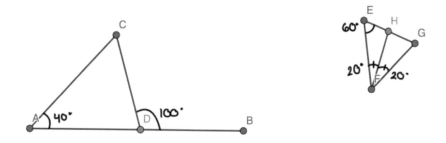

2. The side lengths of a triangle are 4 centimeters, 6 centimeters, and 9 centimeters. One of the side lengths of a similar triangle is 36 centimeters. What is the maximum number of centimeters possible in the perimeter of the second triangles? *Source: MATHCOUNTS*

3. Is the given diagram possible? Why or why not?

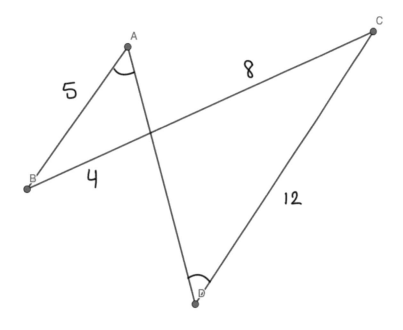

4. Two of the sides in the right triangle in the diagram have length 12 cm and 20 cm, as shown. What is the number of centimeters in the length of the altitude h drawn to the side with length 20 cm? *Source: MATHCOUNTS*

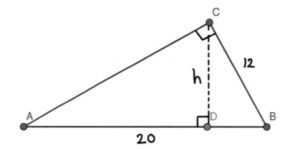

2.4 Right Triangles and Their Properties

2.4.1 Introduction

Now that we've looked at the basics of triangles, let's look specifically at right triangles and their properties. As a quick refresher, in a right triangle, we call the side opposite from the right angle the **hypotenuse**, and the other two sides the legs.

In our first problem, we'll take a stab at proving the **Pythagorean Theorem**, arguably the most important property of right triangles.

2.4.2 Given the following diagram, prove that $a^2 = cd, b^2 = ce$, and finally that $a^2 + b^2 = c^2$.

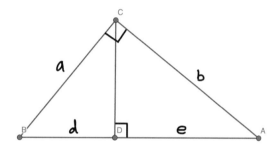

Triangle similarity is going to be our lifesaver in this problem. We can quickly see that $\triangle ADC \sim \triangle ACB$ by AA Similarity, because they both share a right angle and $\angle CAB$. This allows us to set up the proportion $\frac{b}{e} = \frac{c}{b}$. If we multiply both sides by b and e (cross-multiplying), we get that

$$b^2 = ce.$$

In the same manner, we can see that $\triangle BDC \sim \triangle BCA$, giving us the proportion $\frac{a}{d} = \frac{c}{a}$, which cross-multiplies to tell us that

$$a^2 = cd.$$

Now all that's left for us to prove is that $a^2 + b^2 = c^2$. Well, we can say that

$$a^2 + b^2 = cd + ce \longrightarrow a^2 + b^2 = c(d + e).$$

Combining segments d and e gives us segment c, so we have that $d + e = c$. Thus, we have that

$$a^2 + b^2 = c(c) \longrightarrow a^2 + b^2 = c^2.$$

There it is! We've proven the Pythagorean Theorem:

> The Pythagorean Theorem: For any right triangle, the sum of the squares of the legs equals the square of the hypotenuse. Where a and b are the lengths of the legs, and c is the length of the hypotenuse, we have that $a^2 + b^2 = c^2$.

2.4.3   For the following triangles, find the lengths of the missing sides. (Figures may not be drawn to scale.)

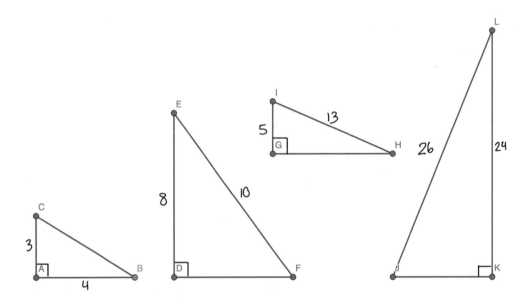

This is just a simple application of the Pythagorean Theorem. Let's go triangle by triangle.

For $\triangle ABC$, we have the lengths of the two legs. Their squares should add up to the square of the hypotenuse, so we can set up that $3^2 + 4^2 = c^2$, where c is the length of $\overline{CB}$. This gives us that $9 + 16 = c^2 \longrightarrow 25 = c^2 \longrightarrow c = 5$.

For $\triangle DEF$, we have the lengths of one leg and the hypotenuse. This allows us to set up the equation $8^2 + b^2 = 10^2$, where b is the length of the second leg. This gives us that $64 + b^2 = 100 \longrightarrow b^2 = 36 \longrightarrow b = 6$.

For $\triangle GHI$, we once again have the lengths of one leg and the hypotenuse. We can then set up the equation $5^2 + b^2 = 13^2$, where b is the length of the second leg. This gives us that $25 + b^2 = 169 \longrightarrow b^2 = 144 \longrightarrow b = 12$.

Finally, for $\triangle JKL$, we have the lengths of one leg and the hypotenuse. This gives us the equation $24^2 + b^2 = 26^2 \longrightarrow 576 + b^2 = 676 \longrightarrow b^2 = 100 \longrightarrow b = 10$.

That was good practice! However, we can also glean some important information from the work we just did.

Looking a little more closely at the triangles, we can see that $\triangle ABC \sim \triangle DEF$, and $\triangle GHI \sim \triangle JKL$, both by SSS Similarity. The side lengths were simply multiplied by some factor to get the lengths in the second triangle.

This leads us to an important discovery: **Pythagorean triples**.

IMPORTANT: A Pythagorean triple is a set of three integers that satisfy the Pythagorean Theorem as sides of a right triangle. We've just worked with two of the most common ones;

$$3, 4, 5 \text{ and } 5, 12, 13.$$

Another common triple is $7, 24, 25$.

Let's continue looking at some right triangles that are a bit special.

2.4.4 In the following diagram, $\triangle ABC$ is an isosceles right triangle. From the given information, find all angles and side lenghts of $\triangle ABC$.

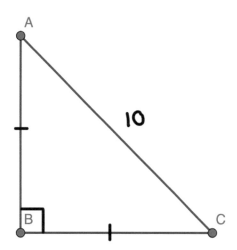

Let's try to get the angles out of the way first. We can use the fact that the angles in any triangle add up to $180°$. We know that one of them is a right angle ($90°$,) and the other 2 are the same. We can set a equal to $m\angle BAC$ and $m\angle BCA$. This gives us that

$$90 + a + a = 180 \longrightarrow 90 + 2a = 180 \longrightarrow 2a = 90 \longrightarrow a = 45.$$

Therefore, we have that

$$m\angle BAC = m\angle BCA = 45°.$$

Now for the sides, we can use the Pythagorean Theorem. We know that

$$a^2 + b^2 = c^2,$$

where a and b are the lengths of the triangle's legs, and c is the length of the triangle's hypotenuse. Well, in this case, our two legs are the same. Let's set the length of a leg equal to b. This gives us that

$$b^2 + b^2 = c^2 \longrightarrow 2b^2 = 10^2 \longrightarrow 2b^2 = 100 \longrightarrow b^2 = 50 \longrightarrow b = \sqrt{50} = 5\sqrt{2}.$$

Thus,

$$AB = BC = 5\sqrt{2}.$$

These discoveries lead us to important information regarding isosceles right triangles.

> **IMPORTANT: An isosceles right triangle is also commonly known as a $45 - 45 - 90$ triangle, because its angles will always be equal to $45°, 45°$, and $90°$. Additionally, the legs are equal, and the hypotenuse is equal to $\sqrt{2}$ times the leg.**

2.4.5 For the following diagram of equilateral triangle ABC, find the area of $\triangle ABC$.

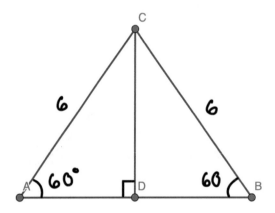

We'll need to find the length of $\overline{CD}$ to get the area of the triangle. Let's see how we can do that.

We can quickly see that $\triangle ACD \cong \triangle BCD$ by AAS similarity. This tells us that $AD = BD$, and since we know that $AD + BD = AB = 6$, we can say that $AD = BD = \frac{6}{2} = 3$.

From here, it's a simple matter of applying the Pythagorean Theorem. We can use $\triangle ACD$. $\overline{AD}$ and $\overline{CD}$ are the legs, and $\triangle AC$ is the hypotenuse. We know the lengths of one leg and the hypotenuse, so we can find the last leg: CD.

We can set up the equation $3^2 + b^2 = 6^2$, where $b = CD$. This continues to give

$$9 + b^2 = 36 \longrightarrow b^2 = 27 \longrightarrow b = 3\sqrt{3}.$$

Now we can finally find the area of $\triangle ABC$. We know that the formula for triangle area is half the base times height. Now that we've found CD, we have both the base and the height! This gives us that the area is

$$\frac{6 \times 3\sqrt{3}}{2} = \frac{18\sqrt{3}}{2} = 9\sqrt{3}.$$

This brings us neatly to our discussion of our next set of special triangles.

2.4.6 **In the previous problem, we discussed an equilateral triangle that had been cut in half. Now, we'll explore the properties of each half-triangle, known as $30-60-90$ triangles. If the original equilateral triangle had side length $2x$, what would the length of both legs be?**

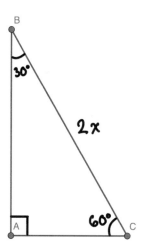

Looking more closely at each half-triangle we created, it's easy to see that because two of the angles are $90°$ and $60°$, the last one will be $30°$. Hence, the triangle's name: $30 - 60 - 90$ triangle!

Now for the sides. Keeping in mind that this triangle was half of an equilateral triangle, we can deduce that the leg serving as the base of the triangle in our diagram has a length of x, because it is simply a side of the equilateral triangle cut in half.

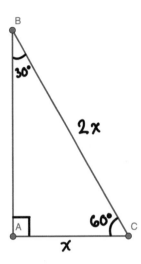

Now that we know the lenghts of the hypotenuse and one leg, we can find the length of the final leg by applying the Pythagorean Theorem. Letting b be the length of the unknown leg, we can set up the equation

$$x^2 + b^2 = (2x)^2 \longrightarrow x^2 + b^2 = 4x^2 \longrightarrow b^2 = 3x^2 \longrightarrow b = \sqrt{3x^2} = x\sqrt{3}.$$

Therefore, the length of the last leg is $x\sqrt{3}$.

Because we proved this algebraically, it's easy to see how this can be applied to any $30 - 60 - 90$ triangle.

> **IMPORTANT: A** $30 - 60 - 90$ **triangle has angles of** $30°, 60°$, **and** $90°$. **Its sides are in the ratio** $1 : \sqrt{3} : 2$, **with the right angle opposite of the longest side, and the** $30°$ **angle opposite of the shorter leg.**

2.4.7   Conclusion

Those are the basic principles of right triangles, plus some special right triangles that you should remember. We explored the Pythagorean Theorem, Pythagorean triples, $45 - 45 - 90$ triangles, and $30 - 60 - 90$ triangles. With practice, you won't even need to recall these specific types; you'll just know what type the triangle is by looking at the problem.

2.4.8   Practice

1. For each triangle in the following diagram, find the length(s) of the missing side(s).

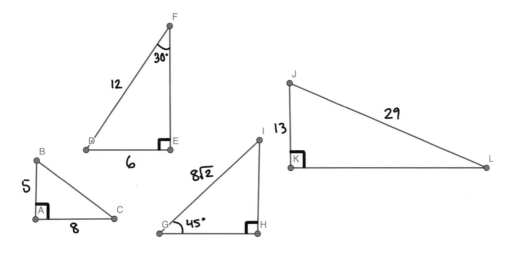

2. What is the area of a triangle with sides $\sqrt{10}$, $\sqrt{13}$, and $\sqrt{23}$?

3. What is the area of an isosceles triangle with legs 4 units long, and a base of length 5?

4. Find the length of all sides of all triangles in the following diagram.

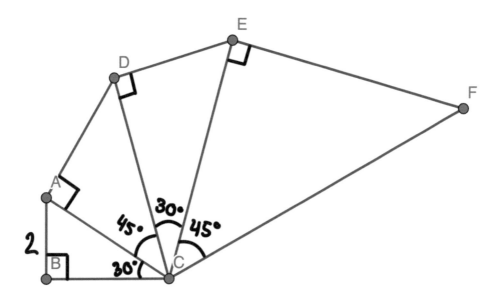

5. Find AC, BC, and BD in the following diagram, as well as $m\angle BCD$ and $m\angle CDB$.

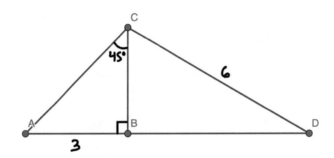

6. Which Pythagorean triples are triangles of the following side lengths based off of?

   (a) $60, 80, 100$

   (b) $10, 24, 26$

   (c) $21, 72, 75$

2.5 Special Parts of Triangles

2.5.1 Introduction

Triangles contain many points, lines, and even circles that can be very useful for figuring out their properties. In specific, we'll be exploring **perpendicular bisectors**, **angle bisectors**, **medians**, **altitudes**, **circumcenters**, and **incenters**.

For context, here are examples of perpendicular bisectors, angle bisectors, medians, and altitudes:

Perpendicular Bisector: the line passing through the midpoint of a segment so the two are perpendicular

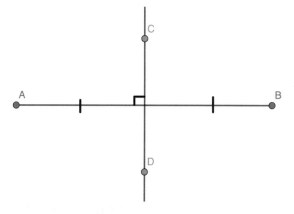

Figure 2.16: line CD is the perpendicular bisector of $\overline{AB}$

Angle Bisector: the ray that divides an angle into two equal angles

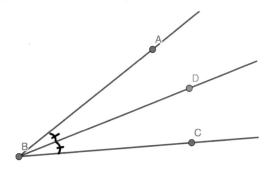

Figure 2.17: ray BD is the angle bisector of $\angle ABC$

Median: the line connecting a vertex of a triangle to the midpoint of the opposite side

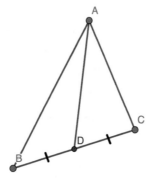

Figure 2.18: $\overline{AD}$ is a median

Altitude: the perpendicular segment from a vertex of a triangle to the opposite side

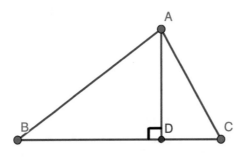

Figure 2.19: $\overline{AD}$ is the altitude

In a triangle, the points where all three perpendicular bisectors, angle bisectors, medians, or altitudes intersect have special properties.

Circumcenter: the point at which all three perpendicular bisectors of the sides of a triangle intersect; the circumcenter is the center of the circumcircle of the triangle, which passes through all three vertices of the triangle

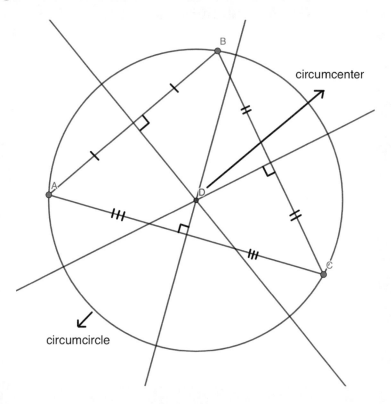

Figure 2.20: Point D is the circumcenter, and the circle with center D is the circumcircle

Incenter: the point at which all three angle bisectors of the angles of a triangle intersect; the incenter is the center of the incircle of the triangle, which is tangent to all three sides of the triangle

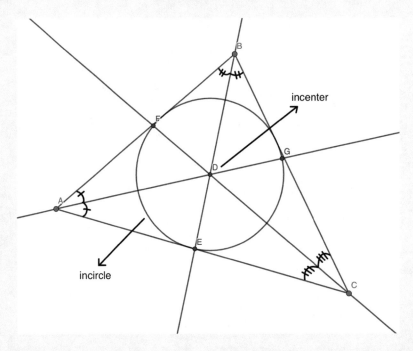

Figure 2.21: Point D is the incenter, and the circle with center D is the incircle

Centroid: the point at which all three medians of a triangle intersect; the three medians divide the triangle into 6 smaller triangles of equal area

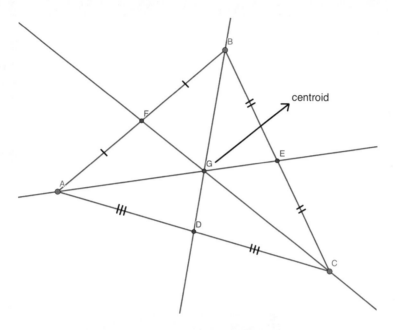

Figure 2.22: Point G is the centroid

Orthocenter: the point at which all three altitudes of a triangle intersect

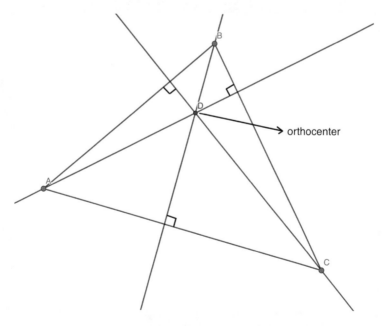

Figure 2.23: Point D is the orthocenter

Connecting the midpoints of the sides of a triangle divides it into 4 congruent triangles, which are all similar to the original triangle. The central triangle created is called the medial triangle.

Now that we know all this let's take a closer look at a few special cases.

2.5.2   Find the circumcenter of a right triangle, using the diagram below. What is the circumradius of the triangle?

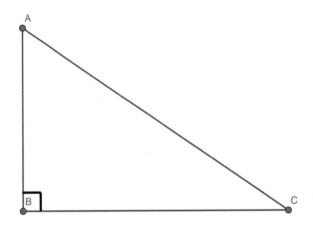

To start, let's draw in the perpendicular bisector of $\overline{AB}$:

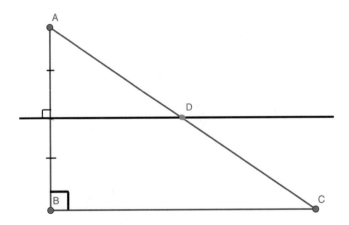

The bisector intersects $\overline{AC}$ at point D. Let's call the intersection of the bisector and $\overline{AB}$ point E. $\overline{ED}$ and $\overline{BC}$ are both perpendicular to $\overline{AB}$, so we know that $\overline{ED}||\overline{BC}$.

Therefore, we can see that $\triangle AED \sim \triangle ABC$ by AA similarity, meaning that $\frac{AD}{AC} = \frac{AE}{AB}$. Since we know that $\frac{AE}{AB} = \frac{1}{2}$, we then know that $\frac{AD}{AC} = \frac{1}{2}$ as well. Thus, we have that point D is the midpoint of $\overline{AC}$! We also know that point D is on the perpendicular bisector of $\overline{AC}$ because it's the midpoint, so D must, in fact, be the point at which all three perpendicular bisectors of $\triangle ABC$ intersect. We have thus proven that D is the circumcenter of $\triangle ABC$.

The endpoints of the hypotenuse, $\overline{AC}$, are on the circumcircle, and since the midpoint of the hypotenuse is the circumcenter, we can deduce that the hypotenuse is the diameter. From this, we can tell that the circumradius is half the length of the hypotenuse of the right triangle!

> **IMPORTANT:** The hypotenuse of a right triangle is the diameter of its circumcircle. The circumcenter is the midpoint of the hypotenuse, and the circumradius equals half the length of the hypotenuse.

2.5.3   In the diagram below, prove that $\frac{AB}{AE} = \frac{CB}{CE}$.

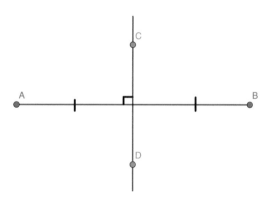

The diagram tells us a few things: $\overline{AC} \| \overline{DB}$, and $\overline{CD}$ is the angle bisector of $\angle ACB$. We can also recognize that $\overline{CD}$ is a transversal, so $\angle CDB$ is also congruent to angles ACD and DCB. Because we now know that $\angle BCD \cong \angle BDC$, we can see that $\triangle BCD$ is isosceles, and $BC = BD$. The parallel lines also give us similar triangles: $\triangle ACE \sim \triangle BDE$. Thus, we have the equation $\frac{AC}{AE} = \frac{BC}{BE}$. From here, since we know that $BC = BD$, we can say that $\frac{AC}{AE} = \frac{BC}{BE}$.

IMPORTANT: In situations such as those portrayed in the diagram below, if D is on $overline{AC}$ such that $\overline{BD}$ is the angle bisector of $\angle ABC$, then $\frac{AB}{AD} = \frac{CB}{CD}$. This is known as the **Angle Bisector Theorem.**

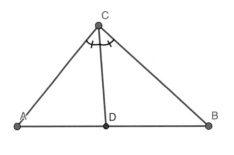

2.5.4 Prove that the centroid of any triangle divides each median in a $2:1$ ratio, with the longer portion consisting of the segment from the centroid to the vertex.

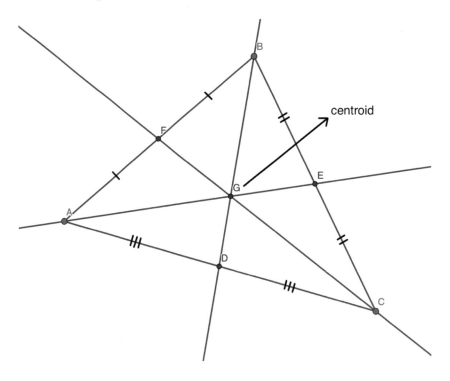

We know that each of the 6 triangles created by the medians have the same area. We know that $\triangle AGC$ consists of two of the small triangles, so we can say that the area of $\triangle AGC$ is double the area of $\triangle GEC$. The two triangles share an altitude; the one from point C to the extension of $\overline{AE}$. Thus, we can say that $\frac{AG}{GE} = \frac{\text{area of } \triangle AGC}{\text{area of } \triangle GEC} = 2$. This works for any median!

> **IMPORTANT: The centroid of a triangle divides its medians in a $2:1$ ratio.**

2.5.5 Conclusion

In this chapter, we explored the properties of perpendicular bisectors, angle bisectors, medians, altitudes, and their corresponding concepts, including circumcenters and circumcircles, incenters and incircles, centroids, and orthocenters. We also saw a few special properties, such as how the hypotenuse of a right triangle is the diameter of its circumcircle, the Angle Bisector Theorem, and that the centroid of a triangle divides its medians in a $2:1$ ratio.

2.5.6 Practice

1. Triangle ABC has the following properties: $AB = 6, \angle B = 90°$, and $BC = 10$. Find the circumradiusof $\triangle ABC$.

2. If the altitudes of a triangle are all the same length, is it true that the triangle must be equilateral? Why or why not?

3. Point D is on side BC of $\triangle ABC$ such that $\angle BAD = \angle CAD$. Given that $AC = 8, BD = 3$, and $DC = 4$, find AB.

4. For a given triangle, the medians $\overline{AD}, \overline{BE}$, and $\overline{CF}$ meet at G. The area of $\triangle ABC$ is 48. Find the areas of $\triangle ADC, \triangle AGC, \triangle GFB$, and $\triangle DEF$.

5. In triangle ABC, altitude $\overline{AD}$ intersects angle bisector $\overline{BE}$ at point X. If $\angle BAC = 117°$ and $\angle ACB = 35°$, then determine $\angle DXE$.

2.6   Area and Perimeter

2.6.1   Introduction

Area and perimeter are both properties of two-dimensional geometric figures. Area is a measure of the number of unit squares needed to cover a figure, and perimeter is a measure of the distance along its boundary all the way around once.

As a refresher, here are some of the fundamental area.

The area of a closed figure can be described as the number of 1×1 unit squares needed to completely cover the figure. Formulas for area that you should already know include the following, where b is the base and h is the height. For circles, r is the radius.

Square / rectangle / parallelogram: $A = b \cdot h$

Triangle: $A = \frac{b \cdot h}{2}$

Trapezoid: $A = \frac{b_1 + b_2}{2} \cdot h$

Circle: $A = \pi \cdot r^2$

2.6.2   The length of one side of a rectangle is 5 more than twice the length of an adjacent side. Keeping in mind that the perimeter of the rectangle is 58, find the area of the rectangle.

This is a good problem to solve using algebra. Let x equal the length of the adjacent side. Then, the original side would have a length of

$$5 + 2x.$$

The total perimeter of the rectangle would equal

$$x + (5 + 2x) + x + (5 + 2x) = 2(x + (5 + 2x)) = 2x + 10 + 4x = 6x + 10.$$

We know that the rectangle has a perimeter of 58, so we have that

$$6x + 10 = 58 \longrightarrow 6x = 48 \longrightarrow x = 8.$$

Thus, the adjacent side has a length of 8, and the original side has a length of $2 \times 8 + 5 = 16 + 5 = 21$. From here, finding the area is as simple as multiplying our two side lengths together:

$$21 \times 8 = 168.$$

2.6.3 What is the area of an equilateral triangle if its perimeter is 48?

The sides of an equilateral triangle are all of equal length, so each side in this triangle will have a length of $\frac{48}{3} = 16$. We can then recall that an equilateral triangle can be split into two $30 - 60 - 90$ triangles, and we can use the special properties of those triangles to deduce that our equilateral triangle has a height of $\frac{16}{2} \times \sqrt{3} = 8\sqrt{3}$. Thus, the area of the triangle is

$$\frac{16 \times 8\sqrt{3}}{2} = 64\sqrt{3}.$$

2.6.4 A square poster is replaced by a rectangular poster that is 2 inches wider and 2 inches shorter. What is the difference in the number of square inches between the area of the larger poster and the smaller poster? *(Source: MATHCOUNTS)*

Note that the problem did not give us any definite side lengths. We'll have to do this algebraically.

Let the original side length of the square poster be x. Thus, the area of the original poster is simply x^2.

The rectangular poster will then have side lengths of $x + 2$ and $x - 2$, making for an area of

$$(x + 2)(x - 2) = x^2 - 4.$$

We now have both areas. It's clear to see that the difference in the area is simply 4 square inches.

2.6.5 In the following diagram, the area of $\triangle ABE$ is 24, the area of $\triangle BCE$ is 15, and the area of $\triangle CDE$ is 10. Find the area of triangle ADE.

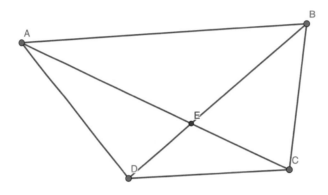

It's clear that triangles ABE and CBE share an altitude from B, so we can set up the ratio

$$\frac{AE}{CE} = \frac{\text{area of } \triangle ABE}{\text{area of } \triangle CBE} = \frac{8}{5}.$$

Similarly, we know that the ratio of the areas of triangles ADE and CDE is equal to

$$\frac{AE}{CE} = \frac{8}{5}.$$

Thus, we have that the area of $\triangle ADE$ is equal to $\frac{8}{5}$ times the area of $\triangle CDE$, which is 16.

If two triangles share a base, the ratio of their areas is the ratio of their altitudes to that base. If two triangles share an altitude, the ratio of their areas is the ratio of the bases to which that altitude is drawn.

2.6.6 Conclusion

In this section, we explored basic concepts of area and perimeter for quadrilaterals and triangles. We saw how changing the dimensions of figures affects these properties, and saw how we can use algebra to find relationships even when no definite properties are given.

2.6.7 Practice

1. A triangle has a perimeter of 45. One of its sides is twice as long as the shortest side, and another side is 50% longer than the shortest side. How long is the shortest side?

2. What is the area of a square if its perimeter is 48?

3. The perimeter of a square garden is 64 meters. The path surrounding the garden has uniform width and has an area of 228 square meters. How many meters of fencing are needed to surround the outer edge of the path? *(Source: MATH-COUNTS)*

4. There is a 20 foot long by 12 foot high wall. Two painters are arguing over how to paint a triangle on the wall. Painter A wants to paint the design on the left, while Painter B wants to paint the design on the right. Whose design will use less paint?

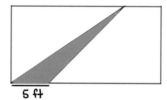
5 ft

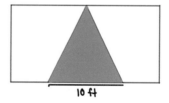
10 ft

5. A gardener plans to build a fence to enclose a square garden plot. The perimeter of the plot is 96 feet, and he sets posts at the corners of the square. The posts along the sides are set 6 feet apart. How many posts will he use to fence the entire plot? *(Source: MATHCOUNTS)*

2.7   All About Quadrilaterals!

2.7.1   Introduction

Quadrilaterals are polygons with four sides, vertices, and angles (all four angles add up to $360°$ in all quadrilaterals). Some common types of quadrilaterals are squares, rectangles, parallelograms, and trapezoids.

A parallelogram is a quadrilateral with two pairs of opposite sides being parallel. Its area is computed by multiplying the base and the height. Opposite sides have equal length, and opposite angles are equal as well. The diagonals from corner to corner bisect each other.

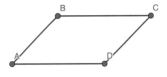

A rhombus is a quadrilateral in which all four sides are of equal length. All rhombi (plural form of rhombus) are parallelograms. The diagonals of rhombi are perpendicular. The area can be found by taking half of the product of the diagonals, or by simply multiplying the base and the height.

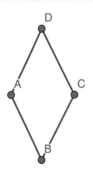

A rectangle is any quadrilateral with four right angles. All rectangles are parallelograms. The area of a rectangle is equal to its base times its height.

A square is a quadrilateral with four right angles and four equal sides. All squares are rectangles, rhombi, and parallelograms. The area of a square is equal to its side length to the second power.

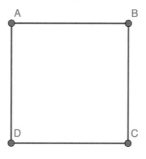

A trapezoid is a quadrilateral with one pair of parallel sides. The segment connecting the midpoints of the sides that are not parallel is called the median. The distance between the two parallel sides is the height. The area of a trapezoid can be found by multiplying the median and the height.

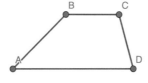

2.7.2   Given that $ABCD$ is a parallelogram, find the values of a and b, and find the measure $\angle D$.

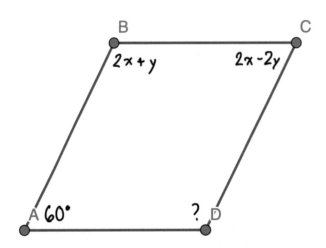

We're given that $ABCD$ is a parallelogram, so we know that its opposite angles are equal. Thus, we know that angles B and D are congruent, so $\angle D$ also has a measure of $2x + y$. From here, we can set up a few equations. For one, we have that angles A and C are equal, so we have

$$2x - 2y = 60.$$

Additionally, we know that all four angles add up to $360°$, so we have that

$$60 + (2x + y) + (2x - 2y) + (2x + y) = 60 + (2x + y) + 60 + (2x + y) = 120 + 4x + 2y$$

$$\longrightarrow 4x + 2y = 240.$$

We have a system of equations! To solve it, we can simply add our two equations, which will cancel the y terms and allow us to solve for x. Adding the two gives us that

$$(2x - 2y) + (4x + 2y) = 60 + 240 \longrightarrow 6x = 300 \longrightarrow x = 50.$$

Knowing that $2x - 2y = 60$, we can solve for y by plugging our value for x into the equation:

$$2(50) - 2y = 60 \longrightarrow 100 - 2y = 60 \longrightarrow -2y = -40 \longrightarrow y = 20.$$

We know that $\angle D$ has a measure equal to $2x+y$, which we now know to be $2(50)+20 = 100 + 20 = 120$ degrees.

We might notice that pairs of angles that lie on the same line, such as angles A and B, or B and C, add up to $180°$. In fact, this applies for all parallelograms.

> **IMPORTANT: In a parallelogram, adjacent angles add up to $180°$.**

2.7.3 Parallelogram $ABCD$ is formed as shown, with the relationships as shown in the diagram. Find the area of $ABCD$, and find the distance between sides $\overline{AB}$ and $\overline{CD}$.

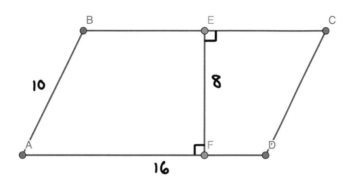

In this case, finding the area is incredibly straightforward, as we know both the base and height. Still, let's see where the ability to find area using base and height comes from. If we draw in the diagonal $\overline{AC}$, we get the following diagram:

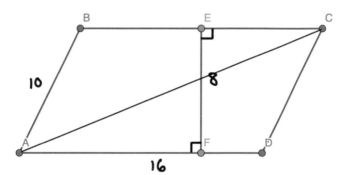

Now it's clear to see: the segment EF has the same length as the height of triangle ACD; 8. Triangles ACD and CAB are congruent by SSS congruence, so they have the same area. Thus, we can say that the area of the parallelogram can be computed as

$$\frac{AD \times EF}{2} \times 2 = AD \times EF = 16 \times 8 = 128.$$

That's the same result we would have gotten if we simply multiplied our known base times the height, but isn't it better to see where that result comes from?

Onto the second part of the problem. We need to find the distance between $\overline{AB}$ and $\overline{CD}$. If we treat $\overline{AB}$ as the base of the parallelogram, then this distance simply becomes the height. We know that the base times the height equals the area, so we can set up the following equation, with h being the height:

$$10 \times h = 128 \longrightarrow h = 12.8$$

Thus, the distance between $\overline{AB}$ and $\overline{CD}$ is 12.8.

2.7.4 $ABCD$ **is a rhombus with diagonals** $AC = 16$ **and** $BD = 8$. **Find the area and perimeter of** $ABCD$.

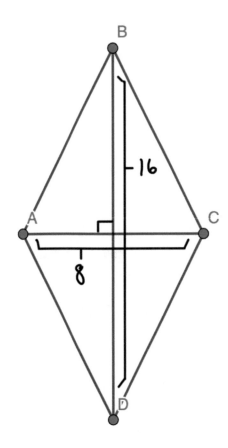

Just like in the last problem, we could simply apply the formula: multiply the lengths of the diagonals, and divide by 2. Still, it's much better to know where that formula comes from.

Either way we look at it, both diagonals, on their own, split the rhombus into two congruent triangles. Let's take diagonal $\overline{AC}$. It forms the pair of congruent triangles ABC and CDA. Adding their two areas should give us the total area of the rhombus, so let's do just that. The area of a triangle is half the base times the height. We know that the height of each triangle will be half the length of diagonal $\overline{BD}$, so $\frac{16}{2} = 8$. This gives us that the area of the rhombus equals

$$2 \times \frac{AC \times \frac{BD}{2}}{2} = 2 \times \frac{AC \times BD}{4} = \frac{AC \times BD}{2} = \frac{8 \times 16}{2} = \frac{128}{2} = 64.$$

And just like that, we see how multiplying the diagonals and dividing by 2 works!

As for the perimeter, we can apply what we know about right triangles. Taking the two diagonals together, we can see that they form 4 congruent right triangles, each with legs length $\frac{8}{2} = 4$ and $\frac{16}{2} = 8$. Using the Pythagorean Theorem allows us to get the hypotenuse, which is also the side length of the rhombus. From this, we see that the hypotenuse, and each side of the rhombus, is equal to

$$\sqrt{4^2 + 8^2} = \sqrt{16 + 64} = \sqrt{80} = 4\sqrt{5}.$$

All four sides are the same, so to get the perimeter, we simply multiply that side length by 4 :

$$4 \times 4\sqrt{5} = 16\sqrt{5}.$$

2.7.5 The width of a rectangle is 2 less than half its length. If the perimeter of the rectangle is 26, find its area.

Let the length of the rectangle equal x. Then we know that the width is equal to $\frac{x}{2} - 2$. The perimeter is equal to twice the sum of the length and width, so we have that

$$2(x + \frac{x}{2} - 2) = 26 \longrightarrow x + \frac{x}{2} - 2 = 13 \longrightarrow x + \frac{x}{2} = 15 \longrightarrow \frac{3x}{2} = 15 \longrightarrow 3x = 30$$

$$\longrightarrow x = 10.$$

Thus, we know that the width is equal to

$$\frac{10}{2} - 2 = 5 - 2 = 3.$$

The area is equal to the length times the width, which in this case is simply $10 \times 3 = 30$.

2.7.6 Find the area and perimeter of a square with diagonals of length 10.

Even in your head, you can visualize how a diagonal divides a square: into two congruent $45 - 45 - 90$ right triangles. We can use our knowledge of these special triangles to find the side length of the square. Let the side length be s. Then, our equation becomes

$$s^2 + s^2 = 10^2 \longrightarrow 2s^2 = 100 \longrightarrow s^2 = 50 \longrightarrow s = 5\sqrt{2}.$$

Squaring the side length gives the area of the square; doing that gives us that the area is equal to $(5\sqrt{2})^2 = 50$.

The perimeter is simply four times the side length, or $4 \times 5\sqrt{2} = 20\sqrt{2}$.

> **IMPORTANT: In a square with side length s and diagonal length d, $d = s\sqrt{2}$, the perimeter is equal to $d(2\sqrt{2})$, and the area is equal to $\frac{d^2}{2}$.**

2.7.7 **In trapezoid** $ABCD$, **we have that** $\overline{BC}\|\overline{AD}, \angle B = 160°$,
and $\angle C = 70°$. **Find** $\angle A$ **and** $\angle D$.

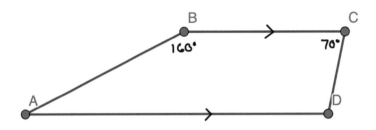

Knowing that $\overline{BC}\|\overline{AD}$, we know that $\angle C + \angle D = 180$. Since $m\angle C = 70°$, we know
that $m\angle D = 180° - 70° = 110°$.

Since $ABCD$ is a quadrilateral, the sum of all its angles should be $360°$. Setting up an
equation involving this fact will allow us to solve for $\angle A$. Doing so gives us that

$$m\angle A + 160 + 70 + 110 = 360 \longrightarrow m\angle A + 340 = 360 \longrightarrow m\angle A = 20°.$$

2.7.8 **For trapezoid** $ABCD$, $\overline{AD}\|\overline{BC}, \angle B = \angle C$, **and** $\angle B < 90°$.
Prove that $AB = CD$.

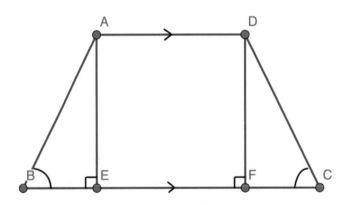

We know that $AE = DF$ because $\overline{AD}\|\overline{BC}$, so we know that $\triangle ABE \cong \triangle DCF$ by
AAS congruence. Thus, by CPCTC, $AB = CD$.

This problem is a quick way to get introduced to isosceles trapezoids.

> **IMPORTANT: An isosceles trapezoid has two pairs of equal base angles,
> equal leg (the sides that are not parallel) lengths, and equal diagonal
> lengths.**

2.7.9 Conclusion

In this section, we explored the major types of quadrilaterals (parallelograms, rhombi, rectangles, squares, and trapezoids), and their various properties. We saw how their sides and angles relate, as well as how their diagonals come into play.

2.7.10 Practice

1. $ABCD$ is a rhombus with $AB = 25$ and $AC = 48$. Find BD, the area of $ABCD$, and the distance between $\overline{AB}$ and $\overline{CD}$.

2. Gerald has a 36 foot by 24 foot garden. He wants to build a path that is 2 feet wide around the garden. If the bricks for the path cost $\$15$ per square foot, how much will the bricks for the path cost?

3. The area of square $ABCD$ is 40. Find AB and AC.

4. Find the area of a trapezoid with bases of lengths 32 and 22, with height 16.

5. The area of trapezoid $ABCD$ is 42. One base is 6 units longer than the other, and the height of the trapezoid is 2. Find the length of the longer base.

6. Each side of an equilateral triangle is 8 inches long. An altitude of this triangle is used as the side of a square. What is the number of square inches in the area of the square? *(Source: MATHCOUNTS)*

7. One of the angles in a rhombus is $120°$. The shorter diagonal has length 2. What is the area of the rhombus?

8. A quadrilateral $ABCD$ is known to be a parallelogram. $AB = 2x - 3, BC = x + 7$, and $CD = 3x - 8$. Find the perimeter of $ABCD$.

2.8   All About Circles!

2.8.1   Introduction

Circles are defined as the set of all points a certain distance from one point; the center. Circles have area, just like polygons, but the concept of perimeter is a little different. A circle's perimeter is its **circumference**. An **arc** is the part of a circle that connects two points on its circumference. An arc is measured by what fraction of the circle's circumference it is. There are $360°$ in a whole circle.

In circles, the irrational number π is of extreme importance. π is the ratio of a circle's circumference to its diameter, which always comes out to $3.14159265...$ It is irrational, so the decimal never ends.

Here are some basic formulas dealing with circles:

> The area of a circle with radius r: πr^2

> The circumference of a circle with radius r: $2\pi r$

2.8.2   A certain circle has area 121π. What is its diameter?

We know that the area of a circle of radius r is equal to πr^2. We can use this and our given area to solve for the radius of the circle, which will then let us find the diameter. We thus have that:

$$\pi r^2 = 121\pi \longrightarrow r^2 = 121 \longrightarrow r = 11.$$

The diameter is simply twice the length of the radius, so the diameter of this circle has length $2 \times 11 = 22$.

2.8.3   A $120°$ arc of a circle has length 18π. What is its area?

Similarly to the last problem, we'll look for the circle's radius, which will then allow us to find its area. $120°$ is $\frac{120}{360} = \frac{1}{3}$ of the total $360°$ in a circle, so we know the arc's length of 18π is $\frac{1}{3}$ of the circle's circumference. Using c to represent the circumference, we thus have that

$$\frac{c}{3} = 18\pi \longrightarrow c = 54\pi.$$

Since we know that the circumference of a circle is $2\pi r$, we can then say that

$$2\pi r = 54\pi \longrightarrow 2r = 54 \longrightarrow r = 27.$$

Finally, the area of a circle is πr^2, so we know that the area of this circle with radius 27 is $\pi(27^2) = 729\pi$.

2.8.4   **For the following circle with center O, chord $\overline{AB}$ has a length of 15. The circumference of the circle is 30π. What is the length of arc AB?**

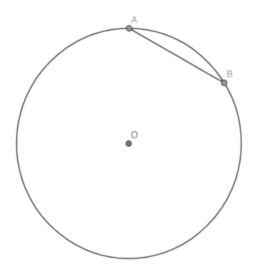

From the circumference, we know that the diameter of the circle is 30. We can notice that the length of chord $\overline{AB}$ is half the length of the diameter. This tells us that it is the same length as a radius! From here, we can note that a triangle formed by points A, B, and O would be an equilateral triangle! We know that the angles of an equilateral triangle are all $60°$. Now we know that arc AB has an angle measure of $60°$, so it should have a length of $\frac{60}{360} = \frac{1}{6}$ of the circumference, which turns out to be $\frac{1}{6} \times 30\pi = 5\pi$.

2.8.5   **A farmer has 30 meters of fence, with which they want to enclose a semicircular space adjacent to a barn. The barn will form one side of the enclosure. What is the area of the space enclosed by the barn and the fence?**

Handily, we don't have to consider the straight side of the semicircle, because the barn takes care of that. Therefore, we know that the 30 meters is formed solely by the fence. This length is a semicircle, so it would be half the length of total circumference of a full circle. Since we know that the circumference of a circle is its diameter times π, we can see that half that length would simply be the radius times π! Thus, we have that

$$30 = r\pi \longrightarrow r = \frac{30}{\pi}.$$

From here, we use the formula for area of a circle, which is πr^2. However, since we only want the area of half of a circle, our formula becomes

$$\frac{\pi r^2}{2} = \frac{\pi(\frac{30}{\pi})^2}{2} = \frac{\frac{900}{\pi}}{2} = \frac{450}{\pi}.$$

2.8.6 **Circle O has radius 6. The region within the circle formed by segments OA and OB in combination with arc AB is called a sector. The shaded region between chord $\overline{AB}$ and the circle is called a circular segment. Find the area of the shaded circular segment.**

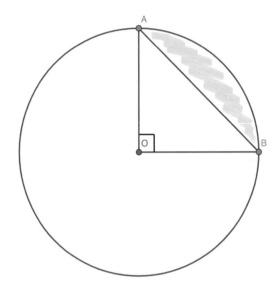

A good strategy we can use would be to find the area of sector AOB, and to then subtract from that the area of triangle AOB. This would leave us with the area of the shaded circular segment.

The area of sector AOB is a fraction of the total area of circle O. What fraction? That would be the fraction of the measure of the arc, divided by $360°$. We can see from our diagram that arc AB has a measure of $90°$, so the fraction in our case is $\frac{90}{360} = \frac{1}{4}$. The circle has radius 6, so it has radius $\pi \times 6^2 = 36\pi$. The area of sector AOB is thus $\frac{1}{4} \times 36\pi = 9\pi$.

Now for the area of triangle AOB. That's easy, we can clearly see that it is an isosceles right triangle with legs of length 6. Thus, the area is $\frac{6 \times 6}{2} = \frac{36}{2} = 18$.

Finally, we can subtract our two areas to find the area of the circular segment, giving us a final result of $9\pi - 18$.

IMPORTANT: The area of a sector of a circle is equal to the area of the circle, times the fraction equal to $\frac{\text{central angle of the sector}}{360°}$.

> **IMPORTANT:** Often, irregular areas can be found by either adding or subtracting areas that are easier to find.

Now that we've looked at various aspects of circles' circumferences and areas, it's time to move on to some more advanced topics. In the next few problems, we'll explore the properties of various types of angles formed by lines interacting with circles. As a prerequisite, here are some terms and relationships you should know.

> **An inscribed angle in a circle has its vertex on the circumference, and its sides intersecting the circle as shown in the diagram.**

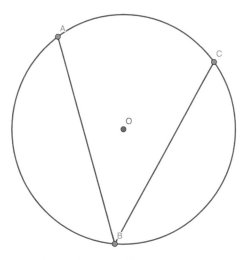

Figure 2.24: $\angle ABC$ is an inscribed angle

A secant is a line that intersects a circle in two points.

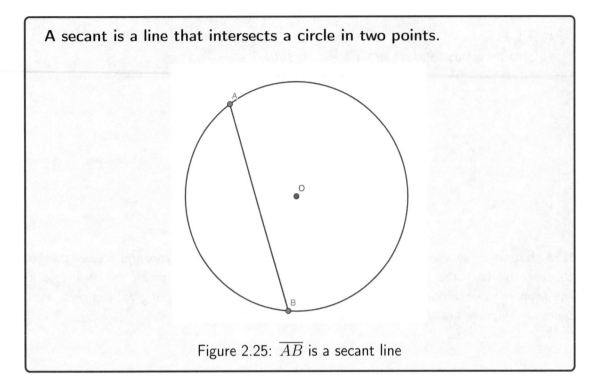

Figure 2.25: $\overline{AB}$ is a secant line

A tangent line is a line that touches a circle at exactly one point. The tangent line is perpendicular to the radius through the intersection point.

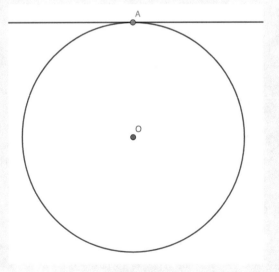

Figure 2.26: The line through A is a tangent line

Two tangents to a circle from the same point outside the circle are always equal in length.

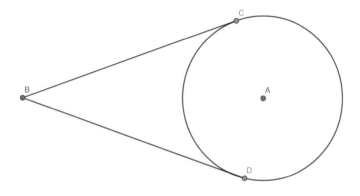

Figure 2.27: Tangents $\overline{BC}$ and $\overline{BD}$ are equal in length

A cyclic quadrilateral is one that has all four vertices on the same circle.

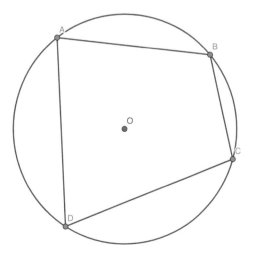

Figure 2.28: Quadrilateral $ABCD$ is a cyclic quadrilateral

2.8.7   **When an inscribed angle cuts off a** $180°$**, it is inscribed in a semicircle. Using the following diagram, prove that all such inscribed angles are right angles.**

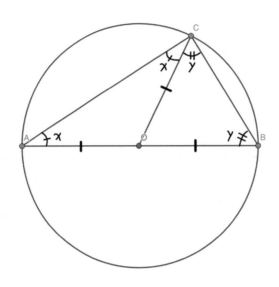

In order to prove that the inscribed angle ACB is a right angle, we need to prove that $x + y = 90°$. We know that triangles AOC and BOC are isosceles, so we have that $x = \angle OAC = \angle OCA$ and $y = \angle OBC = \angle OCB$. Taking triangle ABC as a whole, we see that $\angle A + \angle B + \angle ACB = 180°$, so we know that $x + y + (x + y) = 180°$. This simplifies to $2(x + y) = 180° \longrightarrow x + y = 90°$. This proves that $\angle ACB$ is a right angle.

> IMPORTANT: All angles inscribed in semicircles are right angles.

2.8.8   **Prove that for all angles ACB such that the center of the circle, O, is inside $\triangle ABC$, $\angle ACB$ is half the measure of arc AOB.**

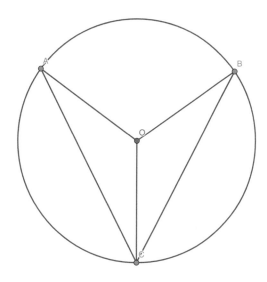

Let $\angle OCA = x$ and $\angle OCB = y$. From here, we see that $\angle ACB = x + y$. Triangles AOC and BOC are isosceles, so we know that $\angle OAC = x$, and $\angle OBC = y$. Thus, we have that $\angle AOC = 180° = 2x$, and $\angle BOC = 180° - 2y$. We can use this information to now find $\angle AOB$.

$$\angle AOB = 360° - \angle AOC - \angle BOC = 360° - (180° - 2x) - (180° - 2y) = 2x + 2y = 2(x+y).$$

Thus, we have that arc AB is equal to $2(x + y)$, so $\angle ACB$ is half the measure of arc AOB.

> **IMPORTANT:** The measure of an inscribed angle is half the measure of the arc it intercepts.

2.8.9   **Given that** $\angle AOB = 2x, \angle ACD = x,$ **and arc** $BC = x,$ **find the value of** $x.$

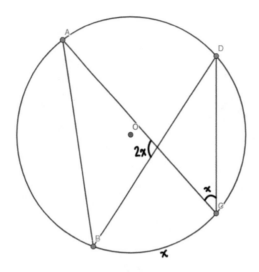

$\angle B$ and $\angle C$ are inscribed in the same arc, they must both be equal to half the measure of the arc. Thus, we know that

$$\angle B = \angle C = x.$$

$\angle A$ is inscribed in arc BC, so we have that $\angle A = \frac{BC}{2} = \frac{x}{2}$. We also know that

$$\angle A + \angle AOB + \angle B = 180° \longrightarrow \frac{x}{2} + 2x + x = 180°.$$

Solving this equation for x gives us that

$$\frac{7x}{2} = 180° \longrightarrow 7x = 360° \longrightarrow x = \frac{360°}{7}.$$

IMPORTANT: Two angles that are inscribed in the same arc are always equal.

2.8.10 Chords $\overline{CD}$ and $\overline{AB}$ intersect at B. Arc DE is equal to x, and arc AC is equal to y. Find an algebraic formula for $\angle DEB$ in terms of x and y.

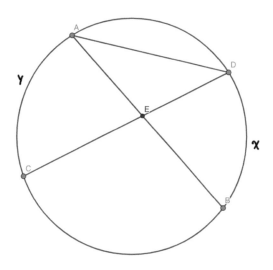

The convenient addition of chord $\overline{AD}$ forms some nice inscribed angles for us to use. We know that $\angle DAB$ is inscribed in arc DB, so we have that

$$\angle DAB = \frac{x}{2}.$$

Applying this logic, we also have that $\angle ADC = \frac{y}{2}$. Finally, using the knowledge that $\angle DEB$ is an exterior angle of $\triangle ADE$, we know that

$$\angle DEB = \angle ADE + \angle DAE = \frac{x}{2} + \frac{y}{2} = \frac{x+y}{2}.$$

> **IMPORTANT:** The measure of an angle formed by two intersecting chords is the average of the measures of the arcs intersected by the two chords.

2.8.11   **In the diagram below, arc EF and DC have measures a and b, respectively. Prove that $\angle B = \frac{b-a}{2}$.**

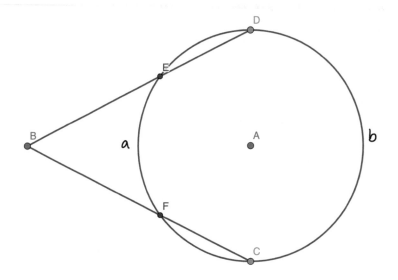

One thing we can do to make this problem easier is to draw an additional line, namely $\overline{EC}$, as shown below.

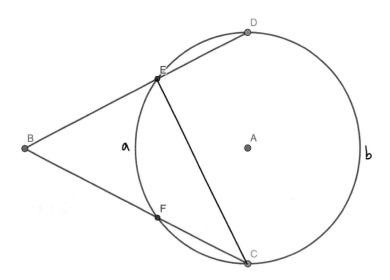

From here, we can see that $\angle ECF = \frac{a}{2}$ and $\angle DEC = \frac{b}{2}$. Similarly to in the previous problem, we can observe that $\angle DEC$ is an exterior angle of $\triangle CEB$, telling us that

$$\angle DEC = \angle B + \angle ECB.$$

Thus, we can say that

$$\angle B = \angle DEC - \angle ECB = \frac{b-a}{2}.$$

> **IMPORTANT:** Two secants that meet at a point outside of a circle make an angle that has a measure half that of the difference of the arcs they intercept.

2.8.12 Conclusion

In this section, we explored many properties of circles. We saw how to find area, circumference, diameter, arc length and measure, and much more. We also discovered new properties of chords and tangent lines. Finally, we saw a few examples of finding irregular lengths, angles, and areas within circles.

2.8.13 Practice

1. Find the area of a circle that has circumference 16π.

2. Find the diameter of a circle that has a circumference equal to its area.

3. Find the area of the shaded region in the circle, given that $\angle AOB = 120°$ and the radius of the circle is 4.

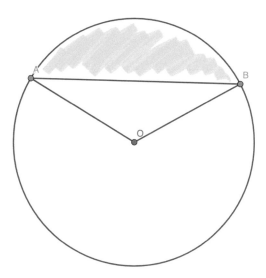

4. $\triangle ABC$ is equilateral, and has side length 10. What is the area of the region within the circumcircle of $\triangle ABC$, but outside the triangle?

5. In the following diagram, quarter-circles are centered at vertices A and C in square $ABCD$. The side length of square $ABCD$ is 5. What is the area of the shaded region?

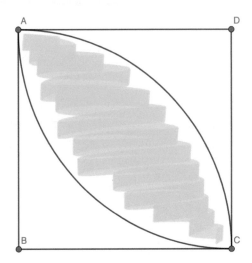

6. In the diagram below, we have that arc $CE = 40°$, arc $CD = 103°$, and arc $DB = 83°$. Point X is the intersection of segments $\overline{CB}$ and $\overline{ED}$. What is the measure of $\angle EXB$?

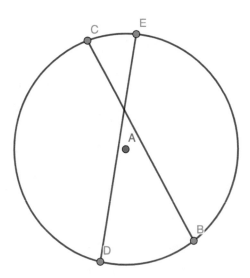

7. Point T is outside circle O. Point X is on circle O such that $\overline{TX}$ is tangent to circle O. The radius of circle O is 6, and $TX = 12$. Find TO.

2.9 3-D Figures

2.9.1 Introduction

So far, our geometric work has been in either zero dimensions (working with points), one dimension (lines), or two dimensions. Now, it's time to move into the third dimension. In this section, we'll explore the properties of prisms, pyramids, cylinders, cones, and spheres; some of the most fundamental three-dimensional figures.

> For this section, instead of working through problems, you'll be presented with material that you should know. When encountering 3-D figures in problems, these formulas and relationships will generally be enough to work through the problem. You'll be able to practice on your own using the provided practice problems, which, as always, have solutions at the end of the book.

2.9.2 Prims

The kinds of **prisms** most of us are familiar with are rectangular prisms, like the one below. It is made up of **bases**, which we colloquially call the "top" and "bottom" of the prism. The boundaries of the prisms are all rectangles, and each of these boundaries are known as **faces**. We call this prism a rectangular prism because the "top" and "bottom" faces (the bases) are rectangles.

Using what we know about the rectangular prisms we are familiar with, let's define what a prism is, in general. A prism is a 3-D figure with two *congruent* parallel faces, and parallelograms as all the other faces (also known as **sides**). If a prism is referred to as "regular", that just means that its bases are regular polygons. If a prism is referred to as "right", that means that the edges connecting the bases form right angles with the bases. Here are some more prisms, so you can better visualize different types.

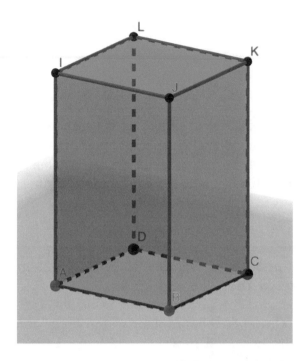

Figure 2.29: Faces $ABCD$ and $IJKL$ are bases of this rectangular prism

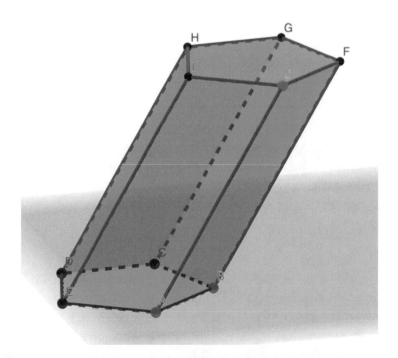

Figure 2.30: A regular pentagonal prism

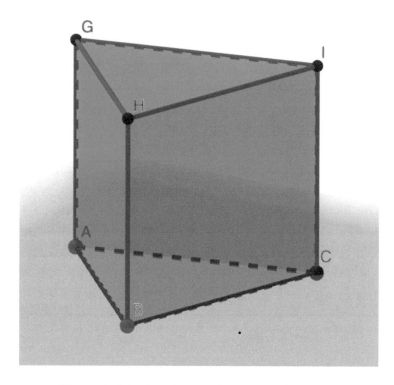

Figure 2.31: A right regular triangular prism

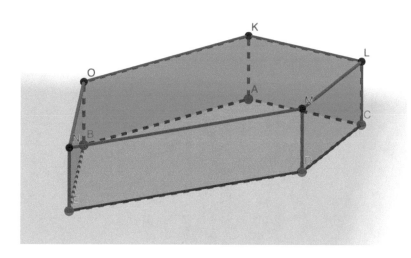

Figure 2.32: A right pentagonal prism

In terms of area and volume, prisms have special formulas.

To find the volume of a prism, multiply the area of a base (b) by the prism's height (h):
$$b \cdot h$$

The total surface area of a prism (or any other 3-D figure) is the sum of the areas of all the surfaces that create the borders of the figure.

The lateral surface area of the prism is the total area of the faces, excluding the areas of the bases.

When a problem simply says "surface area" and does not specify total or lateral, assume that it is referring to total surface area.

2.9.3   Pyramids

On to pyramids! A **pyramid** is what is formed if we connect all vertices of a polygon to a point in a separate plane from the original polygon. This point is known as the **apex**, and the original polygon is the pyramid's **base**. The non-base faces of a pyramid are always triangles. Similarly to a prism, the lateral surface area of a pyramid is the sum of the areas of these triangles, while the total surface area includes the area of the base, as well. While we are most familiar with triangular and square pyramids, just like prisms, pyramids can have any polygon as their base. Here are some examples:

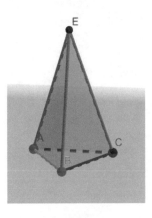

Figure 2.33: A triangular pyramid

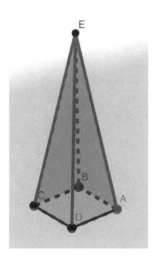

Figure 2.34: A square pyramid

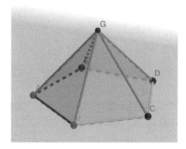

Figure 2.35: A pentagonal pyramid

The formula for the volume of a pyramid is a little peculiar, so make sure to memorize it:

> **To find the volume of a pyramid, multiply the area of the base (b) by the pyramid's height (h), then divide by 3:**
>
> $$\frac{b \cdot h}{3}$$

2.9.4 Cylinders

Next up are cylinders. Put simply, cylinders are prisms with congruent circles as bases, instead of congruent polygons. The line connecting the centers of the bases is known as the **axis**. Similarly to a prism, a cylinder is "right" if the axis forms right angles with the bases. When discussing cylinders, we will almost always be talking about right circular cylinders, like the one below.

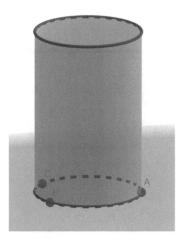

The volume of a cylinder with bases of radius r and height h is the area of its base (πr^2) multiplied by its height:

$$h\pi r^2$$

The lateral surface area of a cylinder with bases of radius r and height h is the circumference of the base ($2\pi r$) multiplied by its height:

$$2\pi rh$$

The total surface area of a cylinder with bases of radius r and height h is the circumference of the base ($2\pi r$) multiplied by its height, plus the areas of both the bases ($2 \cdot \pi r^2$):

$$2\pi rh + 2\pi r^2$$

2.9.5   Cones

Now for cones. Just like cylinders were just prisms with circles as bases, a cone is simply a pyramid with a circle as the base. The tip of the cone is its **vertex**, and the distance from the base to the vertex is its height. Similarly to with the cylinder, the axis of a cone is the line connecting its vertex to the center of the base. Here is an example of a cone:

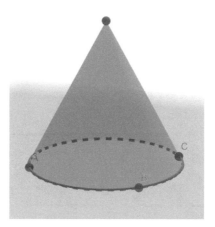

> The volume of a cone is the area of its base (πr^2) multiplied by its height (h):
> $$\pi r^2 h$$

2.9.6   Spheres

Finally, spheres! We defined a circle as the set of all points in a plane the same distance from a point, and spheres are quite similar. A **sphere** is defined as the set of all points in space (any plane) that are the same distance from a point. The sphere's **radius** is the the distance from the sphere's center to any point on its surface. Here's an example (it's just a ball!):

> The volume of a sphere of radius r is:
> $$\frac{4\pi r^3}{3}$$

> **The surface area of a sphere of radius r is:**
>
> $$4\pi r^2$$

2.9.7 Conclusion

In this section, we covered the volumes, surface areas, and different relationships for prisms, pyramids, cylinders, cones, and spheres. The formulas explored in this section should be sufficient for you to succeed at the lower levels. Make sure you know them well to build a strong foundation for the properties you will explore in the future.

2.9.8 Practice

1. A cube has diagonals of its faces with length 3. What is the volume of the cube?

2. A right rectangular prism has volume 36 and two sides of lengths 2 and 3. What is the length of the third dimensions? What is the total surface area of the prism?

3. A right square pyramid has a base of area 10 and a volume of 80. What is its height?

4. A right circular cylinder has radius 4 and height 5. What is its volume? What is its total surface area?

5. A right cone has radius 2 and height volume 12π. What is its height?

6. A sphere's volume and surface area are equal. What is its radius?

7. A sphere has diameter 10. What is its volume? What is its surface area?

Chapter 3

COMBINATORICS & PROBABILITY!

3.1 Introduction

Here comes a topic often not covered in depth at most schools, if it is even covered at all: **combinatorics**, also known as **counting**, and probability. The name "counting" is deceptively simple - we all know how to count, right? The type of counting you'll see in this section, though, is not so easy. For these problems, we'll have to determine first what we want to count, and then determine how we can count those. "$1, 2, 3$" is not going to cut it here!

As for **probability**, it is related to combinatorics in many ways. In fact, many probability problems are simply combinatorics problems in disguise. To put it as simply as possible, in probability problems, we count the number of equally likely scenarios there are for a problem, and then count how many of these scenarios are what we deem a "solution," or a "success". Probability, from here, is just the ratio of the number of "success" scenarios to the total number of scenarios. With this definition, it becomes a bit easier to see how we are really just counting the total number of possibilities, then counting the number of those possibilities that satisfy our requirements for the problem.

While algebra and geometry are certainly not easy, this section is likely to be where you may struggle quite a bit, both because the material is new, and the material is difficult. Don't stress! Take it slow, step by step. Soon, you'll be able to tell your friends you know how to count! They might laugh, but they don't know what you do.

3.2   Let's count things!

3.2.1   Introduction

We're going to kick off combinatorics by starting small: counting in simple scenarios. You may be able to figure out these problems just by looking at them, but take the time to read through the explanations. The concepts here are the backbone of what you will need to solve harder problems down the road.

3.2.2   Count the number of integers in the following list: $1, 2, 3,$ $4, 5, 6, 7, 8, 9, 10, 11, 12.$

Wow... what a hard problem! No, you're not being tricked; it really is that easy. There are 12 numbers. It's that easy.

> **The number of numbers in a list of integers from 1 to some integer n with a difference of 1 between each integer is simply n.**

Because counting the integers from 1 to a certain n is so easy, a good strategy for other problems is to manipulate what we're counting into this kind of format.

3.2.3   Count the number of integers in the following list: $10, 11,$ $12, 13, 14, 15, 16, 17, 18, 19, 20, 21, 22, 23, 24, 25, 26, 27.$

While still simple, this problem is a bit harder than the last one. Yes, we could go through and count the numbers one by one, but there's a much easier way. Let's try to reduce this problem to a list of numbers from 1 to some n.

To do this, we can simply subtract 9 from each number in the list, so that the first number is now 1, and the list is now

$$1, 2, 3, 4, 5, 6, 7, 8, 9, 10, 11, 12, 13, 14, 15, 16, 17, 18.$$

Now it's clear to see: there are 18 numbers in this list.

3.2.4   Count the number of multiples of 5 between 13 and $166.$

Oof. We've been thrown into the deep end a little bit. Never fear! We can reduce this problem to one that we know how to do.

To begin, let's find the first and last multiples of 5 from 13 to 166. These are 15 and 165, so those are the first and last numbers in the list we want to count. Our list is now

$$15, 20, 25, \ldots 155, 160, 165.$$

What can we do to turn this into a list that we can count easily? Well, we can start by dividing everything by 5, since by definition, these numbers are all multiples of 5! Performing this division gives us our new list:

$$3, 4, 5, \ldots 31, 32, 33.$$

We know how to do this! We just did it in the last problem, after all. Subtracting 2 from each number in the list gives us a list starting at 1:

$$1, 2, 3, \ldots, 29, 30, 31.$$

Thus, the answer is simply 31.

3.2.5 In a parking lot, there are 30 vehicles, which are all either sedans or SUVs, and either red or blue. 11 are sedans, and 16 are red. 4 are red sedans. How many blue SUVs are there?

We can solve this problem just by working through the different parameters, being sure to keep track of our logic along the way.

Let's start with the most specific piece of information we're given: there are 4 red sedans. From here, we can note that there are 11 total sedans, and the only other choice of color is blue. Thus, we can deduce that there are $11 - 4 = 7$ blue sedans. Following a similar train of thought, there is only one other choice of blue vehicles: blue SUVs! We don't know the total number of blue vehicles, but we can find it! We have 30 total vehicles, and 16 of them are red, so we must have $30 - 16 = 14$ blue vehicles. Of these, we now know that 7 of them are sedans, so therefore, we must have $14 - 7 = 7$ blue SUVs.

3.2.6 In an ice cream shop, there are 3 choices for the ice cream flavor and 2 choices for the size. How many different ice cream combinations of flavor and size can you create?

As is going to be a recurring theme in this section, we can solve this problem by working logically and keeping track of our steps. We have 3 ways to choose an ice cream flavor. For each ice cream flavor, we will have 2 choices of size, for a total number of choices of $3 \times 2 = 6$.

3.2.7 **How many different outfits can you make from a choice of 4 shirts, 3 pairs of pants, 2 pairs of socks, and 5 pairs of shoes, if you must include one of each element in the outfit?**

This problem is simply a larger, more complex version of the one we just did. Once again, let's work logically.

We have 4 ways to choose a shirt. For each choice of shirt, we have 3 choices for a pair of pants to match it with, giving us $4 \times 3 = 12$ options for a shirt-pants combo. For each one of these combos, we have 2 choices for a pair of socks to add, giving us $12 \times 2 = 24$ shirt-pants-socks combos. Finally, we throw shoes into the mix. For each one of those combos, we have 5 choices of shoes to complete the outfit, giving us a total of $24 \times 5 = 120$ shirt-pants-socks-shoes combos.

3.2.8 **You have 6 different books. You want to place 3 of them on a shelf. How many different ways can you arrange 3 books in this manner?**

For this problem, we must realize that once a book has been chosen for a particular position, it can go in no other position. We must also realize that the number of choices we have for each position is the same, regardless of which book we choose to fill it.

Keeping these facts in mind, we start the problem. We have 3 slots to fill for the books on the shelf. There are 6 ways to fill the first slot, as there are 6 books to choose from. For the second slot, we now have 5 choices, because we have already used 1 book to fill the first slot. Similarly, for the third slot, we then have 4 books, after using 2 to fill the first two slots.

This gives us a total number of combinations of $6 \times 5 \times 4 = 120$ ways to arrange three of the six books on the shelf.

> **This problem is an example of a permutation, which is a problem in which we must choose several items one at a time from a larger group.**

Let's try a more complicated permutation problem.

3.2.9 A club has 15 members. There are four officer positions: president, vice president, secretary, and historian. How many ways can the four officer be chosen if each member can hold at most one officer position? What if each member can hold any number of officer positions?

Let's tackle the first scenario: each member can hold at most one position. This just becomes a simple permutation problem: we have 15 choices for the first officer, 14 for the second, 13 for the third, and 12 for the last. This gives us a total of

$$15 \times 14 \times 13 \times 12 = 32,760$$

ways.

For the second scenario, members can hold as many officer positions as they wish. Instead of complicating the problem, this, in a way, simplifies it! We now have the same number of choices for every position: 15, because even if a member already holds a position, they can hold another one! Thus, the total number of ways is $15 \times 15 \times 15 \times 15 = 15^4 = 50,625$ ways.

3.2.10 Conclusion

In this section, we explored a few basic types of counting problems: straight-up counting a list, counting with items in overlapping sets, counting multiple events, and counting arrangements. It cannot be stressed enough how important the concepts in this section are: you must know them to go on. Review these problems and the practice problems, as well as others you can find from other sources, until you are sure that there are no gaps in this part of your knowledge.

3.2.11 Practice

1. How many multiples of 7 are between 31 and 467?

2. How many 3 digit numbers are perfect squares?

3. In a particular adoption center, there are 35 dogs. 15 of them have short hair, and 18 of them are puppies. If there are 7 long-haired adult dogs, how many short-haired puppies are there?

4. How many ways can you create a car with 4 choices of body style (sedan, coupe, SUV, or truck), 3 choices of engine, 6 choices of color, and 3 trim levels?

5. You have 8 books. Three of them are about science. How many ways can you stack these 8 books on a shelf if there must be a science book on both ends of the stack?

6. There are 16 balls, numbered 1 through 16 in a bin. How many ways can 4 balls be drawn from the bin if the balls are not put back into the bin after they have been drawn? How about if the balls are put back into the bin after they are drawn?

3.3 Counting Strategies

3.3.1 Introduction

Now that we've seen some basic counting problems and covered some fundamental techniques, let's dive into the strategies that will build on those techniques. We'll talk about casework, complementary counting, and constructive counting.

3.3.2 In a particular language, the alphabet has 7 letters. Each word has at most 4 letters in it. There is no word with 0 letters. How many words are possible in this language?

For this problem, we'll use casework. As its name might suggest, in casework, we split what we want to count into categories.

> **In casework, we split what we want to count into categories and compute them separately, then combine the answer in the end.**

In this problem, our cases are relatively easy to spot: our words can have either $1, 2, 3,$ or 4 letters, so we'll tackle each of those cases separately.

Counting the number of 1 letter words, we see that there are just 7: each letter is itself a word.

As for 2 letter words, we have 7 choices for the first letter, and 7 for the second. The problem never said that the letters in a word must be different, so there are $7 \times 7 = 492$ letter words.

Similarly for 3 letter words, we have $7^3 = 343$ words.

Finally, for 4 letter words, we have $7^4 = 2401$ words.

Adding up the results of our four cases, we get that there are $7 + 49 + 343 + 2401 = 2800$ words!

> **You may notice that in this problem, all we did was divide and add. Still, while these are simple operations, the key is knowing when to do what.**

3.3.3 How many pairs of positive integers (x, y) are there such that $x^2 + y \leq 25$?

Let's use casework again. To find our cases, let's let $y = 0$. This tells us that $x^2 \leq 25$, which implies that our choices for x are $1, 2, 3, 4,$ and 5. Once again, we'll look at each case separately.

For the case in which $x = 1$, we thus have that $1 + y \leq 5$, which gives that $y \leq 24$. Thus, our choices for y are simply the consecutive integers from 1 to 24, giving us 24 choices for y, and 24 (x, y) pairs.

When $x = 2$, we have that $4 + y \leq 25$, so $y \leq 21$, giving 21 choices for (x, y) pairs.

When $x = 3$, we have that $9 + y \leq 25$, so $y \leq 16$, giving 16 choices for (x, y) pairs.

When $x = 4$, we have that $16 + y \leq 25$, so $y \leq 9$, giving 9 choices for (x, y) pairs.

Finally, when $x = 5$, we have that $25 + y \leq 25$, so $y \leq 0$. However, y must be a positive integer, so this case gives 0 additional (x, y) pairs.

Thus, to sum up our cases, we get our answer as $24 + 21 + 16 + 9 = 70$ cases.

3.3.4   How many three digit numbers are not multiples of 5?

In this problem, we'll employ complementary counting.

> **In complementary counting, we count what we do NOT want to count, and subtract that from some total.**

As such, we'll be counting the number of three digit numbers that *are* multiples of 5. First, though, we must find the total number of three digit numbers, which is the number of integers between 100 and 999, inclusive. Subtracting 99 from all the numbers in that list gives us that it is the same as the number of numbers from 1 to 900, which is 900.

Now for the number of three digit multiples of 5. The first one is 100, and the last one is 995, for a list of

$$100, 105, 110, ...985, 990, 995.$$

Dividing those by 5 gives that the new list of numbers is

$$20, 21, 22, ...197, 198, 199.$$

Subtracting 19 from all those numbers gives that the final list is

$$1, 2, 3, ...178, 179, 180.$$

The number of integers in that list is simply 180.

Thus, we have a total of 900 three digit numbers, and 180 of them are multiples of 5. Thus, we have $900 - 180 = 720$ three digit numbers that are not multiples of 5.

3.3.5 **You have 7 books that you want to arrange on a shelf. 4 of them are about math, and 3 of them are about science. How many ways can you arrange the books so that at least 2 math books are next to each other?**

Crucial to this problem is realizing that the only way to arrange books so that no two math books are next to each other (where math books are represented by M and science books are represented by S) is

$$MSMSMSM.$$

This is the arrangement that we don't want. For this case, there are $4 \times 3 \times 2 \times 1 = 4! = 24$ ways to order the math books, and $3 \times 2 \times 1 = 6$ ways to order the science books. Thus, for this case, there are $24 \times 6 = 144$ ways to order the books.

Now for the total number of ways to order the books: that is simply

$$7 \times 6 \times 5 \times 4 \times 3 \times 2 \times 1 = 7! = 5040.$$

Thus, the cases that we want to include is simply

$$5040 - 144 = 4896.$$

3.3.6 **In how many four digit numbers is there exactly one zero?**

For this problem, we'll employ constructive counting.

> In constructive counting, we analyze how to construct the items we wish to count, and find a way to count them.

In analyzing how to construct four digit numbers that satisfy the condition of the problem, we deal with the restriction first. This begs the question: We must have a 0 in the number, so where can it go? This leads us to the conclusion that the 0 can either be in the ones, tens, or hundreds digit. Thus, there are 3 ways we can place the 0. Still, for each of the three ways, there are 9 ways that we can place each of the other 3 digits, for a total of $9^3 = 729$ ways for each way we can place the 0. This leads us to our final answer: $3 \times 729 = 2187$ ways to construct a four digit number with exactly one zero.

3.3.7 **Your school's math club has** 15 **members and** 3 **officer positions. However, John is best friends with Jane, and will only serve as an officer if Jane also has a position. How many ways can we fill the offices?**

In this problem, we have a rather severe restriction. Still, we can tackle this problem using casework.

Our two cases: either John and Jane are both officers, or neither are officers.

In the case that John and Jane are both officers, we must first pick what position John has, then Jane, then the last member. There are 3 choices for John's position, 2 remaining for Jane, and then 1 for whoever is left. However, there are then $15 - 2 = 13$ members to choose from for the last position, for a total of

$$3 \times 2 \times 13 = 78$$

total ways to fill the offices if John and Jane are both officers.

If neither John and Jane are officers, the problem becomes rather straightforward. Excluding John and Jane, there are $15 - 2 = 13$ members left in the club. Thus, there are 13 choices for the first position, 12 for the second, and 11 for the third. Thus, there are

$$13 \times 12 \times 11 = 1716$$

ways to fill the offices if neither John and Jane are officers.

Combining our two cases gives a total of $78 + 1716 = 1794$ total ways that your club's officer positions can be filled.

3.3.8   Conclusion

In this section, we saw how to employ the methods of casework, complementary counting, and constructive counting, as well as counting with restrictions. We learned that it is often better to work with restrictions in order of most to least severe.

3.3.9   Practice

1. How many three digit numbers can be made from the digits $1, 2, 3,$ and 4 if digits can be repeated, and the digit 1 must be used at least once?

2. How many different three-digit security codes are possible using the digits $1 - 5$, if the second digit cannot be the same as the first, and third digit cannot be the same as the second? *(Source: MATHCOUNTS)*

3. How many 5 digit numbers have at least 2 zeros?

4. You have 3 shirts, 3 pairs of pants, and 3 pairs of shoes. Each item comes in the same 3 colors. You would rather die than wear an outfit in which all three items are the same color. How many choices for an outfit can you wear?

5. How many license plate numbers can be formed if every license plate has 2 different letters followed by 3 different digits, then 2 letters that are not necessarily different?

6. A particular table with 9 seats in a row must be seated with 6 girls and 3 boys. How many ways can the people be seated such that all 3 boys sit together?

3.4 Overcounting

3.4.1 Introduction

Another strategy in counting is to count more than we want to count, and then subtract what we overcounted. In fact, this method is so common, it has its own section! Sometimes, we even use division for overcounting, whereas we've only seen subtraction used in complementary counting so far.

3.4.2 How many distinct arrangements can possibly be made from the letters in the word "$tree$"?

If this were just any other permutation problem, we might think the answer would simply be

$$4 \times 3 \times 2 \times 1 = 4! = 24.$$

Simple enough, right? Four choices for the first letter, three for the second, two for the third, and one for the last. However, this problem has a bit of a catch.

The issue is that two of the letters we have to work with are identical: the two e's. To demonstrate the impact that this has, let's say that the two e's were distinguishable: we'll call them e_1 and e_2. If this is the case, then we can see how each possible arrangement of the four letters if the e's are indistinguishable is counted twice:

Here are all of the possible cases:

$$tre_1e_2, tre_2e_1 \longrightarrow tree$$
$$te_1e_2r, te_2e_1r \longrightarrow teer$$
$$e_1tre_2, e_2tre_1 \longrightarrow etre$$
$$re_1te_2, re_2te_1 \longrightarrow rete$$
$$e_1e_2tr, e_2e_1tr \longrightarrow eetr$$
$$e_1re_2t, e_2re_1t \longrightarrow eret$$
$$te_1re_2, te_2re_1 \longrightarrow tere$$
$$rte_1e_2, rte_2e_1 \longrightarrow rtee$$
$$e_1rte_2, e_2rte_1 \longrightarrow erte$$
$$e_1te_2r, e_2te_1r \longrightarrow eter$$
$$re_1e_2t, re_2e_1t \longrightarrow reet$$
$$e_1e_2rt, e_2e_1rt \longrightarrow eert$$

From here, we can see that the number of arrangements of tre_1e_2 is simply twice the number of arrangements of $tree$. Therefore, all we need to do to get the number of arrangements of $tree$ is to divide the number of arrangements of tre_1e_2 by 2. Our answer is thus $\frac{24}{2} = 12$.

3.4.3 How many distinct arrangements can possibly be made from the letters in the word "*tatter*"?

This is kind of similar to the last problem, but this time, we have three of the same letter: we have 3 t's.

We'll use a similar strategy. If the three t's were all distinct (call them t_1, t_2, and t_3) then we would have $6! = 720$ possible arrangements of $t_1 a t_2 t_3 e r$.

Instead of listing out all the possibilities like in the last problem, though, we'll apply some logic. For any given arrangement of all the letters, the three t's can be rearranged in $3! = 6$ ways (the number of possible of arrangements of $t_1 t_2 t_3$). From this, we can see that the 720 arrangements of $t_1 a t_2 t_3 e r$ we found actually counts each arrangement of *tatter* 6 times. To account for this overcounting, we'll simply divide the 720 we found by 6, to get a final answer of 120 arrangements of *tatter*.

3.4.4 How many distinct arrangements can possibly be made from the letters in the word "*mamma*"?

Curveball! This word actually consists of just two letters: three m's and two m's. Let's apply the same strategy we've been using and see what we get.

If all the m's and a's were distinct, $(m_1, m_2, m_3;$ and $a_1, a_2)$ we would have $5! = 120$ arrangements. However, using the logic from the last problem, we can see that for the three m's, each arrangement is counted $3! = 6$ times, and for the two a's, each of these possibilities is also counted $2! = 2$ times, totaling $6 \times 2 = 12$ times. Thus, we divide the 120 we got by 12 to find a total of 10 possible arrangements.

3.4.5 In a round-robin tennis tournament, each player plays every other player exactly one time. How many matches will be held during a 6-person round-robin tennis tournament?

This is an example of a problem involving counting pairs. These come up extremely often (you'll likely get sick of seeing the words round-robin).

To begin, we can examine the following (flawed) logic: each player must play 5 matches; one against each of the other 5 players. There are 6 players, so if each each plays 5 matches, there must be a total of $6 \times 5 = 30$ matches.

Let's take a closer look at the matches that just 2 of our 6 players will play. Call them player A and player B. Thinking logically, we can see that one of player A's five matches is against player B. Similarly, one of player B's five matches is against player B. Therefore, when we counted the total number of matches, we counted the match between players A and B twice!

This fact holds true for any two of the six players, so it becomes clear that every match was counted twice in our total of 30. Thus, we divide by 2 to get a total of 15 matches.

3.4.6   How many ways can 8 people be seated around a round table?

We've solve problems similar to this one before; this problem brings back memories of arranging books and people in rows. If our task was to arrange these 8 people in a row, there would simply be 8! arrangements. However, even a quick inspection of that solution reveals that we have overcounted significantly; many different row arrangements actually correspond to the same round table arrangement. For example, look at the image below: all of those 8 arrangements would count as separate row arrangements!

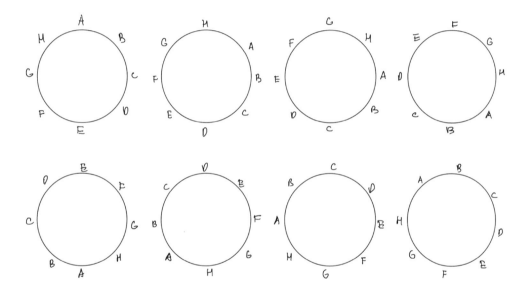

This is an example of a counting problem with symmetry. In this case, the symmetry is rotational: each arrangement can be rotated 8 ways to make other arrangements. Therefore, when we counted our 8! arrangements, we counted each circular arrangement 8 times.

Thus, to get our final answer, we divide our original count of 8! by 8, to get an answer of $8!/8 = 7! = 5040$ arrangements.

3.4.7   Conclusion

In this section, we saw examples of counting arrangements with multiple of the same elements, counting pairs in a scenario, and rotational symmetry. All of these scenarios can be solved using overcounting.

3.4.8 Practice

1. How many arrangements are there of the letters in the word *"tepee"*?

2. How many arrangements are there of the letters in the word *"alabama"* (all lowercase)?

3. How many arrangements are there of the letters in the word *"mississippi"* (all lowercase)?

4. There are 8 spots in a dealership parking lot. The dealership must save 4 spots for SUVs, 3 for sedans, and 1 for trucks. How many ways can the dealership make this arrangement?

5. A bin contains 16 balls numbered 1 through 16. How many ways can 2 balls be selected, if the order in which they are drawn does not matter?

6. At a bowling convention, there are 10 teams in two levels, of 5 groups each. Each team must play every team in its own level twice, and every team in the other division once. How many games will be played?

7. In how many ways can 7 people be seated around a table?

3.5   Combinations and Combinations and More Combinations

3.5.1   Introduction

In this section we'll introduce combinations, then move on to more complicated problems where similar concepts apply. We'll also use combinations in conjunction with other strategies we've learned, such as casework and complementary counting. Additionally, we'll dive into distinguishability, a very common restriction in combination problems. Specifically, the types of problems we'll explore are counting paths, forming committees, and working with different scenarios of distinguishability.

3.5.2   How many ways can a President and Vice President be chosen from a group of 4 people if they cannot be the same person? How many ways can a committee of two people be chosen from a group of four people if the order in which they are chosen does not matter?

We've done a variation of the first problem before: we simply have 4 choices for the first position, leaving us with 3 for the second, for a total of $4 \times 3 = 12$ ways.

The second problem is new. Similar to the first one, we still have to choose two people, but this time, the order doesn't matter. As before, we can see 4 choices for the first person and 3 for the second, but we have overcounted, since choosing a person a first and person b next is the same as choosing person b first and person a second. Dividing by 2 to correct gives us 6 ways to choose such a committee.

> IMPORTANT: Choosing distinct officers and forming a committee are not the same. In choosing officers, order matters; it does not when forming a committee.

3.5.3   How many ways can a 3-person committee be chosen from a group of 8 people?

If order didn't matter (imagine we're choosing 3 officers), we would have $8 \times 7 \times 6 = 336$ ways to do this. However, order does not matter; each possible committee would correspond to $3 \times 2 \times 1 = 3! = 6$ orderings of officers. Thus, we must divide our initla overcount by $3! = 6$, giving a total of $\frac{8 \times 7 \times 6}{3 \times 2 \times 1} = 56$ ways. This leads us to an incredibly important concept.

> **IMPORTANT:** The number of ways to choose a committee of r people from a total of n people is $\binom{n}{r}$, read as "n" choose "r". This is also known as a *combination*.

In this next problem, we'll find a general formula for computing $\binom{n}{r}$.

3.5.4 In a group of n people, how many ways can we choose a committee of r people from those n people?

We can begin by finding the number of ways to choose r people, assuming that order matters. For the first person, there are thus n choices, $n-1$ for the second, $n-2$ for the third, $n-3$ for the fourth, and so on, up until $n-r+1$ for the rth person. Put simply, we have

$$n \cdot (n-1) \cdot (n-2) \cdot (n-3) \cdot \ldots \cdot (n-r+1)$$

ways in which we can choose a committee of r people if n people if order matters.

We're done with that part, but we have to remember that we know there are $r!$ ways to order r people. Thus, we know from past problems that each unordered committee of people corresponds with $r!$ choices of r people. From here, we can see that we need to divide our result by $r!$ to make sure we haven't overcounted.

We now have our final equation:

$$\binom{n}{r} = \frac{n \cdot (n-1) \cdot (n-2) \cdot (n-3) \cdot \ldots \cdot (n-r+1)}{r!}.$$

However, we're not quite finished! We can write this equation in a bit of a simpler manner using factorials. We can take note of the fact that

$$n \cdot (n-1) \cdot (n-2) \cdot (n-3) \cdot \ldots \cdot (n-r+1) =$$

$$\frac{n \cdot (n-1) \cdot (n-2) \cdot (n-3) \cdot \ldots \cdot 2 \cdot 1}{(n-r) \cdot (n-r-1) \cdot (n-r-2) \cdot \ldots \cdot 2 \cdot 1} = \frac{n!}{(n-r)!}.$$

With this improvement, our equation becomes

$$\binom{n}{r} = \frac{\frac{n!}{(n-r)!}}{r!} = \frac{n!}{r!(n-r)!}.$$

> **IMPORTANT:**
> $$\binom{n}{r} = \frac{\frac{n!}{(n-r)!}}{r!} = \frac{n!}{r!(n-r)!}.$$

For this next problem, we'll get a bit of practice in using the combination formula.

3.5.5   Compute $\binom{8}{3}$, $\binom{10}{5}$, and $\binom{7}{2}$.

This is just simple computations, but the purpose is to get you used to using it.

$$\binom{8}{3} = \frac{8!}{3!(8-3)!} = \frac{8!}{3!5!} = \frac{8 \cdot 7 \cdot 6 \cdot 5 \cdot 4 \cdot 3 \cdot 2 \cdot 1}{(3 \cdot 2 \cdot 1)(5 \cdot 4 \cdot 3 \cdot 2 \cdot 1)}.$$

Canceling all of the common terms in the numerator and denominator leaves us with

$$\frac{8 \cdot 7 \cdot 6}{3 \cdot 2 \cdot 1} = \frac{336}{6} = 56.$$

Just as it should be, this is the same result as problem 3.5.3! Make sure you understand why this is the same situation as that problem.

$$\binom{10}{5} = \frac{10!}{5!(10-5)!} = \frac{10!}{5!5!}.$$

Using the same canceling trick as the previous calculation, we can rewrite this as

$$\frac{10 \cdot 9 \cdot 8 \cdot 7 \cdot 6}{5 \cdot 4 \cdot 3 \cdot 2 \cdot 1} = \frac{30240}{120} = 252.$$

$$\binom{7}{2} = \frac{7!}{2!(7-2)!} = \frac{7!}{2!5!} = \frac{7 \cdot 6}{2 \cdot 1} = \frac{42}{2} = 21.$$

Now that you've had some practice, the next question will lead us to an extremely important combinatorial identity.

3.5.6   Compute $\binom{7}{2}$ and $\binom{7}{6}$, then compute $\frac{9}{2}$ and $\frac{9}{7}$.

We know what $\binom{7}{2}$ is, we just computed it in the last problem: it's 21. Let's do $\binom{7}{5}$.

$$\binom{7}{5} = \frac{7 \cdot 6 \cdot 5 \cdot 4 \cdot 3}{5 \cdot 4 \cdot 3 \cdot 2 \cdot 1} = \frac{2520}{120} = 21.$$

Same answer... coincidence?

Our next pair should give us some more insight.

$$\binom{9}{2} = \frac{9 \cdot 8}{2 \cdot 1} = \frac{72}{2} = 36.$$

$$\binom{9}{7} = \frac{9 \cdot 8 \cdot 7 \cdot 6 \cdot 5 \cdot 4 \cdot 3}{7 \cdot 6 \cdot 5 \cdot 4 \cdot 3 \cdot 2 \cdot 1} = \frac{181440}{5040} = 36.$$

The same answer again! What's going on?

To generalize, the pattern we've noticed is that

$$\binom{n}{r} = \binom{n}{n-r}.$$

This is easy to prove, as we know that

$$\binom{n}{r} = \frac{n!}{r!(n-r)!}$$

and

$$\binom{n}{n-r} = \frac{n!}{(n-r)!(n-(n-r))!}.$$

Our two results have the same numerator, so we need to prove that the denominators are the same. Simplifying shows just this: $n - (n - r) = r$, so the denominators are equal! Thus, we have proved that

$$\binom{n}{r} = \binom{n}{n-r}.$$

IMPORTANT:

$$\binom{n}{r} = \binom{n}{n-r}$$

For some practice, the next problem will be helpful.

3.5.7 Compute $\binom{10}{8}$ and $\binom{13}{10}$.

$$\binom{10}{8} = \binom{10}{2} = \frac{10 \cdot 9}{2 \cdot 1} = \frac{90}{2} = 45.$$

$$\binom{13}{10} = \binom{13}{3} = \frac{13 \cdot 12 \cdot 11}{3 \cdot 2 \cdot 1} = \frac{1716}{6} = 286.$$

That last one in particular wasn't great, but imagine how bad it would have been if we hadn't known this identity!

3.5.8 Conclusion

In this section, we dove into combinations and the choose formula through the lens of picking committees out of groups of people. We also saw how distinguishability matters, as well as the importance of knowing whether or not order matters. Along the way, we discovered two crucial identities, shown again below.

> **IMPORTANT:**
> $$\binom{n}{r} = \frac{\frac{n!}{(n-r)!}}{r!} = \frac{n!}{r!(n-r)!}$$

> **IMPORTANT:**
> $$\binom{n}{r} = \binom{n}{n-r}$$

3.5.9   Practice

1. How many ways can 5 different officers be chosen from a club of 11 people?

2. How many ways can a committee of 5 people be chosen from a club of 11 people?

3. From a club of 8 people, the positions of president and vice president must be filled (those are the only positions). There must be 1 president and 3 vice presidents (the vice presidents are interchangeable). How many ways can this be done?

4. Compute $\binom{n}{0}$ for all positive integers n.

5. Compute $\binom{n}{1}$ for all positive integers n.

6. Compute $\binom{n}{1}$ for all positive integers n.

7. Compute $\binom{4}{2}$.

8. Compute $\binom{7}{3}$.

9. Compute $\binom{5}{1}$.

10. Compute $\binom{9}{4}$.

11. Compute $\binom{10}{3}$.

12. Compute $\binom{3}{1}$.

13. Compute $\binom{9}{6}$.

14. Compute $\binom{8}{6}$.

15. Compute $\binom{10}{9}$.

16. Compute $\binom{6}{4}$.

17. Compute $\binom{7}{4}$.

18. Compute $\binom{15}{13}$.

3.6 Basic Probability

3.6.1 Introduction

Now that we've seen a bit on counting scenarios, let's see how this factors into **probability**.

Probability is a bit hard to define, so let's view it through the lens of an example. Take a fair coin with one side as heads and the other as tails. Say we flip the coin, over and over. We would then expect the proportion of flips to land on heads to be $\frac{1}{2}$. Thus, we say that the probability that a coin flip will land on heads is $\frac{1}{2}$. In this way, we can say that probability is the proportion of times that we expect a certain outcome given that we perform the experiment over and over.

The general approach to probability problems is to figure out the total number of equally likely outcomes that are possible, and then count how many of those outcomes fit the required conditions, or are what we consider a "success". The probability is thus the ratio of the successful outcomes to the total number of outcomes.

Some prerequisites that you need are below. They are generally self-explanatory:

> The smallest that the probability of a given event occurring can be is 0.

> The greatest that the probability of a given event occurring can be is 1.

> All probabilities lie between 0 and 1, inclusive.

Let's do a few problems to get you acquainted with the basics of probability.

3.6.2 A fair, six-sided die has the integers 1 through 6 painted on its sides. It is rolled once. What is the probability that it lands on a side that is a prime number?

This one is intuitive, which helps. We see that there are 6 ways that the die can land; one way for each side. Next, we find the ways that we count as "successful". Our range of values for the number the die lands on only goes from 1 to 6, so it's easy enough to see that the only prime numbers in that range are $2, 3$, and 5. That's 3 "successful" cases out of a total of 6 cases, so our answer is $\frac{3}{6} = \frac{1}{2}$.

3.6.3   In a row at a particular parade, there are 4 different red cars and 5 different blue cars. If the row has been arranged randomly, what is the probability that the first two cars are both blue?

A bit of complication gets thrown in here, as we're looking at the first *two* cars. Still, the same general principles apply.

For our total number of cases, that's simply the number of ways to choose any first two cars. We have 9 choices for our first, and 8 remaining for our second, giving us $9 \times 8 = 72$ total cases.

Now for our successful cases. We have 5 ways to pick a blue car first since there are 5 total blue cars, and then 4 ways to pick a second blue car, for a total of $5 \times 4 = 20$ total successful cases.

Therefore, the probability is $\frac{20}{72} = \frac{5}{18}$.

3.6.4   Two fair, six-sided dice have the integers 1 through 6 painted on their sides. They are each rolled once, at the same time. What is the probability that the two numbers they land on have a sum of exactly 8?

Once again, what makes this problem appear trickier is the presence of two dice. Still, we have 6 possibilities for the first die's result, and another 6 for the second; multiplying these two gives $6 \times 6 = 36$ total cases.

For our successful cases, we have to be a bit more careful. Possible sums that add up to 8 written as pairs include $(2, 6); (3, 5);$ and $(4, 4)$. However, we must recognize that both $(2, 6)$ and $(3, 5)$ can be reversed and still work as $(6, 2)$ and $(5, 3)$. This gives a total of $3 + 2 = 5$ cases that work, giving a probability of $\frac{5}{36}$.

Now that you've seen some examples of probability problems, let's see how the counting techniques we've learned apply in more advanced problems.

3.6.5   If a fair coin is flipped a total of 7 times, what is the probability that at least 4 of the flips come up heads?

Read this problem carefully. It doesn't ask for the probability that *exactly* 4 of the flips come up heads, it asks for the probability that *at least* 4 do. Therefore, we also have to consider the scenarios in which $5, 6,$ or 7 come up heads. We can tackle these using casework, like we learned in counting.

Before we start with our cases, though, let's get the total number of outcomes. Each toss can land on either heads or tails, for a total of 2 possibilities, so performing 7 tosses will give $2^7 = 128$ possible outcomes.

In our first case, 4 of the flips come up as heads. To count the number of ways that this can happen, all we need to do is choose 4 of the 7 tosses to land as heads, because the remaining 3 will automatically be tails. We can use our combinations formula, giving us $\binom{7}{4} = \binom{7}{3} = \frac{7 \cdot 6 \cdot 5}{3 \cdot 2 \cdot 1} = 35$ ways.

In our second case, 5 of the flips come up as heads. By the same reasoning as the first case, we can apply our choose formula, giving us $\binom{7}{5} = \binom{7}{2} = \frac{7 \cdot 6}{2 \cdot 1} = 21$ ways.

In our third case, 6 of the flips come up as heads, and this gives us $\binom{7}{6} = \binom{7}{1} = 7$ ways.

In our fourth and final case, all 7 of the flips come up as heads, for a total of 1 way.

Adding up our successful outcomes, we have $35 + 21 + 7 + 1 = 64$ ways. Out of a total of 128 outcomes, the probability that at least 4 tosses come up as heads is thus $\frac{64}{128} = \frac{1}{2}$.

3.6.6 A standard deck of cards consists of 4 suits, each containing 13 cards (for a total of 52 cards). The four suits are hearts, diamonds, spades, and clubs. Hearts and diamonds are painted red, while spades and clubs are black. The 13 cards in each suit are made up of the integers from 2 through 10, one ace, a jack, queen, and king. A card is chosen from a standard deck of 52 cards. What is the probability that the card is a 10 or in the suit of hearts (or both)?

Once again, reading the problem carefully is crucial here: the card is either a 10 *or* in the suit of hearts, but it can also be both.

Once we understand that part of the problem, this seems relatively easy, and it is. There are 4 ways to choose a 10, as there are just 4 in the deck: one in each suit. Then there are 13 ways to choose a card from the suit of hearts, because that's how many there are in the suit.

Here, though, is where we have to remember about overcounting. We have counted the card that is both a 10 and in the suit of hearts (the 10 of hearts) in both our 4 and our 13, so we have overcounted by 1. Thus, there are a total of $4 + 13 - 1 = 16$ successful outcomes.

There are a total of 52 choices, from the 52 cards in the deck. Therefore, the probability is $\frac{16}{52} = \frac{4}{13}$.

IMPORTANT: A standard deck of cards consists of 4 suits, each containing 13 cards (for a total of 52 cards). The four suits are hearts, diamonds, spades, and clubs. Hearts and diamonds are painted red, while spades and clubs are black. The 13 cards in each suit are made up of the integers from 2 through 10, one ace, a jack, queen, and king.

The previous two problems were examples of **probability with addition**, in which we counted probabilities of multiple things and added them up for the answer. This next set of two problems will explore **complementary probabilities**, which is essentially the same as our old technique of complementary counting.

3.6.7   If we roll three fair six-sided dice at the same time, what is the probably that they won't all show the same number?

Ah! So from our experience with counting, we immediately know it would be much easier to calculate the probability that they all *do* show the same number, and then subtract that from the total probability.

Well, there are 6 choices for the numbers they could all show; every number possible on a six-sided die. For each of these numbers, there is just one way that it could be shown on all three dice. Thus, there are a total of 6 outcomes that we want to exclude from our answer.

There are a total of $6^3 = 216$ cases, so the probability that the dice land on an undesirable outcome is thus $\frac{6}{216} = \frac{1}{36}$. Subtracting this from our total probability of 1 gives us $1 - \frac{1}{36} = \frac{35}{36}$.

3.6.8   If 5 coins are flipped, what is the probability of getting at least 1 head?

Here, it would definitely be simpler to calculate the probability of getting no heads, and to subtract that from the total probability.

The only way we can have less than 1 head is to have no heads at all, implying that we have all tails. There is just 1 way to do this, intuitively. Or, we could prove it with math: choosing 5 coins to be tails from 5 coins can be done in $\binom{5}{5} = 1$ way.

Now for the total number of ways: there are 2 choices for each of the 5 coins, so we have $2^5 = 32$ total ways.

Thus, the probability of having no heads is $\frac{1}{32}$, and the probability of satisfying the conditions of the problem are $1 - \frac{1}{32} = \frac{31}{32}$.

Now that you've seen some complementary probability, let's do two problems with **probability and multiplication**, similar to how probability and addition works.

3.6.9 Two fair six-sided dice, one black and one white, are rolled simultaneously. What is the probability that the black die shows a 3 on its top face, and the white die shows a 5?

Intuitively, there is quite literally only one successful outcome: the black die showing 3, and the white die showing 5. There are 6 possible outcomes for the black die and 6 for the white, so multiplying gives us a total of 36 outcomes. Therefore, the probability of success is $\frac{1}{36}$.

Looking at the probabilities individually, we see that the probability of the black die landing on 3 is $\frac{1}{6}$, and the probability of the white die landing on 5 is also $\frac{1}{6}$. Multiplying them gives us the same answer: $\frac{1}{36}$.

3.6.10 A fair, six-sided die is rolled 6 times. What is the probability that an even number is shown in exactly 4 of the 6 rolls?

First, we must recognize that because there are 3 even and 3 odd numbers on a dice, there is a $50/50$ chance that it will be even or odd. Thus, we can essentially treat rolling a dice as a coin flip. Let an even number be heads, and an odd one be tails.

Treating the problem this way, each dice roll effectively has 2 outcomes, for a total of $2^6 = 64$ outcomes. In wanting an even number in exactly 4 rolls, we are essentially asking to choose 4 heads out of 6 coin tosses. Thus, the total number of cases that work is $\binom{6}{4} = \binom{6}{2} = \frac{6 \cdot 5}{2 \cdot 1} = 15$. This leaves us with a probability of $\frac{15}{64}$.

This next, final set of 2 problems explores probability with dependent events. All our previous problems have touched on probability in which all the events involved were independent (they didn't affect each other's outcomes). In these next problems though, the outcome of one will affect the next.

3.6.11 Two cards are drawn from a standard deck of 52 cards. What is the probability that the first card drawn is from the suit of hearts, and the second is from the suit of spades?

With our previous thinking, we might have just multiplied two probabilities, each $\frac{1}{4}$, to get $\frac{1}{16}$. We might assume that both suits make up a quarter of the deck, so they each have a quarter probability of being picked.

However, we must take into account how once we pick the first card, the probability of the suit of the second card being a spade is affected. Sure, the probability that the first card is a heart is $\frac{1}{4}$; our logic holds there. It is for the second draw that things have changed, because we now only have 51 cards to choose from. This makes the probability of drawing a spade $\frac{13}{51}$, not $\frac{13}{52}$. Thus, our final probability is $\frac{1}{4} \times \frac{13}{51} = \frac{13}{204}$.

3.6.12 A bag contains 6 red candies and 3 blue ones, all of identical size and shape. A candy is selected and not replaced. A second candy is then selected. What is the probability that both candies are the same color?

This problem involves a bit of case work - we have one case in which both candies are red, and another case in which both candies are blue. In both cases, we must pay attention to the dependency of the second selection on the first.

In the first case, both candies are red. The probability of selecting a red candy on the first draw is $\frac{6}{6+3} = \frac{6}{9} = \frac{2}{3}$. Then, the probability of drawing another red candy is $\frac{6-1}{9-1} = \frac{5}{8}$, since one red candy has been removed. This lowers both the number of red candies and the total number of candies by one. Thus, the probability of selecting two red candies is $\frac{2}{3} \times \frac{5}{8} = \frac{5}{12}$.

In the second case, both candies are blue. The probability of selecting a blue candy on the first draw is $\frac{3}{9} = \frac{1}{3}$. Then, the probability of drawing another blue candy is $\frac{3-1}{9-1} = \frac{2}{8} = \frac{1}{4}$. Thus, the probability of selecting two blue candies is $\frac{1}{3} \times \frac{1}{4} = \frac{1}{12}$.

From here, we simply add our two cases' probabilities together to get $\frac{5}{12} + \frac{1}{12} = \frac{1}{2}$.

3.6.13 Conclusion

We took a dive right into the deep end of probability in this section. We defined probability as the ratio of successful outcomes to the total number of outcomes, and stated that all probabilities must be between 0 and 1, inclusive. We worked with dice and cards, and explored probability with addition and multiplication. We also saw examples of complementary probability, which is analogous to complementary counting, and probability with dependent events.

3.6.14 Practice

1. If two fair six-sided dice are rolled simultaneously, what is the probability that the sum rolled is a perfect square?

2. One card is randomly drawn from a standard 52-card deck. What is the probability that it is an even number, or a diamond?

3. If 7 coins are flipped, what is the probability of getting at least 2 heads?

4. If 5 fair six-sided dice are rolled, what is the probability that up to 4 of them will show a 2?

5. A fair coin is flipped 8 times. What is the probability that it comes up heads in at least 6 of the flips?

6. A fair coin is flipped 10 times. What is the probability that it comes up heads in at least 7 of the flips?

7. A bag has 4 red marbles and 6 white marbles. Two marbles are drawn from the bag individually, without replacement. What is the probability that the first marble is white, and the second is red?

8. Three cards are randomly drawn from a standard deck of 52 cards. What is the probability that the first card is a 1, the second card is a 2, and the third card is a 3?

3.7   Expected Value

3.7.1   Introduction

Our last topic to touch on before we close out our section on probability is expected value.

To explain expected value, we need a pretty strong understanding of what an average is, or the mean. Generally, the average of the numbers $x_1, x_2, x_3, x_4...x_n$ is calculated as

$$\frac{x_1 + x_2 + x_3 + x_4 + ... + x_n}{n}.$$

This definition of an average can be extended to outcomes of random events. **Expected value** is the average result that would be expected from a large number of trials in an experiment. It can be defined loosely as a weighted average, where the more likely an outcome is, the greater weight it is given when computing the expected value.

For a more formal definition, let's use an event where every possible outcome corresponds to some value. The list of possible outcomes we'll use will be $x_1, x_2, x_3...x_n$. The outcomes all correspond to probabilities that they will happen, so value x_1 will occur with probability p_1, value x_2 has probability p_2, and so on. From here and the definition of probability, we have the relationship that $p_1 + p_2 + p_3 + ... + p_n = 1$.

With this setup, expected value (E) is thus defined as the sum of all the values of outcomes multiplied by their corresponding probabilities, as such:

$$E = x_1 p_1 + x_2 p_2 + x_3 p_3 + ... + x_n p_n.$$

This may seem complex, but with a few examples, you'll be up to speed in no time.

3.7.2   Calculate the expected value of the roll of a fair six-sided die.

So. For expected value, we'll need to know all the possible values of the roll, and their probabilities. Both parts are simple in this case: the possible rolls are a $1, 2, 3, 4, 5$, or 6, and they all have a probability of $\frac{1}{6}$.

Applying our formula, we get that

$$E = 1(\frac{1}{6}) + 2(\frac{1}{6}) + 3(\frac{1}{6}) + 4(\frac{1}{6}) + 5(\frac{1}{6}) + 6(\frac{1}{6}) = (1+2+3+4+5+6)(\frac{1}{6}) = (21)(\frac{1}{6}) = \frac{7}{2}.$$

3.7.3 In a game, a weighted coin is used. It has a $\frac{1}{3}$ chance of landing on heads, which will win the player ten dollars, and a $\frac{2}{3}$ chance of landing on tails, which will lose the player five dollars. What is the expected value of a single coin toss in this game?

Our two possible values in this case are $\$10$ and $\$-5$. The probabilities are $\frac{1}{3}$ and $\frac{2}{3}$, respectively. Setting up our expected value equation gives us

$$E = (10)(\frac{1}{3}) + (-5)(\frac{2}{3}) = \frac{10}{3} - \frac{10}{3} = 0.$$

3.7.4 A group of race cars each have numbers on their roofs. There are 12 cars in total. Some of the cars in the group have a 2 on their roofs, while all the others have a 7. If the expected value for a number on a random car selected is 3.25, how many of the cars have a 7?

Call x the number of cars with a 7 on their roofs. There are then $12 - x$ cars with a 2 on their roofs. The probability of a car having 7 on its roof is then $\frac{x}{12}$, and the probability of it having a 2 is $\frac{12-x}{12}$. The expected value is thus

$$E = (7)(\frac{x}{12}) + (2)(\frac{12-x}{12}) = \frac{24+5x}{12}.$$

From the problem, we know that $E = 3.25$, which gives us the equation

$$3.25 = \frac{24+5x}{12} \longrightarrow 39 = 24 + 5x \longrightarrow 15 = 5x \longrightarrow x = 3.$$

Therefore, we have that 3 cars have a 7 on their roofs.

3.7.5 Conclusion

In this section, we briefly looked into expected value, and how it can be seen as a kind of weighted average. As a reminder, expected value (E) is defined as the sum of all the values of outcomes multiplied by their corresponding probabilities, as such:

$$E = x_1p_1 + x_2p_2 + x_3p_3 + ... + x_np_n.$$

3.7.6 Practice

1. What is the expected value when a fair six-sided die is rolled, and the value shown is squared?

2. A fair six-sided die is rolled. If the roll is n, the player wins n^3. What is the expected value of the win?

3. The numbers on a standard six-sided die are arranged such that numbers on opposite faces always add to 7. The die is rolled, and the product of the numbers appearing on the four lateral faces of the die is calculated (ignoring the numbers on the top and bottom). What is the expected value of this product? *(Source: MATHCOUNTS)*

Chapter 4

NUMBER THEORY!

4.1 Introduction

Number theory, defined in words, is the study of integers. This definition may appear quite simple and almost boring, but the study of integers and their relationships with each other is incredibly important. There's only so much I can do to tell you about how complex this study can get, so you'll just have to keep going and see for yourself. But first, some housekeeping:

Notation

$$a|b$$

The vertical bar denotes divisibility. Instead of writing "a is a divisor of b," we write $a|b$. As an example, $5|20$ translates to "5 is a divisor of 20".

$$\gcd(a, b)$$

This denotes the greatest common divisor of the integers a and b. As an example, $\gcd(9, 15) = 3$.

$$\text{lcm}(a, b)$$

This denotes the least common multiple of the integers a and b. As an example, $\text{lcm}(9, 15) = 45$.

$$\max(a, b)$$

The "max" before a group of real numbers refers to the maximum of that group of real numbers. As an example, $\max(1, 2, 3, 4, 5) = 5$.

$$\min(a, b)$$

The "min" before a group of real numbers refers to the minimum of that group of real numbers. As an example, $\min(1, 2, 3, 4, 5) = 1$.

Definitions
Positive integers, **counting numbers**, and **natural numbers** all refer to the integers on the positive side of zero on the number line.

Negative integers refer to the integers on the negative side of zero on the number line.

Whole numbers include all integers that are positive, or zero.

Perfect squares are integers that are equal to some integer raised to the second power.

Perfect cubes are integers that are equal to some integer raised to the third power.

Perfect powers are integers that are equal to some integer to a power that is at least 2.

Multiples of an integer are products of that integer with any integer.

An integer m is **divisible** by another integer n when $\frac{m}{n}$ is an integer.

An integer d is a **divisor** or **factor** of an integer n if and only if n is divisible by d.

Proper divisors of an integer n are positive divisors of n that are not n.

IMPORTANT: For all integers m and n, their product mn must be both a multiple of m and a multiple of n.

IMPORTANT: For all nonzero integers d, all of the following statements mean the same thing.
n is a multiple of d.
n is divisible by d.
d is a divisor of n.
d divides n.

IMPORTANT: The following statements all mean the same thing.
If a is a divisor of b and b is a divisor of c, then a is a divisor of c.
If b is divisible by a and c is divisible by b, then c is divisible by a.
If b is a multiple of a and c is a multiple of b, then c is a multiple of a.
If $a|b$ and $b|c$, then $a|c$.

IMPORTANT: A prime number is a natural number whose only positive divisors are itself and 1.

IMPORTANT: A composite number is a natural number with some positive divisor(s) other than itself and 1.

IMPORTANT: The only natural number that is neither prime nor composite is 1.

IMPORTANT: If a natural number greater than 1, n, has no prime divisors less than or equal to $\sqrt{n}$, then n is prime.

Phew! Make sure to carefully review any statements that you didn't understand, and take the time to look them up and fully digest them before moving on.

4.2   Multiples and Divisors

4.2.1   Introduction

In this section, we'll explore the relationships that integers have with their multiples and divisors, as well as the relationships between multiples and divisors themselves.

4.2.2   Find all of the positive divisors of 24 and 30. What positive divisors do they have in common?

The divisors of 24 are $1, 2, 3, 4, 6, 8, 12$, and 24. While it might take you a while to find these at first, push through and go in order to make sure you don't miss any. Don't be afraid to take it slow at first. This is a skill that builds with practice; soon, you'll pretty much know them by heart.

The divisors of 30 are $1, 2, 3, 5, 6, 10, 15$, and 30.

Comparing the two lists, we see that the common divisors are $1, 2, 3$, and 6.

4.2.3   Abbie has 42 blue marbles, which she divides into piles that each have n marbles in them. She also has 56 red marbles, which she also divides into n piles with an equal number of marbles in each pile. What is the largest possible value of n?

This problem has a lot of words. Let's break it down.

Abbie is able to split 42 marbles into piles that each contain n marbles, which says that $n|42$. Similarly, she is able to split 56 marbles into piles that each contain n marbles, which says that $n|56$. Now, since we are looking for the largest value of n, we are essentially searching for the greatest common divisor of 42 and 56, or $\gcd(42, 56)$.

Listing out the divisors of 42 gives $1, 2, 3, 6, 7, 14, 21$, and 42. Listing out the divisors of 56 gives $1, 2, 4, 7, 8, 14, 28$, and 56.

The largest possible value of n is thus 14, so we have that $\gcd(42, 56)$ is 14.

> IMPORTANT: Greatest common divisor is also known as greatest common factor, or gcf.

4.2.4   Find all the common multiples of 6 and 15 between 1 and 100, inclusive.

A list of all the multiples of 6 from 1 to 100 gives

$$6, 12, 18, 24, 30, 36, 42, 48, 54, 60, 66, 72, 78, 84, 90, 96.$$

A list of all the multiples of 15 from 1 to 100 gives

$$15, 30, 45, 60, 75, 90.$$

Numbers common to both lists are $30, 60,$ and $90.$

4.2.5   Find the least common multiple (LCM) of 9 and 24.

Our previous approach of listing out multiples and finding the lowest one in common would definitely work, but let's explore a more efficient method.

Instead, we can simply test each multiple of 24 to see if it is also a multiple of 9, as no smaller multiple of 24 could be the LCM of 9 and 24. Thus, the smallest of multiple of 24 that is also a multiple of 9 must be the LCM.

$1 \cdot 24 = 24$, and $9 \nmid 24$, so 24 cannot be a common multiple of 9 and 24.

$2 \cdot 24 = 48$, and $9 \nmid 24$, so 48 cannot be a common multiple of 9 and 24.

$3 \cdot 24 = 48$, and $9|24$. Thus, 72 is a common multiple of 9 and 24. This is the first value we have found to work, so it must be the LCM.

4.2.6   Explain why the difference between any two multiples of 7 is also a multiple of 7.

We can see this relationship with a few examples, and then go from there.

$$49 - 35 = 7 \cdot 7 - 5 \cdot 7 = (7 - 5) \cdot 7 = 2 \cdot 7 = 14$$

$$140 - 119 = 20 \cdot 7 - 17 \cdot 7 = (20 - 17) \cdot 7 = 3 \cdot 7 = 21$$

Each time, we were able to factor a 7 out of the product of each integer times 7 within the differences. This allows us to see that each difference is a multiple of 7.

Let's generalize. For any two multiples of 7, we can express them as $7x$ and $7y$, where x and y are any two integers. Subtracting them gives

$$7x - 7y = 7(x - y).$$

Since both x and y are integers, $x - y$ must also be an integer. Therefore, because $7(x - y)$ is the product of 7 and an integer, it must be a multiple of 7.

This relationship extends to all integers: the difference between any two multiples of n is also a multiple of n.

> **IMPORTANT: The difference between any two multiples of n is also a multiple of n.**

4.2.7 Conclusion

In this section, we explored the properties of multiples and divisors. We saw problems involving the greatest common divisor (GCD) and least common multiple (LCM).

4.2.8 Practice

1. Find all the positive common divisors of 120 and 48.

2. Find all the positive common divisors of 289 and 34.

3. Determine $\gcd(25, 50)$.

4. Determine $\gcd(24, 36)$.

5. Determine $\gcd(12, 23)$.

6. Determine $\gcd(24, 28)$.

7. Find the 4 smallest positive common multiples of 3 and 4.

8. Determine $\operatorname{lcm}(3, 6)$.

9. Determine $\operatorname{lcm}(4, 7)$.

10. Determine $\operatorname{lcm}(18, 42)$.

11. Determine $\operatorname{lcm}(25, 30)$.

12. Show that the sum of 5 multiples of 5 must be a multiple of 5.

4.3   Prime Factorizations

4.3.1   Introduction

Integers are constructed from prime numbers, and this knowledge is crucial to solving many number theory problems. Knowing how an integer breaks down into a product of its prime factors (prime factorization) makes finding common multiples and divisors much easier, which is applicable to an incredibly wide variety of problems.

4.3.2   Find the prime factorization of 20.

What we want to do here is break down 20 into a product of prime numbers. To do this, we'll look for prime divisors of 20 to start with. The most obvious one is 2, because we know that $20 = 2 \times 10$. We can write this in the following chart.

$$2 \begin{array}{|l} 20 \\ \hline 10 \end{array}$$

The leftmost column is the prime factor, and the rightmost column is the number being divided by that factor. In this case, 20 is being divided by the prime 2, which leaves a result of 10 in the next row.

10 is not prime, so we can do the same process again. We know that $10 = 2 \times 5$, so we write a 2 next to the 10, and a 5 in the next row:

$$\begin{array}{l|l} 2 & 20 \\ 2 & 10 \\ \hline & 5 \end{array}$$

5 is prime, so we're done. We now have the prime factorization of 20:

$$20 = 2 \cdot 5 \cdot 5 = 2 \cdot 5^2.$$

> **IMPORTANT: The prime factorization of an integer is the product of primes equal to that integer.**

4.3.3   Find the prime factorization of 120.

Let's do the process again with 120, a larger number.

Once again, we'll start with the smallest prime we can find: we know that $120 = 2 \cdot 60$.

$$2 \begin{array}{|l} 120 \\ \hline 60 \end{array}$$

$60 = 2 \cdot 30$, so we add that to the chart:

$$
\begin{array}{c|c}
2 & 120 \\ \hline
2 & 60 \\ \hline
 & 30
\end{array}
$$

$30 = 2 \cdot 15$, so we add that to the chart as well:

$$
\begin{array}{c|c}
2 & 120 \\ \hline
2 & 60 \\ \hline
2 & 30 \\ \hline
 & 15
\end{array}
$$

Now, $15 = 3 \cdot 5$:

$$
\begin{array}{c|c}
2 & 120 \\ \hline
2 & 60 \\ \hline
2 & 30 \\ \hline
3 & 15 \\ \hline
 & 5
\end{array}
$$

Thus, we have that
$$120 = 2 \cdot 2 \cdot 2 \cdot 3 \cdot 5 = 2^3 \cdot 3 \cdot 5.$$

Now that we've done a few practice problems, we can state a fact.

IMPORTANT: The Fundamental Theorem of Algebra states that every positive integer has exactly one prime factorization.
The proof for this statement is much too complex to get into here, but this is a crucial statement that allows us to solve many number theory problems.

4.3.4   Find a relationship between the prime factorizations of all positive multiples of 12.

Looking at the prime factorizations of various multiples of 12 may allow us to see a pattern:

$$12 = 2^2 \cdot 3$$

$$24 = 2^3 \cdot 3$$

$$36 = 2^2 \cdot 3^2$$

$$48 = 2^4 \cdot 3$$

$$60 = 2^2 \cdot 3 \cdot 5$$

From here, we can see that every multiple of 12 has at least 2 factors of 2 and 1 factor of 3 in its prime factorization.

To prove this relationship, let's denote any positive multiple of 12 as $12n$, where n is some positive integer. Now, let's find the prime factorization of $12n$:

$$
\begin{array}{c|c}
2 & 12n \\ \hline
2 & 6n \\ \hline
3 & 3n \\ \hline
  & n
\end{array}
$$

From here, it can be seen that we can write any positive multiple of an integer x in the form xn for some positive integer n. The first two factors that xn can be split into are $xn = x \cdot n$, and the continued factorization of x ensures that the prime factorization of xn will include the prime factorization of x.

> **IMPORTANT: The prime factorization of any multiple of a natural number x contains the entire prime factorization of x.**

4.3.5   Using prime factorizations, find lcm$(15, 36)$.

The problem said we'd need to use prime factorizations, so let's find the prime factorizations of each:

$$15 = 3 \cdot 5$$
$$36 = 2^2 \cdot 3^2$$

From this, we can see that all multiples of 15 will include 3 to at least the power of 1 and also 5 to at least the power of 1. Similarly, all multiples of 36 will include 2 to at least the power of 2 and also 3 to at least the power of 2.

A multiple of both 15 and 36 will thus need to include at least 2 powers of 2, 2 powers of 3, and 1 power of 5. This gives us

$$2^2 \cdot 3^2 \cdot 5 = 4 \cdot 9 \cdot 5 = 180.$$

The LCM is the smallest positive multiple of 180, so lcm$(15, 36)$ is 180.

> **IMPORTANT: In the LCM of a group of integers, the primes in its prime factorization are the primes present in any of the prime factorizations of the numbers in the group, where the exponent of each prime is the largest exponent of that prime present among the prime factorizations of the number in the group.**

4.3.6   Find lcm$(8, 12, 20)$.

The prime factorization of $8, 12,$ and 20 are as follows:

$$8 = 2^3$$
$$12 = 2^2 \cdot 3$$
$$20 = 2^2 \cdot 5$$

Thus, the LCM of these three integers must include $2^3, 3,$ and 5. The LCM is thus

$$2^3 \cdot 3 \cdot 5 = 8 \cdot 3 \cdot 5 = 120.$$

4.3.7   Find gcd$(36, 48)$.

Let's see if prime factorizations can help with GCDs as well as LCMs.

$$36 = 2^2 \cdot 3^2$$
$$48 = 2^4 \cdot 3$$

From this, we can tell that the prime factorization of a divisor of 36 can have at most 2 powers of 2 and 2 powers of 3. Similarly, the prime factorization of a divisor of 48 can have at most 4 powers of 2 and one power of 3.

Whereas with the LCM, we took the largest exponent of each prime in the prime factorizations, here, we will take the smallest. Any divisor common to 36 and 48 can include at most 2 powers of 2 and 1 power of 3. Thus, the largest possible common divisor of 36 and 48 will be

$$2^2 \cdot 3^1 = 4 \cdot 3 = 12.$$

In this way, the prime factorizations of a group of positive integers can also help us find the GCD.

> **IMPORTANT: In the GCD of a group of integers, the primes in its prime factorization are the primes present in all of the prime factorizations of the numbers in the group, where the exponent of each prime in the GCD's prime factorization is the smallest exponent of that prime present in the factorizations of the numbers in the group.**

4.3.8   Find gcd$(56, 84)$.

$$56 = 2^3 \cdot 7$$
$$84 = 2^2 \cdot 3 \cdot 7$$

The GCD can thus have at most 2 powers of 2 and 1 power of 7, which multiplies out to

$$2^2 \cdot 7 = 4 \cdot 7 = 28.$$

4.3.9   Conclusion

In this section, we explored how to find the prime factorization of an integer, as well as how the prime factorizations of multiple integers can allow us to easily find their GCDs and LCMs. Along the way, we discovered the Fundamental Theorem of Arithmetic, which states that every positive integer has exactly one prime factorization.

4.3.10   Practice

1. Find the prime factorization of 45.

2. Find the prime factorization of 84.

3. Find the prime factorization of 182.

4. Determine $\operatorname{lcm}(10, 25)$.

5. Determine $\operatorname{lcm}(27, 84)$.

6. Determine $\operatorname{lcm}(11, 70)$.

7. Find the 4 smallest positive common multiples of $12, 13$, and 14.

8. Determine $\gcd(144, 96)$.

9. Determine $\gcd(121, 143)$.

10. Determine $\gcd(80, 60)$.

4.4   Counting Divisors

4.4.1   Introduction

Now that we've worked quite a bit with divisors, let's see how to count them. We'll develop a formula for counting the number of positive divisors of an integer.

4.4.2   How many positive integer divisors does 100 have?

We'll solve this using prime factorizations. The prime factorization of 100 shows that

$$100 = 2^2 \cdot 5^2.$$

Thus, a divisor of 100 can only have prime divisors of 2 and 5, so we must be able to express any positive divisor of 100 in the form $2^x \cdot 5^y$. In this case, x must be an integer less than or equal to 2, and y must be an integer less than or equal to 2.

x can thus be $0, 1$, or 2, and y can also be $0, 1$, or 2. Essentially, we have 3 values each for x and y. Using what we learned from counting, this tells us that we have $3 \cdot 3 = 9$ positive divisors of 100.

4.4.3   How many positive integer divisors does 160 have?

We'll use a similar process as the previous problem. The prime factorization of 160 shows that

$$160 = 2^5 \cdot 5.$$

Thus, a divisor of 160 can be expressed in the form $2^x \cdot 5^y$, where x is no greater than 5, and y is no greater than 1. This gives us 6 choices for x $(0, 1, 2, 3, 4, 5)$ and 2 choices for y $(0, 1)$. As for the total number of positive divisors, that is then $6 \cdot 2 = 12$.

4.4.4 n is a number with prime factorization $n = x_1^{y_1} x_2^{y_2} x_3^{y_3} ... x_a^{y_a}$. Find a formula for the number of positive divisors of n.

The prime factorization of n includes powers of x_1 from 0 to y_1, giving $y_1 + 1$ choices for the exponent of x_1 in the prime factorization of a divisor. In a similar manner, there are $y_2 + 1$ choices for the exponent of x_2, $y_3 + 1$ choices for the exponent of x_3, and so on. From this number of choices, the total number of positive divisors of n is thus

$$(y_1 + 1)(y_2 + 1)(y_3 + 1)...(y_a + 1).$$

Put more simply, the total number of positive divisors of a natural number is found by taking the product of 1 more than each of the exponents in its prime factorization.

IMPORTANT: If n **is a natural number with prime factorization**

$$n = x_1^{y_1} x_2^{y_2} x_3^{y_3} ... x_a^{y_a}$$

it has a number of divisors equal to

$$(y_1 + 1)(y_2 + 1)(y_3 + 1)...(y_a + 1).$$

4.4.5   Conclusion

In this section, we briefly explored how to find the number of positive integer divisors a number has, using its prime factorization. We also found a general formula for how to find the number of divisors of a natural number.

4.4.6   Practice

1. How many positive integers does 25 have?

2. How many positive integers does 20 have?

3. How many positive integers does 39 have?

4. How many positive integers does 60 have?

5. How many positive integers does 120 have?

6. How many positive integers does 289 have?

7. How many positive integers does 300 have?

8. How many positive integers does 504 have?

4.5   Base Numbers

4.5.1   Introduction

Everything we have done thus far has been base 10 arithmetic. What does this mean? It's just our standard counting system - we count using 10 digits, and we count using powers of 10.

Think of any number - let's use 527 for example. Well, what do the 5, 2, and 7 really mean? Well, you might be thinking of the fact that the 7 is the units digit, the 2 is the tens digit, and the 5 is the hundreds digit. That is absolutely true. Still, let's break down those definitions further.

In 527, the 7 represents 7 1's, the 2 represents 2 10's, and the 5 represents 5 100's. Thing is, why do we use 1, 10, and 100? The answer is that we are using a base 10 system, in which we count by powers of 10! 1 is 10 to the 0 power, 10 is 10 to the power of 1, and 100 is 10 to the power of 2. Similarly, if we kept going, thousands digit count groups of 10 to the power of 3, and so on.

In this way, we can break down any base 10 number into groups of powers of 10. As another example, the number 146735 :

$$146736 = 1 \cdot 10^5 + 4 \cdot 10^4 + 6 \cdot 10^3 + 7 \cdot 10^2 + 3 \cdot 10^1 + 6 \cdot 10^0.$$

Now that we know how our usual base 10 system works, what would happen if we counted by 6's instead of by 10's? How about by 5's? By 12's? Well, that would be using a base $6, 5$, and 12 system, respectively! In this section, we'll see how to use other base systems, and more.

4.5.2   Write the decimal (base 10) number 66 in base 8.

To solve this problem, let's think about how we broke down base 10 numbers.

Using 66, we see that
$$66 = 6 \cdot 10^1 + 6 \cdot 10^0.$$

In the same way, we can break it down into powers of 8, just as we did into powers of 10.

The largest power of 8 that can go into 66 is $8^2 = 64$. $66 - 64$ leaves a remainder of 2, and that is equivalent to $2 \cdot 8^0$. Thus, we have that

$$66 = 1 \cdot 8^2 + 0 \cdot 8^1 + 2 \cdot 8^0 = 102_8.$$

The subscript of 8 indicates that the number is in base 8.

4.5.3 Convert the decimal number 40 into base 2.

The highest power of 2 that will go into 40 is $2^5 = 32$, which leaves $40 - 32 = 8$ left. 8 is simply equal to 2^3, so we have that

$$40 = 1 \cdot 2^5 + 0 \cdot 2^4 + 1 \cdot 2^3 + 0 \cdot 2^2 + 0 \cdot 2^1 + 0 \cdot 2^0 = 101000_2.$$

4.5.4 Convert the decimal number 200 into base 6.

The highest power of 6 that will go into 200 is $6^2 = 36$, which goes into 200 a total of $\frac{200}{36} = 5$ times, with a remainder of $200 - 5(36) = 200 - 180 = 20$. The next highest power that goes into 20 is $6^1 = 6$, which goes into 20 3 times. This leaves a remainder of $20 - 18 = 2$, which is equal to $2 \cdot 6^0$.

Finally, we have that

$$200 = 5 \cdot 6^2 + 3 \cdot 6^1 + 2 \cdot 6^0 = 532_6.$$

4.5.5 Write the decimal number 35 in base 12.

Wait a second... we haven't seen how to convert to bases higher than 10. We'll run out of digits; we don't have anything higher than 9!

To get around this problem, mathematicians use capital letters, starting with A, to move past 9. In this way, 10 becomes A, 11 becomes B, 12 becomes C, and so on.

Now that we know this fact, we can start the problem. The highest power of 12 that goes into 35 is $12^1 = 12$, which goes into 35 a total of twice. This leaves a remainder of $35 - 2(12) = 35 - 24 = 11$. This is equal to $11 \cdot 12^0$. Thus, we have that

$$26 = 2 \cdot 12^1 + 11 \cdot 12^0 = 2B_{12}.$$

Now that we've had some practice converting decimal numbers into different bases, let's flip the script and try to convert numbers from different bases to decimal.

4.5.6 Write the base 6 number 555_6 in base 10.

The practice we've had converting in the other direction will come in handy here. We know how to break this down:

$$555_6 = 5 \cdot 6^2 + 5 \cdot 6^1 + 6 \cdot 6^0 = 5(36) + 5(6) + 5(1) = 180 + 30 + 5 = 215.$$

4.5.7 Write the base 11 number $A385_{11}$ in base 10.

This one looks a little freaky because of the A, but remember that it represents a 10, nothing more:

$$A385_{11} = 10 \cdot 11^3 + 3 \cdot 11^2 + 8 \cdot 11^1 + 5 \cdot 11^0 = 10(1331) + 3(121) + 8(11) + 5(1)$$

$$= 13310 + 363 + 88 + 5 = 13766.$$

4.5.8   Write the base 8 number 5764_8 in base 5.

So this time, we're not converting to or from decimal. What do we do?

The truth is, we will be converting to decimal - just this time more as an intermediate step. Essentially, we're convert 5764_8 to base 10, then convert that base 10 result to base 5.

$$5764_8 = 5 \cdot 8^3 + 7 \cdot 8^2 + 6 \cdot 8^1 + 4 \cdot 8^0 = 5(512) + 7(64) + 6(8) + 4(1)$$
$$= 2560 + 448 + 48 + 4 = 3060.$$

From here, we break down 3060 into powers of 5. The largest power of 5 that will go into 3060 is $5^4 = 625$, which goes into 3060 4 times with a remainder of $3060 - 4(625) = 3060 - 2500 = 560$. From here, the next largest power that goes into 560 is $5^3 = 125$, which goes into 560 4 times with a remainder of $560 - 4(125) = 560 - 500 = 60$. The next highest power, $5^2 = 25$, goes into 60 twice with a remainder of 10. This is $5^1 = 5$ twice, so our final result is that

$$3060 = 4(625) + 4(125) + 2(25) + 2(5) + 0(1) = 4 \cdot 5^4 + 4 \cdot 5^3 + 2 \cdot 5^2 + 2 \cdot 5^1 + 0 \cdot 5^0 = 44220_5.$$

4.5.9   Conclusion

In this section, we got an introduction into numbers written in different base systems than decimal, which is our usual base 10. We saw how to convert decimal numbers to different bases, including what to do if the base was greater than 10. We then learned how to go in the other direction, converting different base system numbers back to decimal. Finally, we saw how to go from different base to different base, converting to base 10 as an intermediate step.

4.5.10   Practice

1. Convert 564 to base 8.

2. Convert 735 to base 9.

3. Convert 1256 to base 7.

4. Convert 93 to base 2.

5. Convert 110101_2 to base 10.

6. Convert 2120_3 to base 10.

7. Convert $AB35_{12}$ to base 10.

8. Convert 6645_8 to base 10.

9. Convert 2358_9 to base 5.

10. Convert 3120_4 to base 7.

4.6   The Units Digit

4.6.1   Introduction

Units digits can tell us a great deal about the integers they're attached to. We'll dive into how the units digits of integers relate to the units digits of sums, differences, and products of those integers with other integers.

4.6.2   What is the units digit of the sum $7 + 17$?

This one, we can do extremely easily simply by solving the sum: $7 + 17 = 24$, so the units digit is 4.

4.6.3   What is the units digit of the sum $7 + 27$? $7 + 37$? $7 + 47$? $7 + 57$? $7 + 67$? $7 + 77$? $7 + 87$?

Let's make a list:

$$7 + 27 = 34$$

$$7 + 37 = 44$$

$$7 + 47 = 54$$

$$7 + 57 = 64$$

$$7 + 67 = 74$$

$$7 + 77 = 84$$

$$7 + 87 = 94$$

They all have a units digit of 4... What's going on?

Effectively, what we are observing is how the values of the digits with powers of 10 from 10^1 up do not affect the units digit. This is because increasing those digits will never affect the coefficient of 10^0, telling us that we only need to consider the units digits of integers to find the units digit of their sum!

> **IMPORTANT: The sum of two positive integers has a units digit that is the same as the units digit of the sum of their units digits. This can also be applied to sums of groups of integers.**

4.6.4   What is the units digit of $97 - 3$?

Let's see about subtraction: $97 - 3 = 94$, so the units digit is 4.

4.6.5   What is the units digit of $97 - 13$? $97 - 23$? $97 - 33$? $97 - 43$? $97 - 53$? $97 - 63$? $97 - 73$? $97 - 83$?

Once again, we'll make a list:

$$97 - 13 = 84$$
$$97 - 23 = 74$$
$$97 - 33 = 64$$
$$97 - 43 = 54$$
$$97 - 53 = 44$$
$$97 - 63 = 34$$
$$97 - 73 = 24$$
$$97 - 83 = 14$$

What have we here? We see a similar pattern as we did with addition.

> **IMPORTANT:** The difference of two positive integers (subtracting a positive integer from a larger integer) has a units digit equal to the result of subtracting the units digit of the smaller integer from the units digit of the larger integer. This can also be applied to differences of groups of integers.

4.6.6   What is the units digit of 7×3?

Now we move on to multiplication: $7 \times 3 = 21$, so the units digit is 1.

4.6.7   What is the units digit of 7×13? 7×23? 7×33? 7×43?

We'll do our list once more:

$$7 \times 13 = 91$$
$$7 \times 23 = 161$$
$$7 \times 33 = 231$$
$$7 \times 43 = 301$$

From here, we can see that multiplying an integer with a units digit of 3 by an integer with a units digit of 7 results in a product with a units digit of 1. This leads us to a larger relationship:

IMPORTANT: The product of two positive integers has the same units digit as the units digit of the product of their units digit. This can also be applied to products of groups of integers.

Now that we know these relationships, let's tackle some problems that may not be so cut and dry.

4.6.8   Find the units digit of 14^{80}.

We know from our multiplication property that only the units digits of the 14's affects the units digit of the product, so the units digit of 14^{80} is the same as the units digit of 4^{80}.

Let's list a few powers of 4 to see if there's a pattern in the units digits:

$$4^1 = 4$$

$$4^2 = 16$$

$$4^3 = 64$$

$$4^4 = 256$$

$$4^5 = 1024$$

$$4^6 = 4096$$

Luckily, there is a clearly identifiable pattern: the units digits of powers of 4 switch between 4 and 6. Rather than just observe the pattern, let's reason through why it happens this way.

Any time we multiply an integer with a units digit of 4 by the integer 4, the product must then have a units digit of 6. From there, multiplying any integer with a units digit of 6 by the integer 4 results in an integer with a units digit of 4. Thus, we can say that the units digits of the powers of 4.

From our list, we can see that odd powers of 4 have units digits of 4, while even powers of 4 have units digits of 6. 80 is even, so 4^{80} will have a units digit of 6.

4.6.9   The product of two positive integers has a units digit of 3. One of the integers has a units digit of 9. What must be the units digit of the other integer?

We can take note of the fact that the product is odd, as it has a units digit of 3. For a product of two integers to be odd, both of the multiplicands must also be odd. Therefore, the units digit of the integer must be either $1, 3, 5, 7,$ or 9. We can try each of them:

$$1 \times 9 = 9$$
$$3 \times 9 = 27$$
$$5 \times 9 = 45$$
$$7 \times 9 = 63$$
$$9 \times 9 = 81$$

Thus, the units digit of the other positive integer must be 7.

4.6.10   Conclusion

In this section, we saw a bit about units digits, and how they work in patterns through addition, subtraction, and multiplication. We then applied these patterns to problems involving units digits.

4.6.11   Practice

1. What is the units digit of $87 + 91$?

2. What is the units digit of $3 + 2573$?

3. What is the units digit of $1281348 + 1497123$?

4. What is the units digit of $83 - 32$?

5. What is the units digit of $93 - 44$?

6. What is the units digit of $9812838 - 234345$?

7. What is the units digit of 234×2?

8. What is the units digit of 83×134?

9. What is the units digit of 382934×192385?

10. What digit is in the units place of $(3^3)^5$? *(Source: MATHCOUNTS)*

11. I am 3 times as old as my son, who is a teenager. If our ages have the same units digits, how old is my son?

12. When two natural numbers are multiplied, the result has a units digit of 1. If one of the integers has a units digit of 3, what must be the units digit of the sum of the two integers?

4.7   Divisibility Rules

4.7.1   Introduction

This last section is a short one. Think of it as a reward for making it through this entire book :)

This section won't consist of worked problems, per se. It'll be a list of rules for determining divisibility, followed by the usual set of practice problems at the end.

So what is divisibility? Divisibility is whether a given integer is divisible by a particular natural number. There are certain rules for dividing by certain natural numbers which are incredibly handy.

4.7.2   Divisibility by 0

No integers are divisible by 0. Any number divided by 0 is undefined.

4.7.3   Divisibility by 1

Every integer is divisible by 1. This is pretty self-explanatory.

4.7.4   Divisibility by 2

All even integers are divisible by 2. Put another way, if the units digit of an integer is even, it is divisible by 2.

4.7.5   Divisibility by 3

If the sum of the digits of an integer is a multiple of 3, the number is divisible by 3. For an example, the sum of the digits of 456 is $4 + 5 + 6 = 15$. 15 is a multiple of 3, so we know that 456 is divisible by 3.

4.7.6   Divisibility by 4

If the last two digits of an integer (taken together as if to form a new two-digit number) are divisible by 4, the number as a whole is divisible by 4. For example, the last two digits of 724 are 24. We know that 24 is a multiple of 4, so 724 is divisible by 4.

Another variation on this rule is to quickly divide the last two digits of the number by 2, then to divide the result by 2 again. If the result is a whole number, the original number is divisible by 4. Using our example of 724 again, 24 divided by 2 is 12. Dividing by 2 again gives 6, which is still a whole number. Thus, 724 is divisible by 4.

4.7.7   Divisibility by 5

If the units digit of an integer is 0 or 5, it is divisible by 5.

4.7.8   Divisibility by 6

If an integer is even and passes the test for divisibility by 3, it is divisible by 6. Essentially, the integer must pass both the tests for divisibility by 2 and 3 to be divisible by 6.

4.7.9   Divisibility by 7

There is no easily proven or memorizable rule for divisibility by 7.

4.7.10   Divisibility by 8

Similar to the divisibility test for 4, if an integer can be divided by 2 three times and still result in a whole number, it is divisible by 8.

If the number is large enough, an alternate test would be to take the last three digits, and if those are divisible by 8, the number as a whole is divisible by 8.

4.7.11   Divisibility by 9

Similar to the divisibility test for 8, sum the digits of the integer. If the sum is divisible by 9, the number as a whole is divisible by 9.

4.7.12   Divisibility by 10

If the units digit of an integer is 0, it is divisible by 10.

4.7.13   Divisibility by 11

Beyond two-digit numbers, there is no easily proven or memorizable rule for divisibility by 11. For two-digit integers, if the two digits are the same number, the integer is divisible by 11.

4.7.14   Divisibility by 12

If an integer passes the tests for both divisibility by 3 and 4, it is divisible by 12.

4.7.15   Conclusion

In this section, we looked over a list of divisibility rules for dividing by the integers from 0 to 12. Many of these are extremely easy to memorize, and will save massive amounts of time when problem-solving. Try to understand them where you can, but even if understanding why they work isn't possible, these are rules you should memorize. It will help enormously.

4.7.16   Practice

1. Is 864 divisible by 2?

2. Is 75 divisible by 2?

3. Is 80000000004 divisible by 2?

4. Is 128 divisible by 3?

5. Is 936 divisible by 3?

6. Is 129 divisible by 3?

7. Is 136 divisible by 4?

8. Is 194 divisible by 4?

9. Is 10295834 divisible by 4?

10. Is 5555500 divisible by 5?

11. Is 12392 divisible by 5?

12. Is 145 divisible by 5?

13. Is 996 divisible by 6?

14. Is 264 divisible by 6?

15. Is 674 divisible by 6?

16. Is 120 divisible by 8?

17. Is 992 divisible by 8?

18. Is 674 divisible by 8?

19. Is 729 divisible by 9?

20. Is 169 divisible by 9?

21. Is 10002348 divisible by 9?

22. Is 1000 divisible by 10?

23. Is 125 divisible by 10?

24. Is 92836461 divisible by 10?

25. Is 76 divisible by 11?

26. Is 55 divisible by 11?

27. Is 83 divisible by 11?

28. Is 168 divisible by 12?

29. Is 190 divisible by 12?

30. Is 212 divisible by 12?

Chapter 5

Solutions

ALGEBRA!

Introduction

No problems here :)

Linear Equations with One Variable

1. $(2x + 5) - 5 = 15 - 5 \longrightarrow 2x = 10 \longrightarrow \frac{2x}{2} = \frac{10}{2} \longrightarrow \boxed{x = 5}$

2. $(4x - 7) + 7 = 29 + 7 \longrightarrow 4x = 36 \longrightarrow \frac{4x}{4} = \frac{36}{4} \longrightarrow \boxed{x = 9}$

3. $\left(\frac{3x}{5}\right) \times 5 = (x - 8) \times 5 \longrightarrow 3x = 5x - 40 \longrightarrow (3x) - 5x = (5x - 40) - 5x \longrightarrow$
   $-2x = -40 \longrightarrow \frac{-2x}{-2} = \frac{-40}{-2} \longrightarrow \boxed{x = 2}$

4. $(3x + 10) \times 3 = \left(\frac{9x-9}{3}\right) \times 3 + 13 \times 3 \longrightarrow 9x + 30 = 9x - 9 + 39 \longrightarrow 9x + 30 = 9x + 30 \longrightarrow \boxed{\text{Infinite Solutions}}$

5. $(0.2x + 5) - 0.2x = 1.2x - 0.2x \longrightarrow 5 = x \longrightarrow \boxed{x = 5}$

6. $108x - 40 = 36x - 40 + 72x \longrightarrow 108x - 40 = 108x - 40 \longrightarrow \boxed{\text{Infinite Solutions}}$

7. $4a + 3x = 4a + 18 \longrightarrow (4a + 3x) - 4a = (4a + 18) - 4a \longrightarrow 3x = 18 \longrightarrow \frac{3x}{3} = \frac{18}{3} \longrightarrow \boxed{x = 6}$

8. Let x be my age. My brother's current age is thus $x + 4$. In ten years, my age will be $x + 10$, and my brother's will be $x + 4 + 10 = x + 14$. Building our equation, we have

$$x + 14 = \frac{5}{4} \times (x + 10) \longrightarrow 4(x + 14) = 4(\frac{5}{4} \times (x + 10)) \longrightarrow 4x + 56 = 5(x + 10)$$

$$\longrightarrow 4x + 56 = 5x + 50 \longrightarrow (4x + 56) - 4x = (5x + 50) - 4x \longrightarrow 56 = x + 50$$

221

$$\longrightarrow 56 - 50 = (x + 50) - 50 \longrightarrow 6 = x \longrightarrow x = 6.$$

Thus, my current age is $\boxed{6 \text{ years old.}}$

9. Let n be the number of nickels. The number of pennies is thus $2n$. It might be easier to work in cents instead of dollars, to avoid the messy decimals, so our total should be 1750 cents. Our equation is thus

$$n(5) + 2n(1) = 1750 \longrightarrow 5n + 2n = 1750 \longrightarrow 7n = 1750 \longrightarrow \frac{7n}{7} = \frac{1750}{7}$$

$$\longrightarrow n = 250.$$

Thus, there are $\boxed{250 \text{ nickels}}$ in the bag.

10. Let $\frac{1}{x^2}$ equal y. Our equation is then

$$4y + \frac{1}{3} = 7y \longrightarrow \left(4y + \frac{1}{3}\right) - 4y = 7y - 4y \longrightarrow \frac{1}{3} = 3y \longrightarrow \frac{\frac{1}{3}}{3} = \frac{3y}{3} \longrightarrow \frac{1}{9} = y.$$

Now, since $y = \frac{1}{x^2}$, we have that

$$\frac{1}{x^2} = \frac{1}{9}.$$

We can cross-multiply to get

$$9 = x^2 \longrightarrow \sqrt{9} = \sqrt{x^2} \longrightarrow 3 = x \longrightarrow \boxed{\text{x=3 or x=-3.}}$$

> **IMPORTANT: When taking a square root, it is crucial to consider that both the positive and negative square root could be viable solutions.**

11. $5x^2 + 2x - 7 = 2x + 38 \longrightarrow (5x^2 + 2x - 7) - 2x = (2x + 38) - 2x \longrightarrow 5x^2 - 7 = 38 \longrightarrow (5x^2 - 7) + 7 = 38 + 7 \longrightarrow 5x^2 = 45 \longrightarrow \frac{5x^2}{5} = \frac{45}{5} \longrightarrow x^2 = 9 \longrightarrow \sqrt{x^2} = \sqrt{9} \longrightarrow \boxed{x = 3 \text{ or } x = -3.}$

> **IMPORTANT: Once again, we see that considering the sign of the square root is vital.**

12. $4x + 7 = -13 \longrightarrow (4x + 7) - 7 = -13 - 7 \longrightarrow 4x = -20 \longrightarrow \frac{4x}{4} = \frac{-20}{4} \longrightarrow$ $\boxed{x = -5}$
$a(-5) - 30 = 5 \longrightarrow -5a - 30 = 5 \longrightarrow (-5a - 30) + 30 = 5 + 30 \longrightarrow -5a = 35 \longrightarrow \frac{-5a}{-5} = \frac{35}{-5} \longrightarrow \boxed{a = -7}$

13. Let n be the number of each type of coin. Similarly to #9, we will work in cents to eliminate the issue of decimals. Our equation thus becomes

$$n(1) + n(5) + n(25) = \text{some multiple of 50} \longrightarrow 31n = \text{some multiple of 50.}$$

31 and 50 have no common factors besides 1, so their least common multiple will be $31 \times 50 = 1550$. Thus, the smallest possible amount of money in the bag is 1550 cents, or $\boxed{\$15.50.}$

Graphing Lines (Linear Equations)

1. (a) $\boxed{m = -3, \text{ y-intercept} = -5}$

   (b) $\boxed{m = 4, \text{ y-intercept} = -4}$

   (c) $\boxed{m = \text{undefined}, \text{ y-intercept} = \text{DNE}}$

   (d) $\boxed{m = 2, \text{ y-intercept} = 3}$

   (e) $\boxed{m = 0, \text{ y-intercept} = -5}$

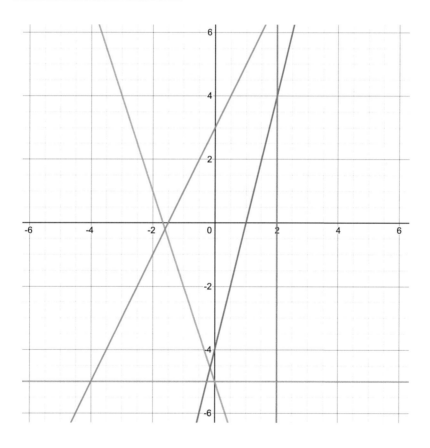

2. y-intercept: -2
   2nd point: $(-4, -3)$ (answers may vary)
   $m = \frac{-2-(-3)}{0-(-4)} = \frac{1}{4}$
   Equation: $\boxed{y = \frac{1}{4}x - 2.}$

3. Slope between points (a) and (b): $m_{a,b} = \frac{0-2}{2-0} = -\frac{2}{2} = -1$
   Slope between points (a) and (c): $m_{a,c} = \frac{-3-2}{4-0} = -\frac{5}{4}$
   The slopes between all combinations of two of these points must be the same for it to be possible that they lie on the same line. We have found two different slopes, so they don't lie on the same line.

4. $3 = (3)(-1) + b \longrightarrow 3 = -3 + b \longrightarrow 3 + 3 = (-3 + b) + 3 \longrightarrow 6 = b \longrightarrow b = 6$
   Equation: $y = 3x + 6$

5. Slope of equation (a): $2x - y = 3 \longrightarrow (2x - y) + y = 3 + y \longrightarrow 2x = y + 3 \longrightarrow$ $(2x - 3) = (y + 3) - 3 \longrightarrow y = 2x - 3 \longrightarrow m_a = 2$ Slope of equation (b): $2x + y = 5 \longrightarrow (2x + y) - 2x = 5 - 2x \longrightarrow y = -2x + 5 \longrightarrow m_b = -2$ The slopes do NOT multiply to -1, so the two lines are not perpendicular.

Inequalities Part 1

1. (a) 7^2; without even calculating, we see that the two values have the same exponent, but 7 is the larger base.

    (b) $\frac{1}{2}$; both fractions have a numerator of 1, so the one with the smaller denominator is larger.

    (c) $\sqrt{456789}$; the numbers look quite scary, but all we need to know is which one is larger; that one has the larger square root.

    (d) $\frac{52635}{52636}$; this one is kind of tricky. Both fractions are extremely close in size, and extremely close to 1. What we can do is figure out which one has a greater difference from 1. Subtracting each from 1 gives us that $1 - \frac{52633}{52634} = \frac{1}{52634}$, while $1 - \frac{52635}{52636} = \frac{1}{52636}$. We know that the smaller denominator is larger, so $\frac{1}{52634}$ is larger, meaning that $\frac{52633}{52634}$ is farther away from 1. Therefore, $\frac{52635}{52636}$ is larger.

2. $(3x - 4) + 4 > 10 + 4 \longrightarrow 3x > 14 \longrightarrow \frac{3x}{3} > \frac{14}{3} \longrightarrow \boxed{x > \frac{14}{3}}$

3. $(4.5x + 10) - 10 \le 55 - 10 \longrightarrow 4.5x \le 45 \longrightarrow \frac{4.5x}{4.5} \le \frac{45}{4.5} \longrightarrow \boxed{x \le 10}$

4. First inequality: $2x - 4 < 4x + 10 \longrightarrow (2x - 4) - 2x - 10 < (4x + 10) - 2x - 10 \longrightarrow -14 < 2x \longrightarrow -\frac{14}{2} < \frac{2x}{2} \longrightarrow -7 < x \longrightarrow x > -7$. Second inequality: $4x + 10 < 3x + 20 \longrightarrow (4x + 10) - 3x - 10 < (3x + 20) - 3x - 10 \longrightarrow x < 10$. x must be greater than -7 and less than 10, so we have that $\boxed{-7 < x < 10}$.

5.

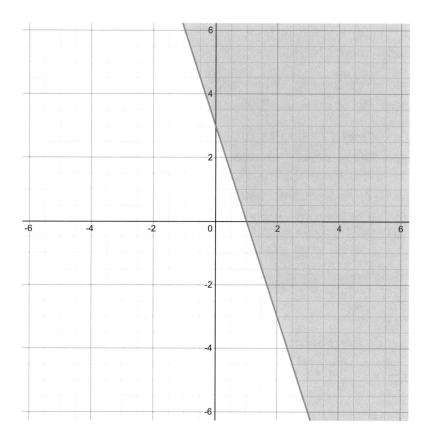

Ratios, Percents, and Proportions

1. For each group of 5 peanuts and 7 almonds, there are 12 nuts total. There are $\frac{96}{12} = 8$ of these groups, in total. The number of almonds in 8 groups is $8 \times 7 = \boxed{56}$.

2. Let x be the total number of questions on the test. $100\% - 85\%$ right $= 15\%$ wrong $\longrightarrow \frac{15}{100} = \frac{6}{x}$. Multiplying both sides by x and 100 gives $\frac{15}{100} \times 100 \times x = \frac{6}{x} \times 100 \times x \longrightarrow 15x = 600$. Dividing both sides by 15 gives $\frac{15x}{15} = \frac{600}{15} = \boxed{40}$.

3. Let the number of blocks in the first box be x. Thus, the number of blocks in the second box is equal to $2x$. The total number of blocks in both boxes is then $x + 2x = 3x$. We know that half the blocks in the first box are blue, so that is $0.5 \times x = 0.5x$ blue blocks in the first box. In the second, 10%, or $\frac{1}{10}$, are blue, which translates to $0.1 \times 2x = 0.2x$ blue blocks in the second box. These two values combine for a total of $0.5x + 0.2x = 0.7x$ blue blocks between the two boxes. The percentage of blocks that are not blue can be found by solving the equation $\frac{0.7x}{3x} = \frac{p}{100}$, with p being our percentage. Simplifying the fractions gives us $\frac{0.7}{3} = \frac{p}{100}$, and multiplying both sides by 100 gives us $\frac{0.7}{3} \times 100 = \frac{p}{100} \times 100 \longrightarrow \frac{70}{3} = p$. To the first decimal place, this gives that $p = \boxed{23.3\%}$.

4. Adding up the fraction values that we are given gives us that $\frac{1}{5} + \frac{1}{4} + \frac{2}{7} + \frac{1}{4} = \frac{69}{70}$. This tells us that $1 - \frac{69}{70} = \frac{1}{70}$ students in the first level, so 20 students are $\frac{1}{70}$ of

the total. Simply multiplying $20 \times 70 = 1400$ gives us the total number of students in the competition: $\boxed{1400}$.

5. There are 180 square feet to be tiled, and each square feet costs $\$24$. Therefore, we will need $\$24 \times 180 = \boxed{\$4320}$.

6. In real time, from $12 : 00$ PM to $1 : 00$ PM, an hour has passed. However, on Cassandra's watch, only 57 minutes and 36 seconds have passed. This translates to 57.6 minutes. From $12 : 00$ PM to $10 : 00$ PM on her watch, 10 hours, or $60 \times 10 = 600$ minutes have passed (according to the watch. This allows us to set up the proportion $\frac{57.6}{60} = \frac{600}{x}$, where x is the real number of minutes that have passed. Multiplying both sides by x and 60, then dividing by 57.6 gives us that $\frac{57.6}{60} \times 60 \times x = \frac{600}{x} \times 60 \times x \longrightarrow 57.6x = 36,000$. Dividing both sides by 57.6 gives that $\frac{57.6x}{57.6} = \frac{36,000}{57.6} \longrightarrow x = 625$. 625 minutes is equivalent to 10 hours and 25 minutes, so the real time when Cassandra's watch says it is $10 : 00$ PM is, in fact, $\boxed{10 : 25 \text{ PM}}$.

7. We can set up the proportion $\frac{2 \text{inches}}{35 \text{miles}} = \frac{x \text{inches}}{945 \text{miles}}$. Multiplying both sides by 945 gives us $\frac{2}{35} \times 945 = \frac{x}{945} \times 945 \longrightarrow 54 = x$. Therefore, the distance on the map is $\boxed{54 \text{ inches}}$.

8. 30 workers is $\frac{30}{48} = \frac{5}{8}$ of 48, so 48 workers should complete the same amount of work in $\frac{5}{8}$ of the time. However, 15 cars is $\frac{15}{10} = \frac{3}{2}$ of 10 cars, so building 15 cars will take $\frac{3}{2}$ as long as building 10. Combining these two changes by multiplying gives us that the 48 workers building 15 cars will take $\frac{5}{8} \times \frac{3}{2} = \frac{15}{16}$ of the time it would take 30 workers to build 10 cars. The 30 workers took 4 days, so the 48 workers will take $\frac{15}{16} \times 4 = \boxed{\frac{15}{4} \text{ days}}$.

9. It is the same distance to Isa's friends house as the return trip, so it doesn't matter the distance she drives. Essentially, the average of the 2 speeds she drives will need to be 35, allowing us to set up the equation $\frac{40+s}{2} = 35$, with s being her speed on the return trip. Multiplying both sides by 2 and then subtracting 40 gives $(\frac{40+s}{2} \times 2) - 40 = (35 \times 2) - 40 \longrightarrow s = 30$. Isa must drive $\boxed{35 \text{ miles per hour}}$ on her way home.

Introduction to Quadratics

1. (a) $(x + 2)(x + 4) = (x)(x) + (2)(x) + (4)(x) + (2)(4) = x^2 + 2x + 4x + 8 = \boxed{x^2 + 6x + 8}$

   (b) $\boxed{x^2 - 2x - 15}$

   (c) $\boxed{x^2 - 8x + 12}$

   (d) $\boxed{2x^2 + 12x - 14}$

(e) $\boxed{3x^2 - 30x + 27}$

(f) $\boxed{4x^2 + 13x - 12}$

2. (a) $(x - 1)(x - 2) \longrightarrow \boxed{x = 1, 2}$

(b) $(x + 1)(x + 3) \longrightarrow \boxed{x = -3, -1}$

(c) $(x - 2)(x - 3) \longrightarrow \boxed{x = 2, 3}$

(d) $(x - 1)(x + 2) \longrightarrow \boxed{x = -2, 1}$

(e) $(2x + 1)(x - 3) \longrightarrow \boxed{x = -\frac{1}{2}, 3}$

(f) $4(2x + 1)(x - 2) \longrightarrow \boxed{x = -\frac{1}{2}, 2}$

3. First, we subtract x from both sides, giving us $\sqrt{x + 7} = 13 - x$. Squaring both sides to get rid of the square root, we get that $x + 7 = (13 - x)^2 = 169 - 26x + x^2$. Subtracting $(x + 7)$ from both sides gives us $0 = x^2 - 27x - 162$. This can be factored as $(x - 18)(x - 9) = 0$. Therefore, the solutions are $\boxed{x = 9, 18.}$

4. (a) $\boxed{x^2 + 8x + 16}$

(b) $\boxed{4x^2 + 20x + 25}$

(c) $\boxed{x^2 - 32x + 256}$

5. (a) $\boxed{(x + 12)(x - 12)}$

(b) $\boxed{(x + 17)(x - 17)}$

(c) $\boxed{(2x + 11)(2x - 11)}$

6. $301^2 - 99^2 = (301 + 99)(301 - 99) = (400)(202) = \boxed{80,800}$

7. (a) $\boxed{(x + 9)(y - 7)}$

(b) $\boxed{-(r - 2)(s + 5)}$

Complex Numbers

1. $(2i)^2 = (2)^2 \times (i)^2 = 4 \times i^2 = (4)(-1) = \boxed{-4}$

2. $-(3i)^2 = -(3)^2(i)^2 = -9 \times i^2 = (-9)(-1) = \boxed{9}$.

3. $(\frac{i}{4})^3 = \frac{i^3}{4^3} = \frac{i^3}{64} = \frac{i^2 \times i}{64} = \boxed{-\frac{i}{64}}$.

4. $(-5i)^4 = (-5)^4 \times i^4 = 5^4 \times (i^2)(i^2) = 5^4 \times (-1)(-1) = 5^4 = \boxed{625}$.

5. $i^{994} = (i^2)^{\frac{994}{2}} = (i^2)^{497} = (i^2) \times (i^2)^{496} = (i^2) \times (i^4)^{\frac{496}{2}} = (i^2) \times (i^4)^{248} = (-1) \times (1^248) = \boxed{-1}$.

6. $(3 + 40i) + (37 - 4i) = (3 + 37) + (40i - 4i) = \boxed{40 + 36i}$.

7. $(-2+8i)(-4-2i) = (-2)(-4-2i) + (8i)(-4-2i) = (-2)(-4) + (-2)(-2i) + (8i)(-4) + (8i)(-2i) = 8 + 4i - 32i - 16i^2 = 8 - 28i - 16i^2 = 8 - 28i + 16 = \boxed{24 - 28i}$.

8. $(1+2i)(1-3i)(2+8i) = [(1+2i)(1-3i)](2+8i) = [1+2i-3i-6i^2](2+8i) = [1-i-6i^2](2+8i) = [1-i+6[(2+8i) = (7-i)(2+8i) = 14 - 2i + 56i - 8i^2 = 14 + 54i - 8i^2 = 14 + 54i + 8 = \boxed{22 + 54i}$.

More Quadratics!

1. (a) $x^2 + 6x + 7 = (x^2 + 6x + 9) - 2 = (x+3)^2 - 2 = 0 \longrightarrow (x+3)^2 = 2 \longrightarrow x + 3 = \pm\sqrt{2} \longrightarrow \boxed{x = -3 \pm \sqrt{2}}$

   (b) $9x^2 - 24x + 13 = (9x^2 - 24x + 16) - 3 = (3x-4)^2 - 3 = 0 \longrightarrow (3x-4)^2 = 3 \longrightarrow 3x - 4 = \pm\sqrt{3} \longrightarrow 3x = 4 \pm \sqrt{3} \longrightarrow \boxed{x = \frac{4\pm\sqrt{3}}{3}}$

   (c) $4x^2 + 28x + 45 = (4x^2 + 28x + 49) - 4 = (2x+7)^2 - 4 = 0 \longrightarrow (2x+7)^2 = 4 \longrightarrow 2x + 7 = \pm 2 \longrightarrow 2x = -7 \pm 2 \longrightarrow x = \frac{-7\pm2}{2} \longrightarrow \boxed{x = -\frac{5}{2}, -\frac{9}{2}}$.

2. (a) $b^2 - 4ac = (-4)^2 - 4(3)(7) \longrightarrow \boxed{\text{negative, so two complex roots}}$

   (b) $b^2 - 4ac = (-25)^2 - 4(6)(37) \longrightarrow \boxed{\text{negative, so two complex roots}}$

   (c) $b^2 - 4ac = (3)^2 - 4(1)(-2) \longrightarrow \boxed{\text{positive, so two real roots}}$

   (d) $b^2 - 4ac = (-12)^2 - 4(1)(36) \longrightarrow \boxed{\text{zero, so one real root}}$

3. (a) $\frac{-(-4)\pm\sqrt{(-4)^2-4(3)(7)}}{2(3)} = \frac{4\pm\sqrt{16-84}}{6} = \frac{4\pm\sqrt{-68}}{6} = \frac{4\pm2i\sqrt{17}}{6} = \boxed{\frac{2\pm i\sqrt{17}}{3}}$.

   (b) $\frac{-(-25)\pm\sqrt{(-25)^2-4(5)(37)}}{2(5)} = \frac{25\pm\sqrt{625-740}}{10} = \frac{25\pm\sqrt{-115}}{10} = \boxed{\frac{25\pm i\sqrt{115}}{10}}$

   (c) $\frac{-(3)\pm\sqrt{(3)^2-4(1)(-2)}}{2(1)} = \frac{-3\pm\sqrt{9+8}}{2} = \boxed{\frac{-3\pm\sqrt{17}}{2}}$.

   (d) $\frac{-(-12)\pm\sqrt{(-12)^2-4(1)(36)}}{2(1)} = \frac{12\pm\sqrt{144-144}}{2} = \frac{12\pm\sqrt{0}}{2} = \boxed{6}$.

Graphing Quadratics

1.

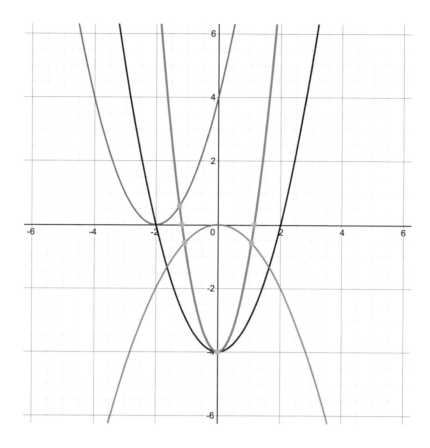

2. We need to put this equation into vertex form. We can do this by completing the square. Factoring a 2 out of the right side gives us $y = 2(x^2 - 6x + 11)$. This can be rewritten as $y = 2[(x^2 - 6x + 9) + 2] = 2[(x - 3)^2 + 2] = 2(x - 3)^2 + 4$. We know that for quadratics of the form $y = a(x - h)^2 + k$, the vertex lies at (h, k). Therefore, the vertex of this graph is at $\boxed{(3, 4)}$.

Functions

1. $3f(3) - f(5) = 3(3(3^2) + 4(3) - 5) - (3(5^2) + 4(5) - 5) = 3(27 + 12 - 5) - (75 + 20 - 5) = 3(34) - 90 = 102 - 90 = \boxed{12}$.

2. $\boxed{\text{domain: all real numbers}}$
   $3x^2 + 4x - 5 = 3(x^2 + \frac{4x}{3} - \frac{5}{3}) = 3(x^2 + \frac{4x}{3} + \frac{4}{9} - \frac{19}{9}) = 3[(x + \frac{2}{3})^2 - \frac{19}{9}] \longrightarrow$
   vertex at $y = -\frac{19}{9}$. $\boxed{\text{range: } y \geq \frac{19}{9}}$

3. $f(x) + g(x) = (3x^2 + 4x - 5) + (8x + 3) = \boxed{3x^2 + 12x - 2}$.

4. $f(x) \cdot g(x) = (2x + 5)(3x^3 - 2) = (2x)(3x^3 - 2) + (5)(3x^3 - 2) = 6x^4 - 4x + 15x^3 - 10 = \boxed{6x^4 + 15x^3 - 4x - 10}$.

5. $f(g(x)) = 3(2x + 3)^2 + (2x + 3) - 4 = 3(4x^2 + 12x + 9) + (2x + 3) - 4 = 12x^2 + 36x + 27 + 2x + 3 - 4 = \boxed{12x^2 + 37x + 26}$.

6. $g(f(x)) = 2(3x^2 + x - 4) + 3 = 6x^2 + 2x - 8 + 3 = \boxed{6x^2 + 2x = 5}$.

7. $y = 3x - 8 \longrightarrow x = 3y - 8 \longrightarrow x + 8 = 3y \longrightarrow y = \frac{x+8}{3} \longrightarrow f^{-1}(x) = \boxed{\frac{x+8}{3}}$.

8. $y = x^2 + 4x + 4 \longrightarrow x = y^2 + 4y + 4 \longrightarrow x = (y+2)^2 \longrightarrow \pm x = y + 2 \longrightarrow y = -2 \pm x \longrightarrow \boxed{f^{-1}(x) = -2 \pm x}$.

Exponential Functions and Their Graphs

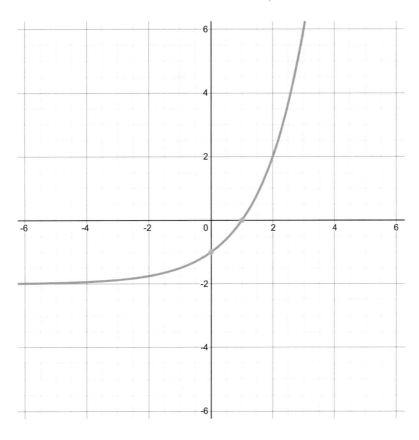

1.

2. $216 = 6^3 \longrightarrow 6^{3x-2} = 6^3 \longrightarrow 3x - 2 = 3 \longrightarrow 3x = 5 \longrightarrow \boxed{x = \frac{5}{3}}$.

3. $9 = 3^2, 27 = 3^3 \longrightarrow 9^{2x+4} = 3^{2(2x+4)}, 27^{x+4} = 3^{3(x+4)} \longrightarrow 3^{2(2x+4)} = 3^{3(x+4)} \longrightarrow$
   $2(2x+4) = 3(x+4) \longrightarrow 4x + 8 = 3x + 12 \longrightarrow x + 8 = 12 \longrightarrow \boxed{x = 4}$.

4. $\boxed{\text{Domain is all real numbers,}}$ because there is no value of x that makes the equation undefined. For the range, we know that 2^x approaches but never reaches a minimum value of 0 as x gets more negative. Adding $4 + 0$ indicates that the minimum value for y would be 4. The function can have any value greater than 4. Thus, the $\boxed{\text{range is all real numbers greater than } 4.}$

Absolute Value Functions and Their Graphs

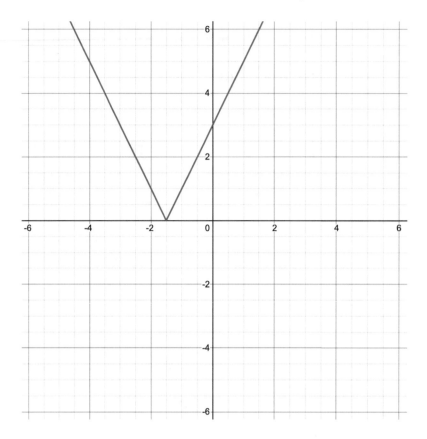

1.

2. $|x + 4| + 30 = 36 \longrightarrow |x + 4| = 6$. This gives us that $x + 4 = 6$, or $-(x + 4) = 6$. If we have $x + 4 = 6$, this gives us $x = 2$. If we have $-(x + 4) = 6$, this gives us $-x - 4 = 6 \longrightarrow -x = 10 \longrightarrow x = -10$. Thus, we have that $\boxed{x = -10, 2}$.

3. $|4x - 16| + 6 = 0 \longrightarrow |4x - 16| = -6$. This gives us that $4x - 16 = -6$, or $-(4x - 16) = -6$. If we have $4x - 16 = -6$, this gives us that $4x = 10 \longrightarrow x = \frac{10}{4} = \frac{5}{2}$. If we have $-(4x - 16) = -6$, this gives us that $-4x + 16 = -6 \longrightarrow -4x = -22 \longrightarrow x = \frac{-22}{-4} = \frac{11}{2}$. Thus, we have that $\boxed{x = \frac{5}{2}, \frac{11}{2}}$.

4. $\frac{|x+4|}{2} = 3 \longrightarrow |x + 4| = 6$. This gives us the exact same result as problem 1, which is that $\boxed{x = -10, 2}$.

5. Breaking the problem into cases, we have three: both $3x - 5$ and $2x + 4$ are positive, both are negative, or they have opposite signs.

   For the first case, $3x - 5 > 0$ when $x > \frac{5}{3}$, and $2x + 4 > 0$ when $x > -2$, so overall, x must be greater than $\frac{5}{3}$. Solving our equation gives us $|3x - 5| + |2x + 4| = 10 \longrightarrow (3x - 5) + (2x + 4) = 10 \longrightarrow 5x - 1 = 10 \longrightarrow 5x = 11 \longrightarrow x = \frac{11}{5}$. $\frac{11}{5} > \frac{5}{3}$, so it is a solution!

For the second case, $3x - 5 < 0$ when $x < \frac{5}{3}$, and $2x + 4 < 0$ when $x < -2$, so overall, x must be less than -2. Solving our equation gives us $|3x+5| + |2x+4| = 10 \longrightarrow -(3x-5) + [-(2x+4)] = 10 \longrightarrow -3x+5-2x-4 = 10 \longrightarrow -5x+1 = 10 \longrightarrow -5x = 9 \longrightarrow x = -\frac{9}{5}$. $-\frac{9}{5}$ is not less than -2, so it is not a solution.

For the final case, we see that we must have $-2 < x < \frac{5}{3}$. This would make $3x - 5$ negative, and $2x + 4$ positive. Thus, we have $|3x - 5| + |2x + 4| = 10 \longrightarrow -(3x - 5) + (2x + 4) = 10 \longrightarrow -3x + 5 + 2x + 4 = 10 \longrightarrow -x + 9 = 10 \longrightarrow -x = 1 \longrightarrow x = -1$. This satisfies our condition that $-2 < x < \frac{5}{3}$, so it is a solution!

Thus, we have that $\boxed{x = -1, \frac{11}{5}}$.

Polynomials

1. $(4x^4 + 3x^2 - 1) + (x^6 + x^5 - 3x^4 + x) = \boxed{x^6 + x^5 + x^4 + 3x^2 + x - 1}$.

2. $\boxed{4}$ and $\boxed{6}$, respectively

3. $(4x^4 + 3x^2 - 1)(x^6 + x^5 - 3x^4 + x) = (4x^4)(x^6 + x^5 - 3x^4 + x) + (3x^2)(x^6 + x^5 - 3x^4 + x) + (-1)(x^6 + x^5 - 3x^4 + x) = (4x^{10} + 4x^9 - 12x^8 + 4x^5) + (3x^8 + 3x^7 - 9x^6 + 3x^3) + (-x^6 - x^5 + 3x^4 - x) = \boxed{4x^{10} + 4x^9 - 9x^8 + 3x^7 - 10x^6 + 3x^5 + 3x^4 - 3x^3 - x}$.

4. $\boxed{10}$

Sequences and Series

1. This is an arithmetic sequences with common difference of 4. The next two terms are thus $53 + 4$ and $53 + 2(4)$, which compute to $\boxed{57 \text{ and } 61}$.

2. This is an arithmetic sequence with first term 24, common difference of 5, and number of terms equal to 8. We can either add up our pairs, or simply use the formula, which gives us $\frac{8}{2} \cdot [2(24) + 5(8 - 1)] = 4 \cdot [48 + 35] = \boxed{332}$.

3. The problem spells out the information for us to plug into the formula for the sum of an arithmetic series, which gives us that the sum is equal to $\frac{7}{2} \cdot [2(-21) + (-2)(7 - 1)] = \frac{7}{2} \cdot [-42 - 12] = \frac{7}{2} \cdot -54 = \boxed{-189}$.

4. We can set a variable x equal to the first term of the series, and a variable d equal to the common difference. This gives us that the sum of the first three terms are equal to $x + (x + d) + (x + 2d) = 60 \longrightarrow 3x + 3d = 60$. We can further divide both sides by 3, giving us that $x + d = 20$. Similarly, the sum of the first 10 terms is $x + (x + d) + (x + 2d) + (x + 3d) + (x + 4d) + (x + 5d) + (x + 6d) + (x + 7d) + (x + 8d) + (x + 9d) = 210 \longrightarrow 10x + 45d = 235$. We can further divide both sides by 5, giving us that $2x + 9d = 47$. We know that $x + d = 20$, so we must have that $2x + 2d = 40$. Subtracting this quantity from $2x + 9d = 47$ gives us that $(2x + 9d) - (2x + 2d) = 47 - 40 \longrightarrow 7d = 7 \longrightarrow d = 1$. Thus, the common

difference is 1. We can use the equation we found, that $x + d = 20$, to see that $x = 20 - 1 = \boxed{19}$.

5. This is a geometric sequence with common ratio $\frac{1}{3}$. Thus, the next two terms are $\frac{4}{3} \cdot \frac{1}{3}$ and $\frac{4}{3} \cdot (\frac{1}{3})^2$, or $\boxed{4/9 \text{ and } 4/27}$.

6. This is a geometric series with common ratio -2, first term -2, and number of terms being 8. Plugging this into our formula gives us that the sum is equal to $\frac{(-2)[(-2)^8 - 1]}{-2 - 1} = \frac{(-2)[256 - 1]}{-3} = \frac{(-2)[255]}{-3} = \frac{-510}{-3} = \boxed{170}$.

7. This is a geometric series with common ratio $\frac{1}{6}$, first term 1296, and number of terms being 7. Plugging this into our formula gives us that the sum is equal to $\frac{(1296)[(\frac{1}{6})^7 - 1]}{\frac{1}{6} - 1} = \frac{(1296)[(\frac{1}{279936}) - 1]}{-\frac{5}{6}} = \frac{(1296)[(-\frac{279935}{279936}]}{-\frac{5}{6}} = \frac{-\frac{279935}{216}}{-\frac{5}{6}} = \boxed{\frac{55987}{36}}$.

GEOMETRY!

Introduction

No problems here? How generous!

Triangle Congruence

1. $\triangle ABC \cong \triangle CDA$ by SSS

   $\triangle EFG \cong \triangle EHG$ by SSS

   $\triangle IJL \cong \triangle IKL$ by SAS, SSS, or ASA

   $\triangle MNO \cong \triangle PQO$ by AAS

   $\triangle RSV \cong \triangle UTV$ by AAS

Triangle Similarity

1. We know that angles that make up a straight line add up to $180°$. We can use this information to get that $\angle ADC = 180° - \angle CDB = 180° - 100° = 80°$. From here, we can find the final angle in triangle ACD using the fact that the angles in a triangle add up to $180°$. This tells us that $\angle ACD = 60°$. Moving on to $\triangle EFG$, we can add up $\angle EFG + \angle HFG = 20° + 20° = 40°$. Once again, we use the fact that the angles in a triangle add up to $180°$ to find that $\angle EGF = 80°$. Well, would you look at that! Both triangles have the same angles, so we say that $\triangle ACD \sim \triangle EFG$ by AA similarity.

2. We know that corresponding parts of similar triangles have the same ratio when comparing their sizes. Maximizing this ratio will give us the greatest possible perimeter of the second triangle. We can do this by having the 36 centimeter side of the second triangle correspond with the smallest side of the first, namely the one that measures 4 centimeters. This gives us a ratio of $\frac{36}{4} = 9$, so the other two sides of the second triangle would measure $9 \times 6 = 54$ and $9 \times 9 = 81$ centimeters. Adding these up gives us a perimeter of $36 + 54 + 81 = \boxed{171 \text{ centimeters}}$.

3. $\boxed{\text{The diagram is not possible.}}$ Both triangles would share the angle formed by the intersection of $\overline{AD}$ and $\overline{BC}$, as well as the congruent angles BAD and CDA. This means that the two would have to be similar by AA similarity. When checking the ratio between corresponding sides, we see that $\overline{AB}$ corresponds to $\overline{DC}$, and their ratio is $\frac{5}{12}$. However, the ratio between the segments formed by point B and the intersection, and point C and the intersection, the ratio is $\frac{4}{8} = \frac{1}{2}$. The ratio is not equal, so this configuration is not possible.

4. We can see that triangles ABC and CBD share a right angle, as well as $\angle ABC$. This means that they are similar by AA similarity. Using the constant ratio of side lengths, we see that $\frac{DB}{12} = \frac{12}{20} \longrightarrow 20DB = 12 \cdot 12 \longrightarrow 20DB = 144 \longrightarrow DB = \frac{144}{20} = \frac{36}{5} = 7.2$. From here, we can notice another pair of similar triangles! Triangles ACD and CBD share a right angle. Additionally, we know that $\angle DAC + \angle ACD = 180° - 90°$, and $\angle DCB + \angle ACD = 90°$. Therefore, we have that $\angle DAC \cong \angle DCB$. Thus, we have that triangles ACD and CBD are similar by AA similarity. We can then set up the equation $\frac{20-7.2}{h} = \frac{h}{7.2} \longrightarrow 7.2(20-7.2) = h^2 \longrightarrow 7.2(12.8) = h^2 \longrightarrow 92.16 = h^2 \longrightarrow \boxed{h = 9.6}$.

Right Triangles and Their Properties

1. We'll go triangle by triangle.

   (a) For $\triangle ABC$, we know both legs, allowing us to set up the equation $5^2 + 8^2 = c^2 \longrightarrow 25 + 64 = c^2 \longrightarrow 89 = c^2 \longrightarrow \boxed{c = \sqrt{89}}$

   (b) For $\triangle DEF$, we can identify it as a $30 - 60 - 90$ triangle, as it is a right triangle containing a $30°$ angle. Therefore, the last side must have a length of $\boxed{6\sqrt{3}}$.

   (c) For $\triangle GHI$, we can identify it as a $45 - 45 - 90$ triangle, as it is a right triangle containing a $45°$ angle. Thus, the legs are simply the length of the hypotenuse, divided by $\sqrt{2}$, which gives legs of length $\boxed{8}$.

   (d) For triangle JKL, we simply apply the Pythagorean Theorem, as we know the lengths of one leg and the hypotenuse. This gives us the equation $13^2 + b^2 = 29^2 \longrightarrow 169 + b^2 = 841 \longrightarrow b^2 = 672 \longrightarrow b = \boxed{4\sqrt{42}}$.

2. We can notice that squaring these side lengths proves that they satisfy the Pythagorean Theorem; thus, the triangle we're dealing with must be a right triangle. The hypotenuse will be the longest side, so it has length $\sqrt{23}$, and the two legs have lengths of $\sqrt{10}$ and $\sqrt{13}$. We know we can find the area of a right triangle by taking half of the product of the lengths of the legs, which gives us $\frac{1}{2} \times \sqrt{10} \times \sqrt{13} = \frac{1}{2} \times \sqrt{130} = \boxed{\frac{\sqrt{130}}{2}}$.

3. We can draw a diagram, since the problem didn't give us one.

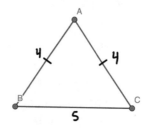

To find its area, we should draw an extra line from the vertex to bisect the base:

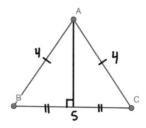

Splitting the triangle in this way gives us two new right triangles, each with one leg of length $\frac{5}{2}$ and hypotenuse of length 4. Now we can set up a formula using the Pythagorean Theorem to find the length of the other leg; the height of the original triangle: $\left(\frac{5}{2}\right)^2 + b^2 = 4^2 \longrightarrow \frac{25}{4} + b^2 = 16 \longrightarrow b^2 = \frac{39}{4} \longrightarrow b = \frac{\sqrt{39}}{2}$. The area of a triangle is half of the base times the height, so the area of our original triangle is thus $\frac{1}{2} \times 5 \times \frac{\sqrt{39}}{2} = \boxed{\frac{5\sqrt{39}}{4}}$.

4. We see that $\triangle ABC$ is a $30 - 60 - 90$ triangle, so $\boxed{BC = 2\sqrt{3},}$ and $\boxed{AC = 4.}$ Next, $\triangle ADC$ is a $45 - 45 - 90$ triangle, so $\boxed{AD = 4,}$ and $\boxed{DC = 4\sqrt{2}.}$ $\triangle DEC$ is another $30 - 60 - 90$ triangle, so $DE = \frac{4\sqrt{2}}{\sqrt{3}} = \boxed{\frac{4\sqrt{6}}{3}}$ and $\boxed{EC = \frac{8\sqrt{6}}{3}.}$ Finally, $\triangle EFC$ is a $45 - 45 - 90$ triangle, so $\boxed{EF = \frac{8\sqrt{6}}{3},}$ and $FC = \frac{8\sqrt{6}}{3} \times \sqrt{2} = \frac{8\sqrt{12}}{3} = \boxed{\frac{16\sqrt{3}}{3}.}$

5. We notice that $\triangle ABC$ is a $45 - 45 - 90$ triangle, so we know that $\boxed{BC = 3}$ and $\boxed{AC = 3\sqrt{2}.}$ We can also notice that because the ratio of $BC : CD$ is $3 : 6 = 1 : 2$, $\triangle BCD$ must be a $30 - 60 - 90$ triangle. Thus, $\boxed{BD = 3\sqrt{3}.}$ $\boxed{m\angle BCD = 60°,}$ and $\boxed{m\angle CDB = 30°.}$

6. (a) $\boxed{3 - 4 - 5}$

   (b) $\boxed{5 - 12 - 13}$

   (c) $\boxed{7 - 24 - 25}$

Special Parts of Triangles

1. It is clear from the given statements that $\triangle ABC$ is a right triangle. Thus, the circumradius is simply half the length of the hypotenuse. We can recognize that this is a $3 - 4 - 5$ triangle, with the hypotenuse having a length of 10. Therefore, the circumradius has a length of $\boxed{5.}$

2. We can reason our way through this. Let our triangle be $\triangle ABC$, and let the heights of the altitudes be $x, y,$ and z, from points $A, B,$ and C, respectively. Then, we must have that the area of $\triangle ABC$ is equal to $\frac{BC \times x}{2} = \frac{AB \times z}{2} = \frac{AC \times y}{2}$. We know that $X = Y = Z$, so we must have that $AB = BC = AC$, meaning that yes, the triangle is equilateral.

3. We know that $\angle BAD = \angle CAD$, so we have that $\overline{AD}$ is the angle bisector of $\angle BAC$. The Angle Bisector Theorem tells us that $\frac{AB}{BD} = \frac{AC}{DC} = 2$. Thus, we know that $AB = 2 \times BD = 2 \times 3 = \boxed{6.}$

4. Medians divide a triangle into six triangles of equal area. Here's a picture for visualization:

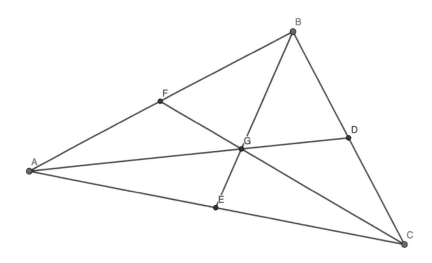

Triangle ADC is made up of 3 of the smaller triangles, which each have an area of $\frac{48}{6} = 8$. Thus, the area of $\triangle ADC$ is $3 \times 8 = \boxed{24.}$ Triangle AGC is made up of 2 of the smaller triangles, so its area is $2 \times 8 = \boxed{16.}$ Triangle GFB consists of just one of the smaller triangles, so its are is simply $\boxed{8}$. Triangle DEF is simply the medial triangle, so its area is a quarter of the total: $\frac{48}{4} = \boxed{12.}$

5. It's a good idea to draw a picture, since the problem didn't give one.

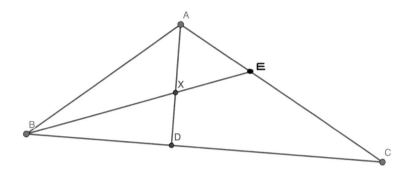

Now it's easier to see that $\angle ABC = 180° - \angle BAC - \angle ACB = 180° - (117° + 35°) = 28°$. We also know that $\overline{BE}$ is an angle bisector, so we have that $\angle DBX = \frac{28°}{2} = 14°$. $\angle DXE$ is an exterior angle of triangle DXB, so we can say that $\angle DXE = \angle DBX + \angle XDB = 14° + 90° = \boxed{104°}$.

Area and Perimeter

1. Let ths shortest side have a length x. Then, the two other sides' lengths become $2x$ and $1.5x$. This gives a perimeter of $2x + 1.5x + x = 45 \longrightarrow 4.5x = 45 \longrightarrow x = 10$. Thus, the shortest side has a length $\boxed{10}$.

2. All four sides of a square have the same length, so each side of this square has a length $\frac{48}{4} = 12$. The area of a square is its side length times itself, which gives $12 \times 12 = \boxed{144}$.

3. The fact that the path has uniform width tells us that the path itself also forms a square. The garden's perimeter gives us that the side length of the garden is $\frac{64}{4} = 16$. Thus, the garden has an area of $16^2 = 256$. The combined garden and path then have an area of $256 + 228 = 484$. Taking the square root of 484 gives us that the side length of the larger square formed by the path is $\sqrt{484} = 22$. Thus, the amount of fencing needed is simply the perimeter of the larger square, or $22 \times 4 = \boxed{88 \text{ meters}}$.

4. The two triangles, though they look quite different, actually have the same height of 12 feet. Thus, all that matters is the size of their bases. Painter A's chosen design on the left has a smaller base, so $\boxed{\text{Painter A's design will use less paint.}}$

5. The square's perimeter of 96 feet tells us that each side has a length of $\frac{96}{4} = 24$ feet. In 24 feet, there are $\frac{24}{6} = 4$ six-foot spaces, necessitating 5 posts. For the top

and bottom of the square, we'll count all 5 posts for a current total of $5 + 5 = 10$. The left and right sides of the square, though, also have 5 posts. However, for each side, we've already counted the topmost and bottom-most post; in actuality, we only count 3 from each of these sides. Therefore, we have a total of $10 + 3 + 3 = \boxed{16 \text{ posts.}}$

All About Quadrilaterals!

1. The problem tells us the length of one side is 25, so the length of all sides is 25. Combining sides $\overline{AB}$ and $\overline{BC}$ with the diagonal $\overline{AC}$ creates an isosceles triangle with legs of length 25, and base of length 48. Splitting it down the middle creates two $7 - 24 - 25$ right triangles. Therefore, we know that half the length of the diagonal $\overline{BD}$ is 7, so $\boxed{BD = 7 \times 2 = 14.}$ The area of $ABCD$ is equal to half the product of the diagonals, so $\frac{14 \times 48}{2} = 7 \times 48 = \boxed{336.}$ We can now use the area to find the distance between $\overline{AB}$ and $\overline{CD}$. Treating $\overline{AB}$ as the base allows us to see this distance as the height (h). This gives us the equation $25h = 336 \longrightarrow h = \boxed{\frac{336}{25}}$.

2. Adding the path effectively creates a bigger rectangle enclosing the original rectangle of the garden, with dimensions $36 + 2 + 2$ feet by $24 + 2 + 2$ feet, or 40 feet by 28 feet. We can find the area of the path by finding the area of this large triangle, and then subtracting from it the area of the garden. The area of the big rectangle is $40 \times 28 = 1120$ square feet, and the area of the garden is $36 \times 24 = 864$ square feet. Subtracting the two gives us that the path has an area of $1120 - 864 = 256$ square feet. Each square foot of bricks cost 15, so the path costs a total of $256 \times 15 = \boxed{3840}$ dollars for the bricks.

3. AB is the length of the square's side. Taking the square root of the area gives us that $AB = \sqrt{40} = \boxed{2\sqrt{10}.}$ AC is the length of the square's diagonal, which can be found using the relationship that $d = s\sqrt{2}$, where d is the diagonal of a square, and s is its side length. Using this relationship gives us that $AC = 2\sqrt{10} \times \sqrt{2} = 2\sqrt{20} = \boxed{4\sqrt{5}.}$

4. The median would have a length that is an average of the two bases, so its length would be $\frac{32 + 22}{2} = \frac{54}{2} = 27$. Multiplying this by the height gives us the area, which is $27 \times 16 = \boxed{432}$.

5. Dividing the area of the trapezoid by its height gives us the length of its median. In this case, it is $\frac{42}{2} = 21$. The median is the average of the two bases. Let the shorter base have length x. Thus, the longer base has length $x + 6$. This gives us the equation $\frac{x + x + 6}{2} = 21 \longrightarrow 2x + 6 = 42 \longrightarrow 2x = 36 \longrightarrow x = 18$. Thus, the longer base has length $18 + 6 = \boxed{24}$.

6. The altitude of the triangle would have length $\frac{8}{2} \times \sqrt{3} = 4\sqrt{3}$. Therefore, the square would have area $(4\sqrt{3})^2 = 16 \times 3 = \boxed{48.}$

7. If one of the angles is $120°$, then the angle adjacent to it has measure $180 - 120 = 60$. Thus, drawing in the shorter diagonal creates two equilateral triangles with side length 2. The area of each of these triangles is $\frac{2 \times \sqrt{3}}{2} = \sqrt{3}$. Adding the areas of the two triangles together gives that the area of the rhombus is $\boxed{2\sqrt{3}}$.

8. Because $ABCD$ is a parallelogram, we have that $AB = CD \longrightarrow 2x - 3 = 3x - 8 \longrightarrow -3 = x - 8 \longrightarrow x = 5$. $BC = AD = 2x - 3$, so the perimeter is equal to $(2x - 3) + (x + 7) + (3x - 8) + (x + 7) = 7x + 3 = 7(5) + 3 = 35 + 3 = \boxed{38.}$

All About Circles!

1. The circumference of a circle is equal to its radius multiplied by 2π. We can thus set up the equation that $2\pi r = 16\pi \longrightarrow 2r = 16 \longrightarrow r = 8$. From here, we can use the fact that the area of a circle is πr^2 to get that our area is $\boxed{64\pi}$.

2. To find the diameter of this particular circle, we can set the formulas for diameter and area equal to each other: $2\pi r = \pi r^2 \longrightarrow 2r = r^2 \longrightarrow 2 = r$. Thus, this circle has a diameter of twice the radius of 2, giving us a final answer of $\boxed{4}$.

3. This problems looks a little complex. Let's come up with a game plan to tackle it. A good plan would be to find the area of the sector formed by points A, B and O, and to subtract the area of $\triangle AOB$ from that. Finding the area of the sector is easy; simply multiplying the area of the circle by the fraction of $360°$ that $120°$ is gives us an area of $\pi(4)^2 \cdot \frac{120}{360} = \frac{16\pi}{3}$. Finding the area of $\triangle AOB$ is a bit more tricky. What we can do is drawn in a perpendicular bisector of $\overline{AB}$ through point O.

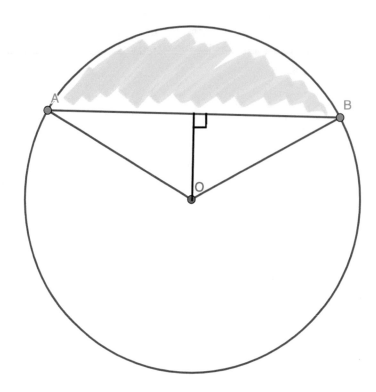

Call the intersection of the bisector and $\overline{AB}$ point X. Now, since the perpendicular bisector acted additionally as an angle bisector of $\angle AOB$, we have created two $30 - 60 - 90$ triangles: $\triangle AXO$ and $\triangle BXO$. Using the side length relationships we learned for these special triangles, we see that $XO = \frac{4}{2} = 2$, and $AX = BX = \frac{4\sqrt{3}}{2} = 2\sqrt{3}$. Thus, we have that the area of $\triangle AOB$ is equal to $\frac{(AX+BX)\cdot(OX)}{2}$, which we can now solve as $\frac{(2\cdot2\sqrt{3})\cdot2}{2} = 4\sqrt{3}$. Finally, we can get the area of the portion in yellow, which is $\boxed{\frac{16\pi}{3} - 4\sqrt{3}}$.

4. To solve this problem, we can find the area of the circumcircle and subtract from it the area of $\triangle ABC$. To find the area of the circumcircle, we need its radius. We can begin to find that by drawing in altitude $\overline{AX}$, which also serves as a median and angle bisector. This makes $\triangle ABX$ a $30 - 60 - 90$ triangle, giving us that $AX = \frac{AB\sqrt{3}}{2} = \frac{10\sqrt{3}}{2} = 5\sqrt{3}$. We know that the circumcenter O is the centroid, so it lies on median AX such that $AO : AX = 2 : 3$. Thus, we have that AO is equal to the radius, which is $\frac{2}{3} \cdot 5\sqrt{3} = \frac{10\sqrt{3}}{3}$. From here, we have that the area of the circumcircle is $(\frac{10\sqrt{3}}{3})^2\pi = \frac{100\pi}{3}$. Now we must find the area of the equilateral triangle, which is easy; that simply becomes $\frac{10\cdot5\sqrt{3}}{2} = 25\sqrt{3}$. Thus, the area of the region is equal to $\boxed{\frac{100\pi}{3} - 25\sqrt{3}}$.

5. To begin, we must recognize that the areas of the regions formed by subtracting quarter-circles ADC and CBA from the area of square $ABCD$ are the same.

Thus, we can find the area of one of those regions, and subtract double its area from the total area of square $ABCD$ to find the area of the desired region. The area of the region formed by subtracting quarter-circle ADC from square $ABCD$ is thus $5^2 - \frac{5^2\pi}{4} = 25 - \frac{25\pi}{4} = \frac{100-25\pi}{4}$. Twice this area is simply $\frac{100-25\pi}{2}$. Thus, the area of the shaded region is $25 - \left(\frac{100-25\pi}{2}\right) = \frac{50-(100-25\pi)}{2} = \boxed{\frac{25\pi-50}{2}}$.

6. We have that arc EB is equal to $360°$ minus the measures of arcs CE, CD, and DB combined. This gives us $360° - (40° + 103° + 83°) = 134°$. We know that $\angle EXB$ is equal to the sum of arcs CD and EB divided by 2, which thus gives us $\frac{103°+134°}{2} = \boxed{\frac{237°}{2}}$.

7. We know that $\overline{TX}$ is tangent of circle O at X, and $\overline{OX}$ is a radius of the circle. This tells us that segments $\overline{TX}$ and $\overline{OX}$ are perpendicular. Using the Pythagorean Theorem to solve for TO gives us that $TO = \sqrt{TX^2 + OX^2} = \sqrt{144 + 36} = \sqrt{180} = \boxed{6\sqrt{5}}$.

3-D Figures

1. We know that the diagonal of a face of a cube is simply the diagonal of a square, because the faces of a cube are squares. Thus, the diagonal splits the square face into two congruent $45-45-90$ triangles. We can use what we know about the side relationships of these special triangles to surmise that the legs of the triangle, and thus the side length of the square face and edge length of the cube, is $\frac{3}{\sqrt{2}} = \frac{3\sqrt{2}}{2}$. Now that we know the edge length, finding the volume is easy; it's just the edge length to the third power. Thus, the volume of the cube is $\left(\frac{3\sqrt{2}}{2}\right)^3 = \frac{54\sqrt{2}}{8} = \boxed{\frac{27\sqrt{2}}{4}}$.

2. We know that the volume of a right rectangular prism is equal to the product of its three different edge lengths. In this case, we know that two of them are 2 and 3, so we can set the third side length equal to s. This gives us the equation that $2 \cdot 3 \cdot s = 36 \longrightarrow 6 \cdot s = 36 \longrightarrow s = 6$. Thus, the length of the third dimension is $\boxed{6}$. As for the total surface area, that is simply $2[(2)(3) + (2)(6) + (3)(6)] = 2(6 + 12 + 18) = 2(36) = \boxed{72}$.

3. We know that the volume of a pyramid is the area of its base times its height, divided by three. Setting the height equal to h, we can set up the equation $\frac{10h}{3} = 80 \longrightarrow 10h = 240 \longrightarrow h = \boxed{24}$.

4. To find the volume, we simply apply the formula of $\pi r^2 h$. This gives us that the volume is $\pi(4^2)(5) = \pi(16)(5) = \boxed{80\pi}$. As for its surface area, we apply the formula $2\pi rh + 2\pi r^2$. This gives us that the total surface area is $2\pi(4)(5) + 2\pi(4^2) = 40\pi + 32\pi = \boxed{72\pi}$.

5. The volume of a cone is given by the area of its base (πr^2) times its height, divided by 3. The area of the base in this case is $\pi(2^2) = 4\pi$. Thus, we can set up the

equation, substituting h for height, that $\frac{4\pi h}{3} = 12\pi \longrightarrow 4\pi h = 36\pi \longrightarrow h = 9$. Thus, the height is $\boxed{9}$.

6. If a sphere's volume and surface area are equal, then we must have the equation that $\frac{4\pi r^3}{3} = 4\pi r^2$, where r is the radius of the sphere. Solving the equation gives that $4\pi r^3 = 12\pi r^2 \longrightarrow 4\pi r = 12\pi \longrightarrow r = 3$. Thus, the radius of the sphere is $\boxed{3}$.

7. If the sphere's diameter is 10, then its radius is simply $\frac{10}{2} = 5$. Thus, its volume is $\frac{4\pi(5^3)}{3} = \frac{4\pi(125)}{3} = \boxed{\frac{500\pi}{3}}$, and the surface area is $4\pi(5^2) = 4\pi(25) = \boxed{100\pi}$.

COMBINATORICS & PROBABILITY!

Introduction

Count the number of problems in this section... it's 0? Easiest counting problem ever! You're welcome :)

Let's count things!

1. To begin, we must find the first and last multiples of 7 in our range. These would be 35 and 462. From here, the list of numbers we wish to count becomes $35, 42, 49, ...448, 455, 462$. Dividing all elements of the list by 7 gives us a list of consecutive integers: $5, 6, 7, ..., 64, 65, 66$. Finally, subtracting 4 from each element makes our list start at 1, giving us a final list of $1, 2, 3, ..., 60, 61, 62$. Thus, there are $\boxed{62}$ multiples of 7 between 31 and 467.

2. Once again, let's find the first and last acceptable elements in this range: the first 3 digit square is 100. The last is a bit harder to find, but we know that $30^2 = 900$, so the last square must be the square of a number not much larger than 30. A bit of trial and error reveals that the last square is $31^2 = 961$. Our list of squares is now $100, 121, 144, ...841, 900, 961$. This is a bit of a mess, so we can rewrite this list in the format of their square roots squared: $10^2, 11^2, 12^2, ...29^2, 30^2, 31^2$. This is much easier to count! And hey, the bases are even consecutive integers. This is essentially like counting the consecutive integers from 10 to 31, which we know how to do. To reflect this scenario, we can rewrite the list as simply $10, 11, 12, ...29, 30, 31$. We can subtract 9 from each element in the list to make it start with 1, giving us $1, 2, 3, ...20, 21, 22$. Thus, there are $\boxed{22}$ 3 digit squares.

3. Let's use the information we have to figure out a bit more. If 15 of the dogs have short hair, then $35 - 15 = 20$ of them must have long hair. Similarly, if 82 of the dogs are puppies, then $35 - 18 = 17$ of them must be adult dogs. From here, we can see that if there are 7 long-haired adult dogs, then there must be $17 - 7 = 10$ short-haired adult dogs. Using the fact that there are 15 short-haired dogs in total, we see that there are $15 - 10 = \boxed{5}$ short-haired puppies.

4. There are 4 choices of body style, and for each choice of body style, 3 choices of engine. This gives $4 \times 3 = 12$ body style-engine combinations. Next, there are 6 choices of color for each of those combinations, giving $12 \times 6 = 72$ body style-engine-color combos. Finally, we add in the trim levels, giving us $72 \times 3 = \boxed{216}$ total combinations.

5. We have the restriction that the books on either end of the stack must be about science. We will take care of this restriction first, by choosing the books to go on each end. 3 of our books are about science, so we have 3 choices for the first end, and thus 2 choices for the second. This gives us a total of $3 \times 2 = 6$ choices for the end combinations. We can treat the remaining 6 books in the interior separately,

giving us a total of $6 \times 5 \times 4 \times 3 \times 2 \times 1 = 720$ ways to arrange the interior books. Combining this with the 6 ways of arranging the end books, we have a total of $6 \times 720 = \boxed{4320}$ ways.

6. In the first scenario, if the balls remain outside of the bin after they have been drawn, we have 16 choices for the first ball, 15 for the second, 14 for the third, and 13 for the last, for a total of $16 \times 15 \times 14 \times 13 = \boxed{43,680}$ ways. However, in the second scenario, the balls are replaced after they have drawn, giving us 16 choices for each draw. This gives a total of $16 \times 16 \times 16 \times = 16^4 = \boxed{65,536}$ ways.

Counting Strategies

1. We can split the problem into cases, based on the number of ones. There are thus 3 cases. If there is just one 1, it can be placed in any of the 3 slots available. In any of these three cases, the other two digits have $3 \times 3 = 9$ choices for how to fill them. Thus, if there is one 1, there are $3 \times 9 = 27$ ways to create a three digit number. If there are 2 ones, there are once again 3 arrangements: the two ones together in the hundreds and tens places, the two ones together in the tens and ones places, and the two ones separate in the hundreds and ones places. For each of these three cases, there are 3 remaining choices for the final digit, giving a total of $3 \times 3 = 9$ ways to create a number. Finally, if there are 3 ones, there is only one possible number: 111. Thus, this adds 1 to the total number of ways. The total number of ways is thus $27 + 9 + 1 = \boxed{37}$.

2. There are 5 choices for the first digit, 4 for the second because it has to be different from the first, and then 4 again for the third, since it must be different for the second. Thus, there are a total of $5 \times 4 \times 4 = \boxed{80}$ choices.

3. For this problem, we'll use complementary counting. There are a total of $9 \times 10 \times 10 \times 10 \times 10 = 90,000$ ways to construct a five digit number with no restrictions. Now we need to find the number of ways to construct such a number with less than 2 zeros. If the number has 1 zero, it can go in any position other than the ten-thousands. Thus, it has 4 positions. There are then 9 choices for each of the other positions, for a total of $9^4 = 6561$ choices. Taking into account the 4 possible positions, we now have $4 \times 6561 = 26,244$ choices for a number with one zero. Now for a number with no zeros, there are simply 9 choices for all 5 digits, for a total of $9^5 = 59,049$ choices. Therefore, we have a total of $26,244 + 59,049 = 85,293$ choices for numbers that contain fewer than 2 zeros and have five digits. Finally, we have our answer: $90,000 - 85,293 = \boxed{4707}$ five digit numbers with at least 2 zeros.

4. In this problem, we can use complementary counting by finding the number of outfits that we cannot wear. In this case, it is simply the outfits in which all the elements are the same color. There are 3 choices of color, and thus 3 outfits that are not acceptable. As for the total number of outfits, there are $3^3 = 27$ choices. Thus, there are $27 - 3 = \boxed{24}$ acceptable outfits.

5. Let's use constructive counting. In forming the first 2 letters, we have 26 choices for the first letter, then 25 for the second, since they must be different. As for the 3 digits that follow, they must all be different, so we have 10 choices for the first, 9 for the second, and 8 for the third. Finally, for the last two letters, we have 26 choices for both, since they can be the same. This gives us a total of $26 \times 25 \times 10 \times 9 \times 8 \times 26 \times 26 = \boxed{316,368,000}$ possible license plate numbers.

6. Using constructive counting, let's create scenarios in which all three boys sit together. If we treat them all as one collective unit, which we call a "superboy," we see that this then becomes a problem of seating the 6 girls and the superboy. In this case, we have $7! = 5040$ ways of seating the girls and the superboy. However, remembering that the superboy is made up of 3 different boys, which can be seated in $3! = 6$ ways, we see that our final answer is $6 \times 5040 = \boxed{30,240}$ ways.

Overcounting

1. Treating all five letters as distinct, we would have $5! = 120$ arrangements. However, we have 3 e's, which are all the same. In any given arrangement of the letters, the three e's can be arranged $3! = 6$ ways if treated as distinct, meaning each true arrangement is counted 6 ways in our total of 120. Therefore, the true number of arrangements is $\frac{120}{6} = \boxed{20}$.

2. The word has 7 letters, leading to a total of $7! = 5040$ arrangements if all the letters were distinct. However, the word has 4 a's, for a total of $4! = 24$ arrangements of the four a's if treated as distinct. Therefore, each true arrangement is counted 24 times in our total of 5040. The true number of arrangements is thus $\frac{5040}{24} = \boxed{210}$.

3. If we treat all 11 letters as distinct, then we have a total of $11!$ arrangements. however, the word contains four i's, four s's, and two p's. This means a total of $4! \times 4! \times 2! = 24 \times 24 \times 2 = 1152$ arrangements of all the duplicate letters if treated as distinct. Thus, each true arrangement is counted 1152 times in our total of $11!$. The true number of arrangements is thus $\frac{11!}{1152} = \boxed{34,650}$.

4. We're more familiar with arranging letters in a word, so we can treat this scenario as an eight-letter word with 4 of one letter, 3 of another, and 1 of a last letter. Thus, the total number of arrangements if all letters were distinct would be $8! = 40,320$. However, the duplicate letters lead to overcounting by a factor of $4! \times 3! \times 1! = 24 \times 6 \times 1 = 144$. Thus, our true number of arrangements is $\frac{40,320}{144} = \boxed{280}$.

5. If the order were to matter, we would simply pick the first ball, of which we have 16 choices, and then the second, of which we have 15 choices, for a total choice of $16 \times 15 = 240$. However, because the order doesn't matter; each pair is counted twice. For a pair of numbers a and b, the orders ab and ba are the same according to the guidelines of this problem, so we've overcounted by a factor of 2. Therefore, the answer is $\frac{240}{2} = \boxed{120}$.

6. We'll split this problem up into two parts: dealing with games within each level,

and games between different levels. For games within a level, there will be a total of $\frac{5 \times 4}{2}$ individual games between teams in the same level. However, since there are two games between each team, there will then be a total of $5 \times 4 = 20$. Now, for the games between levels. For each team in one level, there will be 5 individual games; one between each of the 5 teams in the other level, for a total of $5 \times 5 = 25$ games. However, each team plays the other teams twice, so we must double our result to 50 games. Combined, the teams play a total of $20 + 25 = \boxed{45}$ games.

7. In a row, there would be 7! ways to arrange the people. However, in a circle, there are 7 arrangements in a row for one equivalent arrangement in a circle. Therefore, we must divide our total by 7, giving us a total of $7!/7 = 6! = \boxed{720}$ arrangements.

Combinations and Combinations and More Combinations

1. In this problem, the officers are distinguishable, so we 11 choices for the first officer, 10 for the next, and so on. This gives us $11 \cdot 10 \cdot 9 \cdot 8 \cdot 7 = \boxed{55,440}$.

2. While this problem looks similar to the previous one, this time, the committee is not distinguishable. Thus, we employ our choose formula, getting that $\binom{11}{5} = \frac{11 \cdot 10 \cdot 9 \cdot 8 \cdot 7}{5 \cdot 4 \cdot 3 \cdot 2 \cdot 1} = \frac{55440}{120} = \boxed{462}$.

3. Let's choose the one president first, to get them out of the way: there are simply 8 ways to do this, leaving 7 people left from which to choose the vice presidents. Since they are interchangeable, we use our choose formula, getting $\binom{7}{3} = \frac{7 \cdot 6 \cdot 5}{3 \cdot 2 \cdot 1} = \frac{210}{6} = 35$ ways. Multiplying by the 8 ways we can choose a president, we get $8 \times 35 = \boxed{280}$ ways.

4. One way to do this problem is to simply apply reason, which says that there is just 1 way to choose 0 people. However, we can prove this with our choose formula, giving $\binom{n}{0} = \frac{n!}{n!0!} = \frac{1}{0!}$. Recall that $0! = 1$, and we get that $\binom{n}{0} = \frac{1}{1} = \boxed{1}$ for all positive integers n.

5. $\binom{n}{1} = \frac{n}{1} = \boxed{n}$.

6. $\binom{n}{n} = \frac{n!}{n!} = \boxed{1}$.

7. $\binom{4}{2} = \frac{4 \cdot 3}{2 \cdot 1} = \frac{12}{2} = \boxed{6}$.

8. $\binom{7}{3} = \frac{7 \cdot 6 \cdot 5}{3 \cdot 2 \cdot 1} = \frac{210}{6} = \boxed{35}$.

9. $\binom{5}{1} = \frac{5}{1} = \boxed{5}$.

10. $\binom{9}{4} = \frac{9 \cdot 8 \cdot 7 \cdot 6}{4 \cdot 3 \cdot 2 \cdot 1} = \frac{3024}{24} = \boxed{126}$.

11. $\binom{10}{3} = \frac{10 \cdot 9 \cdot 8}{3 \cdot 2 \cdot 1} = \frac{720}{6} = \boxed{120}$.

12. $\binom{3}{1} = \frac{3}{1} = \boxed{3}$.

13. $\binom{9}{6} = \binom{9}{3} = \frac{9 \cdot 8 \cdot 7}{3 \cdot 2 \cdot 1} = \frac{504}{6} = \boxed{84}$.

14. $\binom{8}{6} = \binom{8}{2} = \frac{8 \cdot 7}{2 \cdot 1} = \frac{56}{2} = \boxed{28}$.

15. $\binom{10}{9} = \binom{10}{1} = \frac{10}{1} = \boxed{10}$.

16. $\binom{6}{4} = \binom{6}{2} = \frac{6 \cdot 5}{2 \cdot 1} = \frac{30}{2} = \boxed{15}$.

17. $\binom{7}{4} = \binom{7}{3} = \frac{7 \cdot 6 \cdot 5}{3 \cdot 2 \cdot 1} = \frac{210}{6} = \boxed{35}$.

18. $\binom{15}{13} = \binom{15}{2} = \frac{15 \cdot 14}{2 \cdot 1} = \frac{210}{2} = \boxed{105}$.

Basic Probability

1. The total number of cases is $6 \times 6 = 36$. The least possible sum is 2 (two 1's), and the greatest possible sum is 12 (two 6's). Thus, the only possible sums that are squares are 4 and 9. A 4 can be achieved through a 1 and a 3, a 3 and a 1, or a 2 and a 2, for a total of 3 ways. A 9 can be achieved through a 3 and a 6, a 6 and a 3, a 4 and a 5, or a 5 and a 4, for a total of 4 ways. Thus, there are $3 + 4 = 7$ ways that work out of 36 total ways, giving a probability of $\boxed{\frac{7}{36}}$.

2. The choices for an even number to drawn are $2, 4, 6, 8,$ or 10, for a total of 5 choices. However, these cards exist in 4 suits, so there are then $4 \times 5 = 20$ ways to get an even number. There are 13 cards that are diamonds, but that includes the 5 even diamonds that we've already counted. Thus, there are 8 more cards that we need to add to our existing 20, for a total of 28. This gives a probability of $\frac{28}{52}$, which simplifies to $\boxed{\frac{7}{13}}$.

3. Counting the probability of *not* getting at least 2 heads will be easier. This entails getting 1 head, or none at all. Getting 1 head can happen in $\binom{7}{1} = 7$ ways, and getting none happens in 1 way, for a total of 8 successful ways. Each coin toss has 2 possibilities, so there are a total of $2^7 = 128$ possibilities. This gives a probability of $\frac{8}{128}$, which simplifies to $\frac{1}{16}$. Subtracting this from our total gives an answer of $1 - \frac{1}{16} = \boxed{\frac{15}{16}}$.

4. It will be easier to calculate the probability that all 5 show a 2, which has one way of happening. There are a total of $6^5 = 7776$ ways, so the probability that all 5 show a 2 is $\frac{1}{7776}$. Thus, the probability that up to 4 of them show a 2 is $1 - \frac{1}{7776} = \boxed{\frac{7775}{7776}}$.

5. If the coin comes up heads in 6 flips, that can happen in $\binom{8}{6} = \binom{8}{2} = 28$ ways. In 7 flips, that happens in $\binom{8}{7} = \binom{8}{1} = 8$ ways. In 8 flips, that happens in just 1 way. Thus, there are $28 + 8 + 1 = 37$ successful ways. There are a total of $2^8 = 256$ ways, so the probability is $\boxed{\frac{37}{256}}$.

6. If the coin comes up heads in 7 flips, that can happen in $\binom{10}{7} = \binom{10}{3} = 120$ ways. In 8 flips, that happens in $\binom{10}{8} = \binom{10}{2} = 45$ ways. In 9 flips, that happens in

$\binom{10}{9} = \binom{10}{1} = 10$ ways. In 10 flips, that happens in one way. This comes together for a total of $120+45+10+1 = 176$ ways that work. The total number of choices is $2^{10} = 1024$, so the probability is $\frac{176}{1024}$, which simplifies to $\boxed{11\ 64}$.

7. The probability that the first marble is white is $\frac{6}{10} = \frac{3}{5}$. Then, the probability that the second marble is red is $\frac{4}{9}$, with the total number of marbles now being lower by 1 to account for the white marble that was just drawn. Multiplying the two probabilities gives an answer of $\frac{3}{5} \times \frac{4}{9} = \frac{12}{45}$, which simplifies to $\boxed{\frac{4}{15}}$.

8. There are 4 ones, twos, and threes, in the deck, each, at the start of the problem. Therefore, the probability of first drawing a 1 is $\frac{4}{52} = \frac{1}{13}$. Then, the probability of drawing a 2 is $\frac{4}{51}$, with one card removed from the total. The probability of drawing a 3 is then $\frac{4}{50} = \frac{2}{25}$, with another card removed from the total. Multiplying the probabilities gives an answer of $\frac{1}{13} \times \frac{4}{51} \times \frac{2}{25} = \boxed{\frac{8}{16575}}$.

Expected Value

1. We have 6 possible values: $1^2, 2^2, 3^2, 4^2, 5^2$, and 6^2, so $1, 4, 9, 16, 25$, and 36. They each have the same probability of occurring: $\frac{1}{6}$. Therefore, our expected value is $\frac{1}{6}(1 + 4 + 9 + 16 + 25 + 36) = \frac{1}{6}(91) = \boxed{\frac{91}{6}}$.

2. We have 6 possible values: $1^3, 2^3, 3^3, 4^3, 5^3$, and 6^3, so $1, 8, 27, 64, 125$, and 216. They each have the same probability of occurring: $\frac{1}{6}$. Therefore, our expected value is $\frac{1}{6}(1 + 8 + 27 + 64 + 125 + 216) = \frac{1}{6}(441) = \frac{441}{6} = \boxed{\frac{147}{2}}$.

3. In this scenario, the products of opposite faces can only be $1 \cdot 6 = 6$, $2 \cdot 5 = 10$, and $3 \cdot 4 = 12$. Therefore, the outcomes after rolling of $6 \cdot 10 = 60$, $6 \cdot 12 = 72$, and $10 \cdot 12 = 120$ are equally likely. Thus, the expected value of these three values is $\frac{60+72+120}{3} = \frac{252}{3} = \boxed{84}$.

NUMBER THEORY

Introduction

Nothing to see here!

Multiples and Divisors

1. The positive divisors of 120 are $1, 2, 3, 4, 5, 6, 8, 10, 12, 15, 20, 24, 30, 40, 60$, and 120. The positive divisors of 48 are $1, 2, 3, 4, 6, 8, 12, 16, 24$, and 48. The positive common divisors are thus $\boxed{1, 2, 3, 4, 6, 8, 12, \text{ and } 24}$.

2. This one might take some time, just to go through all the possibilities. Still, in the end, the positive divisors of 289 are $1, 17$, and 289. The positive divisors of 34 are $1, 2, 17$, and 34. The positive common divisors are thus $\boxed{1 \text{ and } 17}$.

3. The positive divisors of 25 are $1, 5$, and 25. The positive divisors of 50 are $1, 2, 5, 10, 25$, and 50. The GCD is thus $\boxed{25}$.

4. The positive divisors of 24 are $1, 2, 3, 4, 6, 8, 12$, and 24. The positive divisors of 36 are $1, 2, 3, 4, 6, 9, 12, 18$, and 36. The GCD is thus $\boxed{12}$.

5. The positive divisors of 12 are $1, 2, 3, 4, 6$, and 12. The positive divisors of 23 are 1 and 23. The GCD is thus $\boxed{1}$.

6. The positive divisors of 24 are $1, 2, 3, 4, 6, 8, 12$, and 24. The positive divisors of 28 are $1, 2, 4, 7, 14$, and 28. The GCD is thus $\boxed{4}$.

7. The 4 smallest positive common multiples of 3 and 4 will be the first positive multiples of 4 that are also divisible by 3. Some multiples of 4 are $4, 8, 12, 16, 20, 24, 28, 32, 36, 40, 44, 48, 52$, and 56. The first 4 that are divisible by 3 are $\boxed{12, 24, 36, \text{ and } 48}$.

8. The LCM will be the first multiple of 6 that is also divisible by 3, which in this case is simply $\boxed{6}$.

9. The LCM will be the first multiple of 7 that is also divisible by 4. Some multiples of 7 are $7, 14, 21, 28$, and 35. The first one to be divisible by 4 is $\boxed{28}$.

10. The LCM will be the first multiple of 42 that is also divisible by 18. Some multiples of 42 are $42, 84, 126$, and 168. The first one to be divisible by 18 is $\boxed{126}$.

11. The LCM will be the first multiple of 30 that is also divisible by 25. Some multiples of 30 are $30, 60, 90, 120, 150$, and 180. The first one to be divisible by 25 is $\boxed{150}$.

12. The 5 multiples of 5 can be expressed as $5a, 5b, 5c, 5d$, and $5e$, where a, b, c, d, and e are all integers. Adding them gives us $5a + 5b + 5c + 5d + 5e$. From here, we can factor out the 5 to get $5(a + b + c + d + e)$. Since a, b, c, d, and e are all integers, $a + b + c + d + e$ is also an integer. Thus, we are left with a product of 5 and an integer, which therefore must be a multiple of 5.

Prime Factorizations

1.

$$
\begin{array}{r|l}
3 & 45 \\
\hline
3 & 15 \\
\hline
 & 5 \\
\hline
\end{array}
$$

$$\boxed{45 = 3^2 \cdot 5}$$

2.

$$
\begin{array}{r|l}
2 & 84 \\
\hline
2 & 42 \\
\hline
3 & 21 \\
\hline
 & 7 \\
\hline
\end{array}
$$

$$\boxed{84 = 2^2 \cdot 3 \cdot 7}$$

3.

$$
\begin{array}{r|l}
2 & 182 \\
\hline
7 & 91 \\
\hline
 & 13 \\
\hline
\end{array}
$$

$$\boxed{182 = 2 \cdot 7 \cdot 13}$$

4. $10 = 2 \cdot 5, 25 = 5^2$. Thus, the LCM must contain 1 power of 2 and 2 powers of 5, for an LCM of $2 \cdot 5^2 = 2 \cdot 25 = \boxed{50}$.

5. $27 = 3^3, 84 = 2^2 \cdot 3 \cdot 7$. Thus, the LCM must contain 2 powers of 2, 3 powers of 3, and 1 power of 7, for an LCM of $2^2 \cdot 3^3 \cdot 7 = 4 \cdot 27 \cdot 7 = \boxed{756}$.

6. $11 = 11, 70 = 2 \cdot 5 \cdot 7$. Thus, the LCM must contain 1 power of 2, 1 power of 5, 1 power of 7, and 1 power of 11, for an LCM of $2 \cdot 5 \cdot 7 \cdot 11 = \boxed{770}$.

7. $12 = 2^2 \cdot 3, 13 = 13, 14 = 2 \cdot 7$. Thus, any multiple of these 3 integers must have at least 2 powers of 2, 1 power of 3, 1 power of 7, and 1 power of 13, for an LCM of $2^2 \cdot 3 \cdot 7 \cdot 13 = 4 \cdot 3 \cdot 7 \cdot 13 = 1092$. The smallest 4 positive multiples of 1092 are thus $\boxed{1092, 2184, 3276, \text{ and } 4368}$.

8. $144 = 2^4 \cdot 3^2, 96 = 2^5 \cdot 3$. Thus, the GCD can have 4 powers of 2 and 1 power of 3, for a GCD of $2^4 \cdot 3 = 16 \cdot 3 = \boxed{48}$.

9. $121 = 11^2, 143 = 11 \cdot 13$. Thus, the GCD can have 1 power of 11, for a GCD of $\boxed{11}$.

10. $80 = 2^4 \cdot 5, 60 = 2^2 \cdot 3 \cdot 5$. Thus, the GCD can have 2 powers of 2, for a GCD of $2^2 = \boxed{4}$.

Counting Divisors

1. $25 = 5^2 \longrightarrow 2 + 1 = \boxed{3}$ divisors.

2. $20 = 2^2 \cdot 5 \longrightarrow (2+1)(1+1) = (3)(2) = \boxed{6}$ divisors.

3. $39 = 3 \cdot 13 \longrightarrow (1+1)(1+1) = (2)(2) = \boxed{4}$ divisors.

4. $60 = 2^2 \cdot 3 \cdot 5 \longrightarrow (2+1)(1+1)(1+1) = (3)(2)(2) = \boxed{12}$ divisors.

5. $120 = 2^3 \cdot 3 \cdot 5 \longrightarrow (3+1)(1+1)(1+1) = (4)(2)(2) = \boxed{16}$ divisors.

6. $289 = 17^2 \longrightarrow (2+1) = \boxed{3}$ divisors.

7. $300 = 2^2 \cdot 3 \cdot 5^2 \longrightarrow (2+1)(1+1)(2+1) = (3)(2)(3) = \boxed{18}$ divisors.

8. $504 = 2^3 \cdot 3^2 \cdot 7 \longrightarrow (3+1)(2+1)(1+1) = (4)(3)(2) = \boxed{24}$ divisors.

Base Numbers

1. $564 = 1(512) + 6(8) + 4(1) = 1 \cdot 8^3 + 0 \cdot 8^2 + 6 \cdot 8^1 + 4 \cdot 8^0 = \boxed{1064_8}$.

2. $735 = 1(729) + 6(1) = 1 \cdot 9^3 + 0 \cdot 9^2 + 0 \cdot 9^1 + 6 \cdot 9^0 = \boxed{1006_9}$.

3. $1256 = 3(343) + 4(49) + 4(7) + 3(1) = 3 \cdot 7^3 + 4 \cdot 7^2 + 4 \cdot 7^1 + 3 \cdot 7^0 = \boxed{3443_7}$.

4. $93 = 1(64) + 1(16) + 1(8) + 1(4) + 1(1) = 1 \cdot 2^6 + 0 \cdot 2^5 + 1 \cdot 2^4 + 1 \cdot 2^3 + 1 \cdot 2^2 + 1 \cdot 2^0 = \boxed{1011101_2}$.

5. $110101_2 = 1 \cdot 2^5 + 1 \cdot 2^4 + 0 \cdot 2^3 + 1 \cdot 2^2 + 0 \cdot 2^1 + 1 \cdot 2^0 = 32 + 16 + 4 + 1 = \boxed{53}$.

6. $2120_3 = 2 \cdot 3^3 + 1 \cdot 3^2 + 2 \cdot 3^1 + 0 \cdot 3^0 = 2(27) + 1(9) + 2(3) = \boxed{69}$.

7. $AB35_{12} = 10 \cdot 12^3 + 11 \cdot 12^2 + 3 \cdot 12^1 + 5 \cdot 12^0 = 10(1728) + 11(144) + 3(12) + 5(1) = 17280 + 1584 + 36 + 5 = \boxed{18905}$.

8. $6645_8 = 6 \cdot 8^3 + 6 \cdot 8^2 + 4 \cdot 8^1 + 5 \cdot 8^0 = 6(512) + 6(64) + 4(8) + 5(1) = 3060 + 384 + 32 + 5 = \boxed{3481}$.

9. $2358_9 = 2 \cdot 9^3 + 3 \cdot 9^2 + 5 \cdot 9^1 + 8 \cdot 9^0 = 2(729) + 3(81) + 5(9) + 8(1) = 1458 + 243 + 45 + 8 = 1754 = 2(625) + 4(125) + 4(1) = 2 \cdot 5^4 + 4 \cdot 5^3 + 0 \cdot 5^2 + 0 \cdot 5^1 + 4 \cdot 5^0 = \boxed{24004_5}$.

10. $3120_4 = 3 \cdot 4^3 + 1 \cdot 4^2 + 2 \cdot 4^1 + 0 \cdot 4^0 = 3(64) + 1(16) + 2(4) = 192 + 16 + 8 = 216 = 4(49) + 2(7) + 6(1) = 4 \cdot 7^2 + 2 \cdot 7^1 + 6 \cdot 7^0 = \boxed{426_7}$.

The Units Digit

1. $7 + 1 = \boxed{8}$

2. $3 + 3 = \boxed{6}$

3. $8 + 3 = 11 \longrightarrow \boxed{1}$

4. $3 - 2 = \boxed{1}$

5. $3 - 4 \longrightarrow 13 - 4 = \boxed{9}$

6. $8 - 5 = \boxed{3}$

7. $4 \times 2 = \boxed{8}$

8. $3 \times 4 = 12 \longrightarrow \boxed{2}$

9. $4 \times 5 = 20 \longrightarrow \boxed{0}$

10. $(3^3)^5 = 3^{3 \cdot 5} = 3^{15}$. $3^1 = 3, 3^2 = 9, 3^3 = 27, 3^4 = 81, 3^5 = 243, 3^6 = 729, etc.$ The digits repeat every 4 iterations. Dividing 15 by 4 gives a remainder of 3, so the units digit must be the same as the units digit of $3^3 = 27 : \boxed{7}$.

11. Let my son's age be x, and my age be $3x$. Because our ages have the same units digit, the units digit of the difference of our ages must be 0, giving us the equation $3x - x = 2x$ and that $2x$ has a units digit of 0. From this, we know that $10 | 2x$, so we must have that $5 | x$. We know that my son's age must be between 10 and 20, so the only age in that range with a units digit of 5 is $\boxed{15}$.

12. Let x be the number with the units digit of 3. Let y be the other natural number. We know that xy ends in 1, so y must have a units digit of 7. From this, we know that adding the two numbers will result in a units digit of $3 + 7 = 10$, which really means a units digit of $\boxed{0}$.

Divisibility Rules

1. The units digit, 4, is even, so $\boxed{\text{yes}}$.

2. The units digit, 5, is odd, so $\boxed{\text{no}}$.

3. The units digit, 4, is even, so $\boxed{\text{yes}}$.

4. The sum of the digits is $1 + 2 + 8 = 11$, which is not a multiple of 3, so $\boxed{\text{no}}$.

5. The sum of the digits is $9 + 3 + 6 = 18$, which is a multiple of 3, so $\boxed{\text{yes}}$.

6. The sum of the digits is $1 + 2 + 9 = 12$, which is a multiple of 3, so $\boxed{\text{yes}}$.

7. The last two digits, 36, are a multiple of 4, so $\boxed{\text{yes}}$.

8. The last two digits, 94, are not a multiple of 4, so $\boxed{\text{no}}$.

9. The last two digits, 34, are not a multiple of 4, so $\boxed{\text{no}}$.

10. The units digit is 0, so $\boxed{\text{yes}}$.

11. The units digit is 2, so $\boxed{\text{no}}$.

12. The units digit is 5, so $\boxed{\text{yes}}$.

13. The sum of the digits is $9 + 9 + 6 = 24$, which is a multiple of 3, so it is divisible by 3. The units digit is even, so it is divisible by 2. Thus, $\boxed{\text{yes}}$, it is divisible by 6.

14. The sum of the digits is $2 + 6 + 4 = 12$, which is a multiple of 3, so it is divisible by 3. The units digit is even, so it is divisible by 2. Thus, $\boxed{\text{yes}}$, it is divisible by 6.

15. The sum of the digits is $6 + 7 + 4 = 17$, which is not a multiple of 3, so it is not divisible by 3. Thus, $\boxed{\text{no}}$, it is not divisible by 6.

16. Dividing 120 by 2 three times gives $\frac{120}{2} = 60 \longrightarrow \frac{60}{2} = 30 \longrightarrow \frac{30}{2} = 15$. The result is a whole number, so $\boxed{\text{yes}}$, it is divisible by 8.

17. Dividing 992 by 2 three times gives $\frac{992}{2} = 496 \longrightarrow \frac{496}{2} = 248 \longrightarrow \frac{248}{2} = 124$. The result is a whole number, so $\boxed{\text{yes}}$, it is divisible by 8.

18. Dividing 674 by 2 three times gives $\frac{674}{2} = 337...$ Whoops. That's already odd, so we won't be able to divide by 2 twice more and get a whole number. Thus, $\boxed{\text{no}}$, it is not divisible by 8.

19. The sum of the digits is $7 + 2 + 9 = 18$, which is a multiple of 9, so $\boxed{\text{yes}}$.

20. The sum of the digits is $1 + 6 + 9 = 16$, which is not a multiple of 9, so $\boxed{\text{no}}$.

21. The sum of the digits is $1 + 2 + 3 + 4 + 8 = 18$, which is a multiple of 9, so $\boxed{\text{yes}}$.

22. The units digit is 0, so $\boxed{\text{yes}}$.

23. The units digit is not 0, so $\boxed{\text{no}}$.

24. The units digit is not 0, so $\boxed{\text{no}}$.

25. The two digits are not the same, so $\boxed{\text{no}}$.

26. The two digits are the same, so $\boxed{\text{yes}}$.

27. The two digits are not the same, so $\boxed{\text{no}}$.

28. The sum of the digits is $1 + 6 + 8 = 15$, which is a multiple of 3, so it is divisible by 3. The last two digits, 68, are a multiple of 4, so it is divisible by 4. Thus, $\boxed{\text{yes}}$, it is divisible by 12.

29. The sum of the digits is $1 + 9 + 0 = 10$, which is not a multiple of 3, so it is not divisible by 3. Thus, $\boxed{\text{no}}$, it is not divisible by 12.

30. The sum of the digits is $2 + 1 + 2 = 5$, which is not a multiple of 3, so it is not divisible by 3. Thus, $\boxed{\text{no}}$, it is not divisible by 12.

Made in United States
Troutdale, OR
09/27/2024

23189934R00155